DATABASE LAW

DATABASE LAW

Edited by
Christopher Rees
and
Simon Chalton

JORDANS
1998

Published by
Jordan Publishing Limited
21 St Thomas Street, Bristol BS1 6JS

British Library Cataloguing-in-Publication Data
A catalogue record for this book is available from the British Library.

ISBN 0 85308 510 2

Typeset by Mendip Communications Ltd, Frome, Somerset
Printed by MPG Books Ltd, Bodmin, Cornwall

Contributor Biographies

BIRD & BIRD

Bird & Bird is a 40-partner law firm with offices in London, Brussels and Hong Kong. The firm is particularly well known for its work in a number of fields, especially information technology, telecommunications, digital media and on-line services.

Bird & Bird's Information Technology ('IT') Group is widely regarded as one of the leading practices of its kind in the UK. The Group acts for users and suppliers of IT on all aspects of computer and electronics law. Although best known for giving advice to companies in the private sector, the Group also has unrivalled expertise in the field of public procurement contracting, outsourcing and facilities management. More recently, the Group has been actively involved in some of the largest IT projects taking place under the Private Finance Initiative.

Within the telecommunications field, Bird & Bird has a long and well-established track record, acting for many substantial UK and international suppliers as well as major financial institutions and users. The firm's Communications Group provides a wide range of corporate and commercial legal advice to businesses in the telecoms and broadcasting sectors: from advising on joint ventures and strategic alliances to procurement, outsourcing, regulatory advice and other specialist areas such as video on demand and voice on the Internet.

Internationally known for its intellectual property expertise, Bird & Bird has one of the largest departments dedicated to this field in Europe. The firm's team of 27 specialist IP lawyers advise on the full range of strategic, commercial and litigious issues associated with patents, trade marks, designs, copyright, trade secrets, confidential information, regulatory issues and related rights in the EU. Drawing together the firm's core skills in telecoms, IT, IP and commercial law, Bird & Bird has been able to establish a strong digital media practice which advises on the full range of issues affecting multimedia businesses and those wishing to exploit on-line opportunities such as the Internet.

In 1998, the firm decided to dedicate an additional focus on the emerging fields of Databases and Privacy and has established a group of partners and assistants who will be focusing on the growth of this important new field of IT law. This book constitutes the first fruits of that group's activities, concentrating on the intellectual property aspects of database law.

CHRISTOPHER REES

Christopher Rees is the founder partner and current co-Chair of Bird & Bird's IT Group. Since his first involvement with computer contracts in 1978, Christopher has developed considerable expertise in the law and practice of the IT industry. His experience includes six years as the European Counsel for a leading American systems supplier where he served for five years on their Board of Directors.

He acts for both suppliers and purchasers on every aspect of international and domestic IT procurement and outsourcing contracts. He acted for the first UK-based virtual reality company when it obtained its Stock Exchange listing. He has also acted for the UK's largest independent video games publishers on all their corporate, commercial and litigious matters. He has always combined his IT practice with corporate transactional work for companies from a wide range of industry sectors with the result that he now often acts as the lead partner in merger and acquisition deals where the target is rich in intellectual property or intellectual capital.

From 1993 to 1996 Christopher served as Managing Partner of Bird & Bird. His current extra-mural activities include the presentation of a two-day seminar on 'Negotiating Computer Contracts' and he sits on the editorial panel of the *Computer Law and Security Report*. He chairs the Legal Affairs Group of the National Computing Centre and is Chairman of the International Bar Association's Computers and Databases Standing Committee.

Christopher was the Herbert Ruse Prizeman in his Law Society Finals and took two degrees from Cambridge.

SIMON CHALTON

Simon Chalton joined Bird & Bird's IT Group as a consultant in 1995 to spearhead Bird & Bird's activity in the increasingly important area of databases, data protection and the developing law of privacy. Simon's experience with computers and the law relating to information technology goes back to the late 1960s. During this period, he has contributed to the specification, design and implementation of several computer application programs.

In the course of his distinguished career, Simon has held the positions of Chairman of the British Computer Society's Intellectual Property Committee, Chairman of the International Bar Association's Computer and Database Committee, Deputy Chairman of the British Computer Society's Professional Issues Board, Chairman of the UK's National Computing Centre's Legal Affairs Group and has been a member of the Society for Information Management's Procurement Working Group.

Simon is a co-editor of Sweet & Maxwell's *Encyclopaedia of Data Protection*, has contributed to Sweet & Maxwell's *Encyclopaedia of Information Technology Law* and writes for a variety of professional journals in the information technology law field.

SIMON TOPPING

Simon Topping is head of Bird & Bird's competition law group. He is resident in and head of the firm's EC Office in Brussels. He has considerable experience of advising on the EC and UK competition law aspects of all types of IT and telecom, often at the leading edge of a new technology's introduction. For example, Simon has advised a major GSM operator on EC regulation relating to mobile telephony.

Simon is a frequent contributor of articles to the *Telecoms Regulation Review* and has also written the competition section in the *European Guide to Telecommunications Liberalisation* published by Horrocks Technology. He is a founder Member of the Brussels Telecoms Forum.

Simon graduated in Politics, Philosophy and Economics from Oxford University before converting to law, no doubt for sound political, philosophical and economic reasons. He qualified as a Barrister in 1988 and spent two years with a major French law firm in Brussels advising purely on EC law and competition law. He has also spent a six-month period working in the Directorate General for Competition of the European Commission (DG IV) in the division dealing with the IT and telecommunications sectors and therefore has a detailed knowledge of the workings of DG IV and the merger task force.

TREVOR M COOK

Trevor Cook joined Bird & Bird in 1974. He was admitted as a solicitor in 1977 and since then has practised in the firm's Intellectual Property Department becoming a partner in 1981, and Head of the Department in 1993.

His practice covers all aspects (contentious and non-contentious) of intellectual property, technology and regulatory law. He is Treasurer of the British Group of the AIPPI (the International Association for the Protection of Industrial Property). He is Secretary to the Intellectual Property Committee of the British Computer Society, and also to the British Copyright Council Working Group on Copyright and New Technology. He is a member of the Licensing Executives Society and of the Pharmaceutical Trade Marks Group and is an associate of the Chartered Institute of Patent Agents.

Trevor contributed to the third and fourth editions of the Chartered Institute of Patent Agents *Guide to the Patents Act 1977* (Sweet & Maxwell, 1990, 1995) and also contributes to the Chartered Institute of Patent Agents *European Patents Handbook* (FT Law & Tax). He contributed to both editions of *Information Technology and the Law* (Macmillan, 1986, 1990) and is co-author of *Pharmaceuticals Biotechnology and the Law* (Macmillan, 1991) and *Practical Intellectual Property Precedents* (FT Law & Tax, 1997). He is on the editorial board of *Managing Intellectual Property* and on the advisory board of *Commercial Judicial Review*.

Trevor graduated in Chemistry from Southampton University.

LORNA BRAZELL

Lorna Brazell is a solicitor in Bird & Bird's Intellectual Property Department. She specialises in intellectual property and technology law, particularly patent litigation in the mechanical and electronic fields and non-contentious and contentious copyright.

Lorna has written widely on topical issues in the fields of copyright, trade marks, designs and patents. She has a first-class honours degree in Geophysics from Edinburgh University and an LLM from King's College London.

HELEN BROWN

Helen Brown is an assistant solicitor in Bird & Bird's IT Group, having joined Bird & Bird from Eversheds, Leeds in January 1998. Helen has experience of a wide range of IT agreements having acted for both supplier and purchaser.

Helen has a degree in law from Oxford University.

HOWARD RUBIN

Howard Rubin joined Bird & Bird's Information Technology Group as a partner in 1998. Since qualifying in 1981, Howard has acted primarily for businesses in the IT and entertainment industries. Having spent four years as Group Legal Director of Sega Europe Limited, Howard has particular experience of the legal issues relating to video and computer games as well as games hardware platforms and entertainment centres. He also has extensive experience of the competition issues which affect the IT and video games industries.

RUTH LOVERSEED

Ruth Loverseed is a member of Bird & Bird's IT Group handling all aspects of IT law from mergers, acquisitions and joint ventures involving technology companies, to software licensing, and facilities management. Ruth has advised on outsourcing transactions for the public and private sector, with recent experience of outsourcing IT on a Europe-wide basis across a group of companies.

Ruth also has particular interests in informational privacy – both as it is protected by data protection and the laws on confidentiality. She has advised a range of businesses on their data protection registrations and policies.

Ruth has a first-class degree in English from Oxford University.

BEVERLEY ANDREE

Beverley Andree is a member of Bird & Bird's IT Group where she specialises in back office transactional support and company secretarial matters. She carries out company secretarial duties for a number of prominent IT companies, including most recently Action 2000, the government-sponsored company responsible for leading the UK's awareness campaign relating to the Millennium Bug.

Beverley has a law degree from the University of London and is a Member of the Institute of Chartered Secretaries and Administrators. She is currently completing an external Masters Degree in European Law with the University of Leicester.

Dedication

For Lisa, Helen and Thomas

Preface

The road from Delhi to Agra is congested, prone to seemingly interminable delays, and allows the traveller a window onto a world containing much of human experience. We mention this not because it might seem an appropriate metaphor for the current state of the Information Super-Highway but because it was on that road that the seeds for the creation of this book were sown last November.

The two of us were attending the International Bar Association's Conference in Delhi and had decided to take a well-deserved break from proceedings in the form of a trip to view the Taj Mahal. Trains are a much more sensible way to travel around in India, but we were told that the two available services were fully booked so we were left with no option but to undertake the five-hour journey by bus.

It is surprising what a broad range of topics can be covered in such a space of time. Having exhausted matters such as (it being India) religion, philosophy and politics on the outward journey, we seemed unaccountably to have drifted into a conversation on developments in the field of law on the return journey. The upshot of our discussion was the conclusion that it would be sensible to focus on two pieces of legislation which were due to be promulgated in 1998, namely the Database Regulations and the Data Protection Bill. We agreed that these two pieces of legislation, concentrating as they do on the content rather than the technology of computer systems, would represent a significant step forward for the state of computer law in the UK. We therefore conceived the idea of holding two seminars to explore these matters in greater depth. Those seminars duly took place at Bird & Bird in January and February of this year. It was our good fortune that a representative of our publishers was present at the first of these seminars on the Database Regulations and approached us afterwards with the idea that we should produce a book to disseminate our learning further. The pages which follow are the result.

We would like to pay tribute to the individual authors who have contributed their pieces in the very demanding timetable placed upon them. We would also like to pay particular thanks to Ruth Loverseed and Beverley Andree whose tireless efforts as sub-editors have helped to give the book much of its polish. It is impossible to achieve a conformity of style across a book where there are a number of contributing authors. However, it is important that the underlying content and quality of those contributions should mesh one with the other. The fact that the outcome in these respects has been so successful is largely due to the care and attention to detail of Ruth and Beverley. Responsibility for any errors which remain may properly be laid at our door.

Christopher W Rees
Simon NL Chalton
Bird & Bird
June 1998

Contents

Table of Cases

References are to paragraph numbers; italic references are to page numbers of Appendices.

Table of Statutes

References are to paragraph numbers; italic references are to page numbers of Appendices. Bold italics refer to pages where materials are set out in full.

Table of Statutory Instruments

References are to paragraph numbers; italic references are to page numbers of Appendices. Bold italics refer to pages where materials are set out in full.

Table of EC Materials

Entries are in chronological order. References are to paragraph numbers. Italic references are to page numbers of appendices. Bold italics refer to pages where materials are set out in full.

Table of International Conventions

Table of Foreign Laws

References are to paragraph numbers.

Table of Abbreviations

Full title	Citation in this book
Agreement on the European Economic Area signed at Oporto on 2 May 1992 as adjusted by the Protocol signed at Brussels on 17 March 1993	EEA Agreement
Agreement on Trade-Related Aspects of Intellectual Property Rights	TRIPs
Berne Convention for the Protection of Literary and Artistic Works of September 1886, Paris Revision, 24 July 1991	Berne Convention
Copyright (Computer Programs) Regulations 1992, SI 1992/3233	Software Regulations
Copyright and Rights in Databases Regulations 1997, SI 1997/3032	Database Regulations
Copyright, Designs and Patents Act 1988	CDPA
Data Protection Act 1984[1]	Data Protection Act
Digital Equipment Corporation	DEC
EC Directive 91/250/EEC on the Legal Protection of Computer Programs	Software Directive
EC Directive 96/9/EC on the Legal Protection of Databases	Database Directive
European Commission	Commission
European Commission Green Paper on Copyright and the Challenge of Technology COM (88) 172 issued on 7 June 1992	Copyright Green Paper
European Communities Act 1972	EC Act

---

1   There will probably be a 1998 Act by the time this book is published.

Full title	*Citation in this book*
European Economic Area	EEA (comprising the Member States of Austria, Belgium, Denmark, Finland, France, Germany, Greece, Ireland, Italy, Luxembourg, Netherlands, Portugal, Spain, Sweden, UK (EU Member States) and Norway, Iceland and Liechtenstein (EFTA-States))
European Economic Area Act 1993	EEA Act
General Agreement on Tariffs and Trade	GATT
in-circuit emulator	ICE
Non-Disclosure Agreement	NDA
Resale Prices Act 1976	RPA
Restrictive Trade Practices Act 1976	RTPA
Small and medium-sized enterprises	SMEs
Treaty on European Union	the Maastricht Treaty
Treaty of Rome	EC Treaty
Universal Copyright Convention of 6 September 1952	UCC
World Intellectual Property Organisation	WIPO
World Trade Organisation	WTO

Chapter 1

INFORMATION AND THE LAW

1.1 The information age – 1.2 Is information capable of being owned? – 1.3 The common law protections for information: contract and confidence – 1.4 The statutory protections for information: copyright and database right – 1.5 Information and the criminal law – 1.6 Databases as property

1.1   THE INFORMATION AGE

Information is the raw material for the new economic era which we entered upon some few short years ago. The fact is acknowledged by its commonly accepted name as the Information Age. In the Agrarian Age, the law developed to facilitate the ownership and use of the most important asset of the time: land. In the Industrial Age, the law developed to facilitate the ownership and use of the chattel. So, in the Information Age, we should expect the law to develop to address the use of information, and in doing so to consider whether it can indeed be owned at all. The Copyright and Rights in Databases Regulations 1997 (the 'Database Regulations'), which are the UK's current expression of the subject of this book, are part of the law's attempt to come to terms with the new economic god: information. In broad terms, the Database Regulations seek to give legal effect to the notion that, just as in previous ages, man recognised that labour with particular raw materials such as land, iron or steel should give rise to protectable rights, so the time and effort that is put into the collection, selection, arrangement and presentation of information should lead to the law protecting the value of that work product.

Yet here we come to a difficulty. Information is the life-blood by which people conduct their daily lives. It might be fascinating to debate whether those societies which have sought to limit their members' right to the access and use of information have proved to be either more creative or more resilient than those which did not seek to exercise such control, but the contemporary consensus within liberal societies is that restraint on the availability and use of information, in any form, has to be strictly justified. Whilst perhaps not articulated as 'the more the merrier', it is certainly the case that information is perceived to be a 'good thing'. For every one complaint of information overload can be found a matching nine which complain that not enough information is being provided, whether by a government, an employer or a commercial enterprise.

So, granted this political orthodoxy, man's insatiable desire for information and information's seminal significance for much modern economic activity, it will be a predictable consequence that if a legal system seeks to import a new property right over the use of information there will be an accompanying wailing and gnashing of teeth. The Database Regulations have created such a right. It now falls to the lot of the lawyers to make sense of the legislation giving effect to the right. Much ink, but hopefully no blood, will therefore be spilt in construing the new right and assessing the way that it fits into the existing framework of law in the field.

This book has been compiled in order to contribute to this process of construction and assessment. The scheme of the book is first to look at the historical background leading up to the passing of the European Union's Directive on the Legal Protection of Databases[1] (the 'Database Directive'), then to consider the UK's implementation of the Database Directive in the form of the Database Regulations, including the impact on the existing legislation in the field, the Copyright, Designs and Patents Act 1988 (the 'CDPA') and the Copyright (Computer Programs) Regulations 1992 (the 'Software Regulations'). We shall then move on to consider the competition law and international ramifications of the legislation, ending with the by no means straightforward subject of the transition from the old order to the new. The various appendices provide annotated versions of all the source material.

Thus, by the end of the book, it is hoped that the patient reader will have a rounded appreciation of the new legislation and some ideas about the likely areas of greatest contention and debate that will arise from it. We will endeavour to keep you entertained and stimulated as you progress through the pages. If the end result is a degree of enlightenment concerning what might otherwise remain a shrouded and difficult subject, we shall be content.

In a spirit of purposeful enquiry, we shall commence our journey with a discussion of the nature of information itself, and then look at the way the law has thus far seen fit to protect those who claim rights over particular granules or parcels of it. This will involve a consideration of some contract law issues, a look at the law of confidence and then the law of copyright. We will then turn to crime, so to speak, and examine the instances where the long arm of criminal law extends its reach to the unsuspecting collar of information. All of this will assist us to see our subject in its proper context, and also perhaps to grasp the revolutionary nature of the new rights granted by the apparently innocuous Database Regulations.

1.2   IS INFORMATION CAPABLE OF BEING OWNED?

Information, so the Oxford English Dictionary tells us, is 'knowledge'. For most purposes this definition might satisfy us. But if we are embarked on a philosophical quest to seek the nature of information it will soon be seen that this definition is too simplistic.

Knowledge itself is an awareness gained by experience. That experience is garnered from the world around us: its creatures, its objects and its attributes. These might be appropriately called the data necessary, but not sufficient, to comprise knowledge.

As we have introduced the term data, it is worth pausing to note its derivation from the Latin (*dare*: to give, *datum*: a thing having been given). Thus, we have the notion that the data upon which we are to base our knowledge of the world are freely given to us

---

1   Council Directive No 96/9/EC, 11 March 1996.

all. This may colour our subsequent view as to the degree to which it is appropriate to prevent those data remaining in the public domain. This notion lies behind the often repeated (and sometimes misunderstood) statement that information cannot be owned. We will explore this statement in some detail in the following sections, as we examine the various means the law allows to protect the value inherent in information, the triple Cs: contract, confidence and copyright. In doing so, we would invite you to bear in mind that not only is a triple stranded rope rarely broken, but that these rights will in future sit alongside, indeed in reserve to, the primary protection which the law will allow for the protection of certain collections of information, namely the 'database right'[1].

In addition to these protections for information, it might bc thought that we should also consider the subject of patents on the grounds that a patent amounts to a restraint on the use of information. This is to misunderstand the nature of the patent right. The grant of a patent secures for the patentee the right, for the period of the patent, to prevent production of articles embodying a particular invention in return for full disclosure of new information relating to his invention. The information itself is made freely (we will not labour the point) available to all others with the intention that by so doing the state of the art and the common wealth will be improved. Thus, it can be seen that the patent process, far from being an inhibitor of the use of information, is a contributor to its greater availability and use.

1.3   THE COMMON LAW PROTECTIONS FOR INFORMATION: CONTRACT AND CONFIDENCE

If we allow that information should not be capable of outright ownership, we should nevertheless admit that there are circumstances when legitimate restraints on its *use* may be imposed on some people. For over two centuries, English law has recognised that if information, not publicly known, is transmitted in such a way as to indicate that it is not to be further used or disseminated, it will be, as it were, stamped ('impressed' in the Anglo-French vernacular favoured by lawyers) with a prohibition against its further use or disclosure by the confidant, and certain others, without the confider's consent[2].

This is a species of negative licence. It can lead to the paradoxical position that in certain circumstances it can be more important to *avoid* receiving information than actually to receive it, as to receive it may mean that one's freedom of action will be circumscribed by virtue of its possession. This is best illustrated by the policy of many research and development departments within companies with regard to the receipt of unsolicited offers of 'new' ideas and inventions. These offers will be politely declined until the potential discloser has signed an agreement which makes clear that no restriction will be placed on the further use of the information by the disclosee. In other words, there will be a studied effort to ensure that the law of confidence will not

---

1   Database Regulations, reg 13(1).
2   The line of cases starts with *Pope v Curl* (1741) 2 Atk 342, which allowed Alexander Pope to restrain use of certain letters written by him. A good analysis of the cases is set out in the Law Commission Report on Breach of Confidence, Cmnd 8388, 1981 at pp 10–18.

apply to the information concerned. Only when this waiver of any claim to confidentiality has been executed will it be safe for the research department to receive the information. The point being that to receive it without first having removed any restriction on its further use would mean that a similar idea or product that is already under development by the department at the time may be said to have benefited from the disclosed information. The consequence of this might be that the ownership of and ability to exploit any intellectual property right in that development would be tainted.

So, generally speaking, when information which is confidential to one organisation is intended to be disclosed to another to carry on a particular business venture, the disclosure will be hedged around with the most elaborate restrictions regarding the scope and duration of the use of the information. This illustrates the way that contract law is increasingly used to buttress the principles of the law of confidence in protecting the value perceived to be inherent in the information disclosed. In certain cases, the preparation of the disclosure agreement will become a considerable exercise in itself. The negotiation of the substantive commercial transaction will not commence until this document has been executed. The parties will not be prepared to release the relevant information, whether it be, for example, market share, customer lists or technological matters, because of the value 'locked up' in that information and the risk that unless it is suitably protected that value will be lost by its disclosure to the other party. However, it would be as well for the parties to bear in mind that even the finest drafting of a disclosure agreement cannot avoid certain elements of value in the information leaking out in the course of a disclosure exercise.

Consider, for example, the position regarding the return of disclosed information, if the intended transaction were not to proceed. This neatly illustrates the point we have been making concerning the impossibility of ever truly owning information in the first place. Usually, the disclosure agreement will provide that all documents and materials which have been disclosed have to be handed back, and the disclosee must certify that he has retained no copies of them. That will be well and good so far as the physical manifestations of the information are concerned, but what about the information which, having become known to the disclosee, has, so to speak, entered his head and become part of his store of knowledge?

For example, let us say that because of information contained in the customer list the disclosee has realised that a number of his largest customers have been doing business with his rival on substantially different terms. He cannot return this information, but can he be prevented from using it? He can in the overt sense of seeking to justify a change in his own dealings with those customers on the basis that he should enjoy the same advantageous terms that he had learnt about from the discloser. However, it would be very odd if he did not use the information he had learnt as part of the disclosure exercise in his future business dealings. If he knows that a particular commercial term has been agreed to by his customers with another supplier he would find it very difficult to put off the change in his own terms that his know-how of the market now dictated he should adopt. The information, therefore, having become transmuted into knowledge in the head of the disclosee, is not susceptible to the same degree of legal control. The restrictions on overt use will remain in accordance with the terms of the disclosure agreement, but covert use of the information as part of the continuing stock-in-trade of his trade or profession cannot be effectively policed.

In case this reasoning is thought to be unduly tendentious, we would direct your attention to the approach of Cross J in *Printers and Finishers Limited v Holloway and Others*[1]. The celebrated Cambridge jurist Dr John Hopkins was fond of saying 'read Upjohn[2]; he's never wrong'. We would not wish to cross swords with Dr Hopkins but we would also like to press the claims of Cross J to join that small band of judges to whom one can turn for reliable judgment.

In *Printers and Finishers*, Cross J, whilst prepared to grant an injunction against a former employee from using written materials (and recognising that in certain instances of flagrant 'memorising' it would be right to extend this to non-written materials), was not prepared to extend the jurisdiction of the court to restrain the ex-employee from putting at the disposal of his new employers his personal skills which necessarily incorporated his memory of particular features of the plaintiff's plant. The reasoning behind this judgment being that the knowledge in question was not readily separable from the employee's general knowledge of his trade. To impose an injunction on his use of the know-how would therefore put him in an impossible position. As the learned judge remarked: 'The law will defeat its own object if it seeks to enforce in this field standards which would be rejected by the ordinary man'.

He went on to say that if there were features 'which can fairly be regarded as trade secrets ... then the proper way for the plaintiffs to protect themselves would be by exacting covenants ... not by asking the court to extend the general equitable doctrine to prevent breaking confidence beyond all reasonable bounds'.

The above discussion might incline the reader to venture further into this field, in which case he is referred to the Law Commission's analysis in its Consultation Paper on the Misuse of Trade Secrets[3], Linda Clarke's *Confidentiality and the Law*[4] and, particularly in relation to the principles which the courts will use in connection with confidential information, where a contract of employment is in place, the judgment of Neill LJ in *Faccenda Chicken Limited v Fowler*[5]. It will be seen from those sources that the matter is by no means as clear-cut as we have, in the interest of brevity, tried to state it. There is, as they say, a contrary view; indeed, this being the common law, several of them. Our reason for wishing to be emphatic about the matter rests on a belief that our argument stems from sound first principles, namely: (i) information about the world should be freely available to all its inhabitants; and (ii) once acquired, information is impossible to unlearn (as opposed to forgetting, which is, of course, an entirely different matter).

It is, therefore, subject to the above limitations that we say that it is entirely possible and appropriate for certain information to become the subject matter of a legally binding relationship (whether established by contract or the law of confidence). In giving effect to the terms of that relationship, the law will seek to import some restrictions on the freedom with which that information may subsequently be used. However, the existence of such relationships should not obscure the clarity of the common sense conclusion that information as such should not be treated as property.

---

1   [1964] 3 All ER 731.
2   Lord Upjohn, Lord of Appeal in Ordinary, 1963–1971.
3   Law Commission Consultation Paper on the Misuse of Trade Secrets, No 150, 1997.
4   Linda Clarke (ed) *Confidentiality and the Law* (Lloyds of London Press Limited, 1990).
5   [1987] Ch 117 at 135–136.

Indeed, we would say that it is impossible to treat it so, as it lacks the necessary quality of exclusivity, whether in terms of the right to possession or the right of enjoyment. This exclusivity of possession or enjoyment is the essence of a property right and information *per se* signally lacks those qualities.

And since we have mentioned Lord Upjohn, we should perhaps leave the last word on the subject to him. In *Boardman v Phipps*[1], he concluded that confidential information 'is not property in any normal sense'. If that was a good enough conclusion for Lord Upjohn, it is a good enough conclusion for us.

1.4   THE STATUTORY PROTECTIONS FOR INFORMATION: COPYRIGHT AND DATABASE RIGHT

We now turn to the statutory protection which the law allows for the protection of information. This is in the form of copyright and the newly created database right.

The CDPA provided for the protection of tables and compilations of information. These were included in the category of 'literary works' and protected as such by copyright. This has been altered by the Database Regulations which provide that a database (as defined in the narrow way prescribed by the Database Regulations) is excluded from that category of copyright protected works. Databases, as defined, are now a new sub-classification of literary works protectable by copyright and also separately protectable under the database right. This, of course, is in line with the central aim of the Database Regulations, which is to provide a new remedy for protecting such collections.

What arises for consideration is that a collection not falling within the definition of a database as set out in the Database Regulations (because, perhaps, it is a collection of materials which are not independent, or items which are not individually accessible) may nevertheless remain protected as a copyright table or compilation under s 3(1) of the CDPA if it satisfies the standard of originality required of such works under English law. The reader may well be aware that this standard of originality is considerably lower than the standard required in many other EU countries, notably Germany. In large part, this very point lay behind the impetus to promulgate the Database Directive which gave rise to the Database Regulations: it was perceived that there was a need to harmonise the standards of originality required in the construction of a database before it would be appropriate to grant EU-wide property rights over such works. These standards now relate to originality, in the form of intellectual creativity (for copyright protection) and investment of financial, technical or human resources (for database right).

There will, therefore, need to be a meticulous analysis of the *nature* of the collection of information in question before it can properly be classified for the purposes of legal protection under either the Database Regulations or the CDPA. This point will no doubt give rise to practical difficulties in due course, and is dealt with in greater detail in Chapter 4 of this book.

---

1   [1966] 2 All ER 721, [1967] 2 AC 46.

The particular point we would like to raise for consideration at this stage concerns the extent to which it is, or should be, possible to use copyright, or the new Database Right, to control information itself. Copyright is not concerned so much with the originality of the information itself as with the manner of expression of that information. This leads some to consider that there is no copyright in ideas or information as such, only in the form of expression in which they are couched.

We would respectfully join the distinguished authors of *The Modern Law of Copyright and Designs*[1] in asserting the incorrectness of this proposition. As the authors of that book show[2], much of the confusion in this area is caused by the fact that the pre-1911 copyright cases which are cited in support of the statement would have been decided differently after the passing of the Copyright Act 1911. A better formulation of the statement would be that information, until reduced to writing or other material form, cannot be susceptible of copyright protection, but that once the information has been set out in the form of a work, whilst any one piece of unelaborated information is not by itself capable of protection, elaboration or an aggregation of various elements of information may amount to a part of an original work in which copyright will subsist. It would then amount to an infringement of that copyright to use that particular elaboration or aggregation of information, whatever different language or mode of expression was to be used in so doing.

Once the law is seen in this way, it can be appreciated that there is no 'bright-line' test that can be used to say that such and such is unelaborated information in the form of an 'idea' and is not protected by copyright, but such and such is elaboration or aggregation of information in the form of expression which *is* therefore protected by copyright. What is necessary is that each case is looked at on its merits to decide whether the elaboration or aggregation of information or ideas which it is alleged have been borrowed constitutes such a substantial part of the copyright work as a whole that its use without permission of the copyright owner would be unjustified. This, it is submitted, is the approach recently adopted by Jacob J in the leading English computer case in the field[3].

So, the conclusion we reach is that copyright does indeed protect information itself and will (in appropriate circumstances) continue to do so, irrespective of whether the information is organised in the form of a database as defined by the Database Regulations. In this context, we would invite you to consider whether copyright might in certain circumstances prove to be an illegitimately wide protection for information giving rise to unfortunate consequences for the use and availability of material of high economic value and critical commercial importance. For example, let us take the case of an interface[4] for an existing, highly successful computer program. If it could be established that there was only one way of expressing the interface for the program then it would be necessary for a person who wished to have his program inter-operate with that existing program to repeat that expression in creating his inter-operable

---

1   Laddie, Prescott and Vittoria *The Modern Law of Copyright and Designs* 2nd ed (Butterworths, 1995).

2   At sections 2.73 and following.

3   *Ibcos Computers Ltd v Barclays Mercantile Highland Finance Ltd* [1994] FSR 275.

4   An interface is that part of a computer program which has to be accessed by another computer program if it is intended that the programs will operate satisfactorily with each other.

program. The US courts[1] have solved this problem by importing a doctrine of 'merger' into their copyright law. That is to say, if it can be demonstrated that there truly is only one way of expressing a given piece of information then the information and the expression are said to have 'merged', and no copyright is allowed to subsist in the merged material.

The position under English law is governed by s 50B of the CDPA. This makes it lawful for copyright to be 'overridden' in accordance with the strict criteria for the decompilation of software laid out in that section, which was introduced into the CDPA as a result of the passing of the Software Regulations. But no one has suggested that the scheme of the Software Regulations should apply to anything other than computer programs. Accordingly, it remains to be seen whether the English courts might adopt the doctrine of merger or some other rule of construction related to the misuse of copyright if it became apparent that copyright was being used to provide an illegitimate restraint on the use of information.

1.5   INFORMATION AND THE CRIMINAL LAW

In our consideration of the law of information we now come to consider how the criminal law has dealt with offences concerning the use of information. This patch of legal turf has been the subject of a valuable recent tilling in the form of the Law Commission's Consultation Paper[2] referred to earlier. That paper would repay careful study by all those interested in pursuing the matter at length from the policy perspective and with a view to seeing how the law may develop. For our present purposes, we shall be content to sketch the state of the present law and give our own views on the best way that things might progress.

Oxford v Moss[3] is the leading case on the subject, being a unanimous decision of a strong Divisional Court of Appeal. It was held in that case that information was not property for the purposes of s 4(1) of the Theft Act 1968[4]. It follows that that which is not property cannot be subject of a charge of theft. Ergo, information cannot be stolen.

A number of commentators have questioned the correctness of this analysis, including Professor Palmer in his interesting chapter in *Confidentiality and the Law*[5], but it should be pointed out that one of the authorities cited by Professor Palmer as contradicting *Oxford v Moss*, namely *R v Stewart*[6] was expressly disagreed with by the Alberta Court of Appeal in *R v Offley*[7] and *Stewart* itself has been reversed by the Canadian Supreme Court[8].

---

1   *Sega Enterprises Limited v Accolade Inc* [1992] 977 F2d 1510.
2   Op cit, fn 6.
3   [1978] 68 Cr App R 183.
4   'Property includes money and all other property, real or personal, including things in action and other intangible property.'
5   Op cit, fn 7.
6   An Ontario case reported at [1984] 149 DLR (3d) 583.
7   [1986] 28 CCC (3d) 1c.
8   [1988] 50 DLR (4th) 1.

The purity of the *Oxford v Moss* approach is best illustrated by the facts of the case. A student (from Liverpool University, not from Oxford as might have been supposed) obtained, without authorisation, access to the examination paper in which he was due to be examined some months later. He did not remove nor did he intend to remove the paper. He merely read it. Whether he profited from it in terms of the class he achieved in the examination is not mentioned in the report of the case. Whatever its ultimate utility to him, the information was unarguably 'taken' by being assimilated by him. Yet, as there was no intention permanently to deprive the owner of the only property (the paper) which the law was prepared to recognise for the purpose of a charge of theft, the prosecution failed.

This approach was followed in the case of *R v Absolom*[1] where the stakes and financial consequences of the taking were significantly higher: the defendant was charged with trying to sell geological data which was said to have cost £13 million to compile. Despite the defendant having in the judge's view acted in 'utmost bad faith', the jury was directed to acquit the defendant as the information concerned could not form the basis of a charge of theft.

Aside from the law of theft there are a number of provisions within the CDPA and the Trade Marks Act 1994 which criminalise dealings in copyright works and trade works. However, it must be appreciated that these deal with conduct relating to the actual intellectual property rights which are themselves property[2]. As the quarry for our present search is the information underlying those property rights and these provisions do not enlighten us regarding the effect or otherwise on that underlying information, we shall not pause to dwell on them.

The Computer Misuse Act 1990, however, is something to which we should direct our attention. Under that Act, it is a criminal offence to gain unauthorised access to data (that is to say, information) if held on a computer[3]. Section 2 of the Computer Misuse Act 1990 goes on to establish a further offence of gaining unauthorised access with intent to commit 'an arrestable offence'[4]. The Computer Misuse Act 1990 therefore appears to give substantial protection to information as such. It only needs to be stored on a computer to enjoy the benevolence of the Computer Misuse Act 1990. However, as was illustrated in *DPP v Bignall*[5], the scope of protection of the Computer Misuse Act 1990 is being restrictively construed. In *Bignall*, information was extracted from the police force's national database for the private purposes of two officers. It was held by the Divisional Court that because the officers were entitled to access the database, they could not be guilty of an offence under the Computer Misuse Act 1990 even if they then used the information for their own private (unauthorised) purposes.

Thus, it is submitted that the Computer Misuse Act 1990 should be seen as a weapon to protect the integrity of a computer system or database, not the information contained in the computer or database itself.

---

1   (1983) *The Times*, 14 September.
2   Section 1(1) of the CDPA; s 2 of the Trade Marks Act 1994.
3   Section 1 of the Computer Misuse Act 1990.
4   By and large, 'arrestable offences' are the more serious types of crimes, punishable with five years or more in prison.
5   (1997) 161 JP 541.

In *Bignall*, the judge suggested that the facts were not appropriate for the case to have been brought under the Computer Misuse Act 1990 at all. He felt the case should have been brought under s 5(2)(b) of the Data Protection Act 1984 (the 'Data Protection Act'). This section makes it a criminal offence to use personal data for a purpose not registered under the Data Protection Act.

The problem with this approach is that in a leading case on the Data Protection Act, *R v Brown*[1] there proved to be a difficulty in fitting the provisions of the Data Protection Act around the difficult concept of what is meant by the 'use' of information. *Brown* was the first case on the Data Protection Act to reach the House of Lords and, like *Bignall*, concerned use of the Police National Computer.

In *Brown*, a police officer called up information from the database but, having assimilated it, appeared to make no further use of it. The House of Lords held that these circumstances did not constitute a use or an attempted 'use' of the information under s 5(2)(b) of the Data Protection Act.

Aside from this, it will be appreciated that there is an inherent limitation to control[2] all information – the Data Protection Act only deals with personal data[3] and therefore leaves a great deal of information outside its ambit. For example, the Data Protection Act does not cover information about dead individuals, corporations or other inanimate objects. The Law Commission has proposed in its Consultation Paper on the Misuse of Trade Secrets[4] that a new offence should be created which criminalises the use or disclosure of an author's trade secret[5] where the 'owner' of the secret does not consent to its disclosure. This will take the English criminal law into new territory in terms of its treatment of the use and abuse of information. It can be anticipated that there will be many voices raised in opposition to the proposals made by the Law Commission due to the proper reluctance to extend the ambit of criminal law into an area of life where the consequences of wrongdoing are essentially financial. However, the Law Commission draws attention to the many foreign jurisdictions (particularly the United States) which have already enacted legislation along the lines they propose.

On balance, we believe it is not appropriate for the footprint of the criminal law to descend upon this area of life. None the less, it has to be conceded that the proposed offence would, in its own way, go no further in the criminal sphere than the Database Regulations have correspondingly gone in the civil arena in broadening the protection afforded to information extracted or re-utilised from a database as defined by the Database Regulations.

---

1   [1996] 1 AC 543.
2   In order to avoid undue sensitivity amongst our law enforcement brethren, we were studious in avoiding the word 'police' in this instance.
3   Ie that relating to living individuals.
4   Op cit.
5   The way that 'trade secret' is defined will, of course, be critical to the proposal, see Part IV of the Report for a full discussion of the policy arguments.

1.6   DATABASES AS PROPERTY

The conclusion that we are drawn towards at the end of this introductory chapter is, therefore, that the ambivalence which the various branches of the English law have up to now taken as to the correct manner in which to protect information and collections of information is in need of a careful restatement. That ambivalence and corresponding need has been shared by the other jurisdictions of the European Union and has been answered in part by the Database Directive. The intention of the Database Directive was that the increasing economic value represented by collections of information or, to bring our book's subject properly into centre stage, databases, should be dealt with in a consistent and appropriate manner by Member States across the European Union.

Whether the intention of the legislators will be realised is not a subject that we care to dwell on overmuch at this early stage in the life history of the subject. Suffice to say that some of the difficulties which are already apparent from the implementation of the Database Regulations in the UK, and which are referred to in later chapters of this book, will be compounded by the slight differences in emphasis and nuance which will inevitably arise in the course of the Database Directive's implementation into the laws of the other Member States. The ultimate goal of complete uniformity is probably neither attainable, nor necessarily that important. What is to be hoped is that the overall framework required by the Database Directive can be made to work in a way which assists the growth and development of the Information Industry, rather than acting as any impediment to it.

It will be assumed that the readers of this book will need little persuasion as to the critical role databases already play in the economics of developed nations and that this role will increase dramatically, perhaps almost unimaginably, as we progress further into the Information Age. We are told that the average hour of work is now 25 times more productive than it was in 1850[1]. Whilst this was substantially the result of mechanisation of physical infrastructure in the earlier part of the twentieth century, latterly the efficiency gains have been the result of speedier access to and processing of information. With greater productivity goes greater profitability, so it is a racing certainty that the availability of greater and greater processing speeds and therefore capabilities for databases[2] will mean that the value of those databases as assets of a business will rise disproportionately compared to the other assets of a business.

Most owners of businesses would inform you that their most valuable asset is the people who work for them. Today they would be correct. We would invite you to consider whether this will be true in 20 or 50 years time. Might it be that the most valuable asset of a business then would be its database: that store of historic data (information) about itself, its products, its markets, its customers, its suppliers, its competitors, which proves to be so reliable, malleable and fertile as a source of old information and therefore new ideas that it gives the business its unique competitive advantage? If that is going to be the case, and we will not risk our readers' indulgence

---

1   *Redefining Work* (Royal Society of Arts, 1998).

2   These increases are guaranteed for the near term by virtue of the incremental improvements which can be foreseen from known semiconductor technology, to say nothing of the possible advances which could be fuelled by as yet unknown developments.

by pretending to a prescience in this vision that we do not properly enjoy, then it will be incumbent on all commercial lawyers to have a good grasp of the property right which the law has established to govern the ownership and use of this most valuable of properties.

It is for this reason that we see the Database Regulations as a massively important piece of legislation. It is the Sale of Goods Act for the new millennium. Unfortunately, the Database Regulations do not enjoy the clarity of drafting that our Victorian forebears gave to their great commercial law statutes. Indeed, some of the provisions of the Database Regulations bear the opacity reserved for Euro-legislation at its worst. None the less, we must, for the reasons explained above, persevere with them. We hope that the pages that follow will assist in making the Database Regulations more intelligible for you and that you will profit from their study and application.

Chapter 2

EU DIRECTIVE 96/9/EC ON THE LEGAL PROTECTION OF DATABASES[1]

2.1 EC Green Paper on Copyright and the Challenge of Technology – 2.2 The first and subsequent proposals for a Database Directive – 2.3 Development of the sui generis *right – 2.4 The compulsory licensing provisions and lawful user and other exceptions – 2.5 The Database Directive as adopted*

2.1 EC GREEN PAPER ON COPYRIGHT AND THE CHALLENGE OF TECHNOLOGY

2.1.1 The Commission's approach

The European Commission's Green Paper on Copyright and the Challenge of Technology (the 'Copyright Green Paper')[2], issued on 7 June 1992, announced the Commission's intention to propose a number of harmonising measures in the field of copyright with a view to eliminating obstacles to the free movement of goods and services and preventing distortion of competition within the internal market. The opening chapter of the Copyright Green Paper referred to the importance of balancing protection of the interests of authors and other creators, the promotion of ready access to information, and the pursuit of cultural goals. The opening chapter also noted that the growing economic importance of industries needing copyright protection against ready misappropriation of their products, particularly by copying, had produced pressure for the modernisation of copyright laws at both national and Community level. Chapter 6 of the Copyright Green Paper sought opinions on a proposal for harmonisation of the legal protection of databases within the Community.

The Commission's view of the Community's fundamental concerns, as expressed in the Copyright Green Paper[3], was fourfold:

(1) to ensure the proper functioning of the Common Market by eliminating obstacles to cross-frontier trade and competition in copyright-protected goods and services within the Community;
(2) to develop intellectual property policies and protection which would improve the competitiveness of the Community's economy in relation to its trading partners;
(3) to prevent misappropriation, outside the Community, of Community members' investments in intellectual property; and

---

1   Hereafter referred to as 'the Database Directive'.
2   COM (88) 172.
3   Copyright Green Paper, para 1.3.

(4) to prevent unduly broad and lengthy copyright protection of, for example, purely functional industrial designs and computer programs which would amount, in practice, to monopolies having a restrictive effect on competition.

The scope of the Copyright Green Paper was limited[1] to six specific areas, namely piracy, home copying of sound and audiovisual works, distribution and rental rights for sound and video recordings, the legal protection of computer programs, the legal protection of databases and the external aspects of copyright protection. The Software Directive, which followed the Copyright Green Paper, was adopted on 14 May 1991 and became the model for a subsequent proposal for a directive on the legal protection of databases. This proposal was to go through two versions, and substantial revisions of its second version, before its final adoption on 11 March 1996 as the Database Directive.

Chapter 6 of the Copyright Green Paper dealt with databases, taking that term to mean a collection of information stored and accessed by electronic means. The reference to information in this definition was broad, and was explained as being intended to include existing copyright works, extracts from works, collections of materials in the public domain, catalogues, timetables, price lists and other reference materials in printed form. However, emphasis was firmly placed on electronic forms and electronic access, either on-line or by means of electronically accessible carriers such as CD-ROMs. It was assumed that the main need for harmonisation of copyright laws related to copyright in electronic databases and not to collections of materials in printed form, which were already protected by copyright under Art 2(5) of the Berne Convention. This Article requires that:

> 'collections of literary or artistic works such as encyclopaedias and anthologies which, by reason of the selection and arrangement of their contents, constitute intellectual creations shall be protected as such, without prejudice to the copyright in each of the works forming part of such collections.'

The Commission also considered whether protection should extend to databases comprising material which was not itself protected by copyright, but concluded that such action should only be taken if the investment which the compilation of such databases represented could not be secured by copyright rather than by other means: here was foreshadowed the possibility of a new *sui generis* right to protect such investment.

2.1.2   The Copyright Green Paper and the Berne Convention

Article 2(5) of the Berne Convention limits copyright protection to collections which, by reason of the selection and arrangement of their contents, constitute intellectual creations. To require Member States to extend their copyright laws to protect collections which are comprehensive (as opposed to creatively selected), or which are ordered non-creatively, for example alphabetically (so avoiding the requirement of creative arrangement), would not have matched the Berne Convention's requirement for the protection by copyright of intellectually creative collections. The only alternative remaining to the Commission was to create a new *sui generis* or

---

1   Copyright Green Paper, para 1.7.

neighbouring right to protect investment in non-creative collections, along the lines of the Danish ten-year catalogue right referred to in the Copyright Green Paper[1].

The Copyright Green Paper was ambivalent about the protection of information as such. The investment involved in the gathering and presentation of new data, in order to make them available for retrieval in the scientific, industrial and business fields, was said to be of greater economic value than the creativity with which the contents of such databases were originally selected and arranged[2], but there was concern whether the retrieval of stored information should constitute a restricted act under copyright law[3]. The Copyright Green Paper seemed to be suggesting that copyright, which protects the expression of ideas and information, was not a proper vehicle for the protection of information as such, especially when that information was not the product of human intellectual creativity. The problem was that such information often necessitates substantial investment if it is to be collected, verified and presented so as to make it accessible and reliable, and that this investment relates to the obtaining, verification and presentation of the information rather than the way in which it is selected and arranged.

The attraction and difficulty of fitting the legal protection of databases, as carriers of information, into the framework of the Berne Convention were apparent. All Member States of the Berne Union are required to protect the works of nationals of other Union Member States under the principle of national treatment: but attempts to shoehorn new classes of work into the Berne Convention's scheme for the protection of literary works might damage the coherence of the protection provided within the Union. Each country would need to extend its own national copyright law to protect such new classes of work, and if any country failed to do so in a manner consistent with the forms of protection adopted by other Union members the principle of national treatment would give varying levels and forms of protection across the Berne Union.

The 1981 Paris Act of the Berne Union made no provision for the protection of computer programs as such, although its definition of literary and artistic works is such as to admit of computer programs being protected by copyright within that classification. The World Intellectual Property Organisation Copyright Treaty, adopted by the Diplomatic Conference held in Geneva in December 1996 as a special agreement within the meaning of Art 20 of the Berne Convention, has provided that computer programs, whatever the mode or form of their expression, are protected by copyright as literary works within the meaning of Art 2 of the Berne Convention. There is no reference either in this Treaty or in the Berne Convention to databases, but, as already mentioned above, Art 2(5) of the Berne Convention provides conveniently for the protection of collections.

The inclusion of both computer programs and databases under the Berne Convention classification of copyright literary works causes tension. Article 2 of the 1996 World Intellectual Property Organisation Copyright Treaty provides that copyright protection extends to expressions and not to ideas, procedures, methods of operation or mathematical concepts as such. While it is diplomatically and commercially

---

1   Copyright Green Paper, para 6.4.5.
2   Copyright Green Paper, para 6.1.5.
3   Copyright Green Paper, para 6.3.2.

convenient to classify computer programs and databases as literary works, there are features of both computer programs and databases which are not appropriate for protection under traditional concepts of copyright. These features include, in the case of computer programs, their functional ability to process information and to produce, without further human creative intellectual intervention, computer-generated productions and works. In the case of databases, their ability to hold and to generate the production of information which has no element of human creativity but which may be of great commercial value is also, arguably, a characteristic which is not appropriate for protection by copyright. An example of the latter is the database which provides negative information, that is to say disclosure of the fact that an item of information is not present in the database. In such a case, the information given is information as such which is not an item of content of the database.

2.1.3   Conclusions on the copyright protection of computer programs and databases

These issues are not clearly presented in the Copyright Green Paper but may be deduced from it[1]. With hindsight, it might have been better for the Commission's harmonisation process had these issues been clearly expressed and succinctly addressed, either in the Copyright Green Paper or in a subsequent document. Meanwhile, it has taken over a decade, and successive draft proposals for directives, to reach a position from which the following broad conclusions may be drawn in relation to copyright in computer programs and databases:

- both computer programs and databases are protectable by copyright within the EEA as literary works, but only if they are their authors' only intellectual creations;
- both computer programs and databases are subject within the EEA to lawful user rights which broadly allow a person in lawful possession of a copy of either a computer program or of a database to use that work for its normal purposes without express permission from the rightholder, and that such use may not be restricted by contract[2];
- if a physical carrier holding a copy of either a computer program or of a database is sold within the EEA with the consent of its rightholder, that action will exhaust within the EEA the rightholder's copyright restricted act of distribution in relation to that copy; and
- transient copying in the course of unauthorised use of either a computer program or a database within the EEA is a copyright restricted act.

The parallels between computer programs and databases reflect the fact that it is not always possible to distinguish between these two forms of production. Apart from their representation in the form of binary codes, which makes them practically difficult to distinguish, it is often the case that a computer program interacts upon a database, and a database upon a computer program, in such a way that neither conveniently and exclusively fits into either classification. To create laws which treat computer programs and databases differently, therefore, creates opportunities for

---

1   See, for example, the problems canvassed in para 6.3 of the Copyright Green Paper.
2   This broad statement over-simplifies the position on lawful user rights, which are considered further at **2.4** below.

uncertainty and potentially conflicting regimes. The Commission's instinct to base the copyright provisions of the Database Directive on the form and principles expressed by the Directive on the Legal Protection of Computer Programs recognises this fact: however, the creation of a *sui generis* right to protect investment in databases but with no equivalent right to protect investment in computer programs may lead to difficulty.

2.2 THE FIRST AND SUBSEQUENT PROPOSALS FOR A DATABASE DIRECTIVE

The Commission's first proposal for a Council Directive on the Legal Protection of Databases was submitted on 15 April 1992 with an Explanatory Memorandum[1]. The Explanatory Memorandum described the proposal as aiming to provide a harmonised and stable legal regime protecting databases created within the Community[2]. It was proposed to establish Community-wide rules for the protection of databases by copyright and a new *sui generis* right which latter right was to be available only to Community makers of databases.

The Explanatory Memorandum referred to the economic importance of information and of electronic information services, including ASCII database services, videotext services, the CD-ROM market and other new delivery media. There were references[3] to raw information material in science, technology and culture, but the emphasis was on electronic information services rather than information as such or to print-on-paper and other forms of manual carriers of collections of information.

The central concern was that, although most Member States already protected collections of works or other materials by copyright either as works under Art 2(1) or as collections under Art 2(5) of the Berne Convention, it was unclear whether in all cases such protection extended to databases and to electronic databases in particular, or to collections of works or materials other than text[4]. There was also uncertainty as to the scope of copyright protection in each of the Member States for electronic databases.

Reference was made in the Explanatory Memorandum to the scope of copyright protection in countries outside the Community, and in particular in the United States. The US Supreme Court's decision in *Feist Publications Inc v Rural Telephone Service Company Inc*[5] had rejected 'sweat of the brow' expended in the production of a white pages alphabetical listing of telephone subscribers as being insufficiently creative to meet the US Copyright Act's criterion of originality. Reference was also made in the Explanatory Memorandum to the Japanese Copyright Law of 1986 which gives protection to 'database works which, by reason of the selection or systematic construction of information contained therein, constitute intellectual creations'[6].

---

1   COM (92) 24 Final SYN 393.
2   Explanatory Memorandum, paras 1.1 and 3.1.1.
3   Ibid, para 2.1.3.
4   Ibid, para 2.2.8.
5   111 S Ct 1282 (1991).
6   Art 12 bis.

In addition to referring to the protection of databases as collections, the Explanatory Memorandum expressed the intention to give limited protection to the contents of a database[1] where such contents were not already protected by copyright. This was to guard against parasitic behaviour by competitors, and to create a climate in which investment in data processing could be stimulated and protected against misappropriation.

The problems inherent in providing protection for information as such were recognised. If a database was the only source of the information contained in it, the Database Directive could, by protecting the database, create a monopoly in the information contained in it: to prevent this consequence, compulsory licences allowing the commercial re-exploitation of relevant information were to be required to be granted by rightholders on fair and non-discriminatory terms. Here there appeared to be echoes of the *Magill* decision of the European Court of Justice[2], where broadcasting companies were not only the holders of copyright in their own broadcasting schedules but were also the sole sources of the information on which those schedules were based: their refusal to grant copyright licences permitting the re-publication of these schedules was held by the European Court of Justice to be an abuse of a dominant position, contrary to Art 86 of the EC Treaty. This issue was essentially one of competition law, and the attempt to resolve it by including a compulsory licensing provision in the proposed directive was subsequently abandoned.

In addition to developing sets of harmonised norms to meet the Community's need to protect databases, the Commission had to take into account discussions then taking place within the World Intellectual Property Organisation in connection with a proposal for a protocol to the Berne Convention directed at protecting databases. The Commission also had to conform to the requirement of Art 10(2) of TRIPs which requires that compilations of data or other material, whether in machine-readable or other form, which by reason of the selection or arrangement of their contents constitute intellectual creations, shall be protected as such.

The first proposal for a directive included features which were subsequently amended or abandoned in later versions and in the final form of the Database Directive. These features included:

– a definition of the term 'database' which referred only to collections of works or materials arranged, stored and accessed by electronic means: printed and other non-electronic forms of database were not included;

– the new *sui generis* right was described as a right to prevent unfair extraction and unfair re-utilisation of material from a database for commercial purposes: the reference to 'unfairness' had overtones of unfair competition and was subsequently dropped;

– a complex definition of 'insubstantial change' was included in the first proposal, but did not appear in later versions;

---

1   Explanatory Memorandum, para 3.2.8.
2   *Radio Telefís Eireann and Independent Television Publications Ltd v Commission of the European Communities* (1995 C-241/91 and C-242/91) [1995] All ER 416.

- originally, the *sui generis* right was to apply to databases which were also protected by copyright but was not to apply to the contents of a database where those contents were themselves protected by copyright. The concept of withholding the *sui generis* right from databases the contents of which were protected by copyright was subsequently dropped;

- provisions distinguishing between electronic materials necessary for the operation of a database, which were to be included within the Database Directive's protection, but excluding computer programs used in the making or operation of a database were dropped from later versions of the proposal. Neither the Software Directive on the legal protection of computer programs[1] nor any version of the proposal for a directive on the legal protection of databases contained a definition of the term 'computer program'. The distinction between databases and computer programs used in the making or operation of databases accessible by electronic means, which latter are excluded from protection under the Database Directive, has been maintained but may be difficult to apply. In particular, a computer program used in the making or operation of databases accessible by electronic means, being excluded from protection under the Database Directive, is excluded from protection under the *sui generis* right[2]. A computer program not so used, which otherwise conforms to the definition of a database in the Database Directive, may be capable of enjoying that protection;

- a reference in the original proposal to a lawful user's right to perform any of the copyright restricted acts 'necessary in order to use [that] database in the manner determined by contractual arrangements with the rightholder' was dropped from later versions. It was difficult to see why it should be necessary to grant a contractual user of a database the right to use the database in accordance with the user's contract. Perhaps underlying this provision was a concern that users with a right to use a database should not be contractually restricted from exercising normal use of it, a point based on concepts of abuse of copyright. However that may be, the lawful user exception from the copyright restricted acts was differently expressed in later versions of the proposal;

- a reference in the original proposal to acts permitted under national laws as derogations from the exclusive rights under copyright[3] would have allowed the fair dealing provisions of the CDPA[4] to have applied to copyright in databases. The final version of the Database Directive does not contain this exception, and expressly prohibits uses of a copyright database for research or teaching which in either case are for commercial purposes[5];

- a requirement in the original proposal that the right to extract and re-utilise the contents of a database be licensed on fair and non-discriminatory terms if the materials in the contents cannot be independently created, collected or obtained from another source, or if the database is made publicly available by a public body under a duty to assemble or disclose the information, was dropped from later versions (see **2.4** below);

---

1   91/250/EEC.
2   Database Directive, Art 1(3).
3   First Proposal, Art 7(2).
4   Section 29 of the CDPA.
5   Database Directive, Art 6(2).

–   the original proposal's ten-year term of protection for the *sui generis* right was subsequently extended in later versions to 15 years.

The Commission's original proposal for a directive was referred by the European Parliament to the Committee on Legal Affairs and Citizen's Rights and to the Economic and Social Committee. Thereafter, the Council of Ministers referred the proposal to a Working Group comprising delegates of all the Member States, with representatives of the Council, as a result of which a second version of the proposal was produced in early 1994. This version was subject to further negotiations between the Member States and emerged, with changes, as a Common Position in July 1995. The Common Position was still further amended, significantly in relation to the definition of 'database', before it was adopted by the European Parliament and the Council as Directive 96/9/EC on 11 March 1996, for transposition into the law of the Member States by 1 January 1998. It was published in the *Official Journal* on 27 March 1996.

2.3   DEVELOPMENT OF THE *SUI GENERIS* RIGHT

Although the Commission's proposal for a directive on the legal protection of databases was aimed at creating a harmonised rule for the protection of databases by copyright throughout the Community, its most significant and innovative contribution was its introduction of a *sui generis* right to protect collections of materials which, although expensive to compile and commercially valuable, lacked any element of human intellectual creativity. They were thus said to be inappropriate for protection by copyright.

In the original version of the Commission's proposal[1], the right to prevent unfair extraction was to be taken to mean the right of a maker of a database to prevent acts of extraction and re-utilisation of material from that database for commercial purposes. This introduced three new concepts:

(1) the maker of a database, to be distinguished from a database's author;
(2) extraction; and
(3) re-utilisation.

These concepts have been carried through to the Database Directive in its final form as adopted, but with additional qualifications and elaboration.

The maker of a database who can show that there has been qualitatively and/or quantitatively a substantial investment in either the obtaining, verification or presentation of the contents of the database is to have a *sui generis* right to prevent extraction and/or re-utilisation of the whole or of a substantial part, evaluated qualitatively and/or quantitatively, of the contents of that database[2]. The *sui generis* right's requirement of substantial investment is the counterpart of the copyright requirement of intellectual creativity. Where the object of protection by copyright is the author's own intellectually creative selection or arrangement of the contents of a

---

1   COM (92) 24 Final SYN 393.
2   Database Directive, Art 7(1).

database, the object of protection by the *sui generis* right is the investment of the database's maker in the obtaining, verification or presentation of the contents of the database. In the Database Directive as adopted, it is immaterial either that the database is itself protectable by copyright, or that its contents should be so protectable, or that there should or should not be any author of the database who may or may not be the maker of the same database: indeed, the interests and rights of the author and of the maker respectively may conflict, and author and maker may be different persons.

The concepts of extraction and re-utilisation are to be compared with the copyright restricted acts, with which they have features in common. In the first proposal for a directive the right to prevent unfair extraction is defined as the right of the maker of the database to prevent acts of extraction and re-utilisation of material from that database for commercial purposes[1]. In the final form of the Database Directive, the reference to fairness did not appear, and the reference to commercial purposes was replaced by exceptions relating to teaching and scientific research for non-commercial purposes.

The terms 'extraction' and 're-utilisation' are themselves defined in the final form of the Database Directive as follows:

- 'extraction' shall mean the permanent or temporary transfer of all or a substantial part of the contents of a database to another medium by any means or in any form; and
- 're-utilisation' shall mean any form of making available to the public all or a substantial part of the contents of a database by the distribution of copies, by renting, by on-line or other forms of transmission. The first sale of a copy of a database within the Community by the rightholder or with his consent exhausts the right to control resale of that copy within the Community[2].

There is an express declaration in the Database Directive that public lending is not an act of either extraction or re-utilisation[3].

The *sui generis* right, like copyright, may be transferred, assigned or granted under contractual licence and is to apply irrespective of eligibility of the contents of a database for protection by copyright or other rights[4].

Although both extraction and re-utilisation apply only to those acts in relation to all or a substantial part of the contents of a database, repeated and systematic extraction or re-utilisation of insubstantial parts of the contents of a database implying acts which conflict with a normal exploitation of that database, or which unreasonably prejudice the legitimate interests of the maker of the database, are not to be permitted[5].

This might appear to leave an unlicensed user of a database free to extract insubstantial parts of the database provided that the extraction is not repeated or systematic: but where the process of extraction of an insubstantial part of a database requires on-line screen display of the database's contents, and this in turn necessitates the permanent or temporary transfer of all or a substantial part of such contents to

---

1   First Proposal, Art 1(2).
2   Database Directive, Art 7(2).
3   Database Directive, Art 7(2).
4   Database Directive, Art 7(4).
5   Database Directive, Art 7(5).

another medium, that act is to be subject to authorisation by the *sui generis* rightholder[1].

This in turn appears to give the *sui generis* rightholder control over the searching of an electronic copy of a database where searching involves the transfer of that or another copy temporarily to machine memory, even though the search process yields discovery of only an insubstantial item of content, or no item at all. However, the position is not certain and existence of the *sui generis* right is expressly stated not to give rise to the creation of a new right in the works, data or materials comprised in the contents of the database[2]: this statement requires to be reconciled with the rightholder's intended control over transfer of substantial parts of such contents to another medium.

It is not clear whether the right to prevent re-utilisation of substantial parts of a database continues to apply to those parts after they have been extracted. Suppose, for example, that a competitor of a *sui generis* rightholder without consent or other justification extracts a substantial part of that rightholder's protected database and adds it to the competitor's own database, where it is not identifiable as having been part of the first rightholder's collection. Suppose also that an innocent third party, with the licence of the competitor, extracts from the competitor's database and re-utilises copies of the same material that was originally and wrongfully extracted from the first rightholder's database. Does the innocent third party infringe the *sui generis* right of the first rightholder? Would recognising the third party's act as an infringement be to create a right over the extracted contents of that database, contrary to Recital 46, and equivalent to creating a right over information as such?

Even without creating a right over the extracted contents of a database, the *sui generis* right is a powerful protection of those contents which protection is not significantly weaker than copyright in a database. The copyright restricted acts under the Database Directive include temporary or permanent reproduction by any means and in any form of the database, in whole or in part[3]. This is to be compared with the *sui generis* restricted act of extraction by permanent or temporary transfer of all or a substantial part of the contents of a database to another medium by any means or in any form.

Both temporary reproduction and temporary transfer to another medium are likely to occur when a copy of a database on an electronic carrier, for example a CD-ROM, is transferred to machine memory in the course of searching the database. The distinction between 'in whole or in part' (copyright) and 'all or a substantial part' (*sui generis* right) is important, but may not be significant when considering potential infringement by searching of a database carried on a CD-ROM. If this is a correct analysis, both copyright and the *sui generis* right potentially control the searching of a database carried on portable electronic media, although the rights to control searching will be vested in different classifications of rightholders: authors, in relation to copyright, and makers, in relation to the *sui generis* right.

Both copyright and the *sui generis* right are subject to exceptions in favour of lawful users: these exceptions are considered in **2.4** below. Each right also has a different

---

1   Database Directive, Recital 44.
2   Database Directive, Recital 46.
3   Database Directive, Art 5(a).

term of protection. For copyright, the current usual term of 70 years from the end of the year of death of the author is applicable, and the Database Directive is expressly without prejudice to Community provisions relating to the term of protection of copyright[1]. For the *sui generis* right, the term of protection is prescribed as 15 years from 1 January of the year following the date of completion of the database[2]. There is an exceptional provision for databases which are made available to the public before expiry of this period: this gives such databases a 15-year term from 1 January of the year following the date when the database was first made available to the public[3].

More significantly, any substantial change, evaluated qualitatively or quantitatively, to the contents of a database, including any substantial change resulting from the accumulation of successive additions, deletions or alterations, which would result in the database being considered to be a substantial new investment, evaluated qualitatively or quantitatively, is to qualify the database resulting from that investment for its own term of protection[4]. In the result, any database requiring regular updating or verification[5] has potential for achieving a succession of 15-year terms through regularly updated editions, so that while an old edition may fall out of protection at the end of 15 years from the year of its completion, a succession of updated editions can be permanently within the *sui generis* right.

Since the *sui generis* right is not a right which conforms or is required to conform to the Berne Convention or any other international treaty, other than the TRIPs agreement, there is no equivalent right yet available outside the EEA. The Database Directive does not provide for application of the principle of national treatment to the *sui generis* right, and the right is only available to database makers or rightholders who or which are nationals of a Member State or have their habitual residence in the territory of the Community[6]. This provision also applies to companies and firms formed in accordance with the law of a Member State or having their registered office, central administration or principal place of business within the Community: however, where such a company or firm has only its registered office in the territory of the Community, its operation must be genuinely linked on an on-going basis with the economy of a Member State[7]. Provision is made for extending the *sui generis* right to databases made in third countries under agreements concluded by the Council, but the term of any such protection is not to exceed that available under Art 10[8], namely 15 years.

The *sui generis* right is to be available in respect of databases the making of which was completed on or after 1 January 1983 and which at 1 January 1998 fulfilled the Database Directive's requirements for *sui generis* right protection[9], but without prejudice to any acts completed or rights acquired prior to 1 January 1998[10].

---

1 Database Directive, Art 2(c).
2 Database Directive, Art 10(1).
3 Database Directive, Art 10(2).
4 Database Directive, Art 10(3).
5 For new investment involving verification, see Database Directive, Recital 55.
6 Database Directive, Art 11(1).
7 Database Directive, Art 11(2).
8 Database Directive, Art 11(3).
9 Database Directive, Art 14(3).
10 Database Directive, Art 14(4).

2.4   THE COMPULSORY LICENSING PROVISIONS AND LAWFUL USER AND OTHER EXCEPTIONS

The Commission's original proposal for a directive included compulsory licensing provisions under the *sui generis* right which were to apply to databases made publicly available:

- if the works or materials contained in the database could not be independently created, collected or obtained from any other source; or
- if the data had been made publicly available by a public body which was either established to assemble or disclose information pursuant to legislation, or was under a general duty to do so[1].

These provisions were explained and justified in Recitals to the original proposal, which referred to the interests of competition and the obligations of public bodies[2].

The compulsory licensing provisions did not appear in the Database Directive as adopted, and the related Recitals were replaced in the Database Directive by a single Recital referring to competition rules and a requirement that the *sui generis* right must not be used in such a way as to facilitate abuses of a dominant position[3]. This Recital appears to indicate that refusals to grant licences on fair and non-discriminatory terms may be at risk of challenge by the Commission under Arts 85 or 86 of the EC Treaty.[4]

Both the Commission's original proposal and the Database Directive as adopted included exceptions to the restricted acts for copyright and the *sui generis* right. These exceptions as expressed in the original proposal were elaborated and extended in later versions and in the Directive as adopted, and may be classified as:

- mandatory exceptions in favour of lawful users (a concept which originated with the Software Directive)[5]; and
- optional exceptions[6] relating to:
  - reproduction or extraction for private purposes from a non-electronic database;
  - reproduction or extraction for the sole purpose of illustration for teaching or scientific research, as long as the source is indicated and to the extent justified by the non-commercial purpose to be achieved; and
  - reproduction or extraction for the purpose of public security or for the purposes of an administrative or judicial procedure.

A Recital makes clear that 'scientific research' is intended to cover both the natural sciences and the human sciences[7].

---

1   First Proposal, Art 8(1) and (2).
2   First Proposal, Recitals 31 to 35.
3   Database Directive, Recital 47.
4   In August 1997, the Court of Appeal of Amsterdam in the Netherlands held in *Denda International v KPN* that a refusal by the Dutch PTT to license its 'White Pages' telephone directories for re-publication on CD-ROM would be an abuse of a dominant market position.
5   Database Directive, Arts 6(1) and 8.
6   Database Directive, Arts 6(2) and 9.
7   Database Directive, Recital 36.

Where other exceptions to copyright which are traditionally authorised under national laws are involved, they may continue but subject to the provisions relating to optional exceptions and to non-commercial purposes referred to above[1].

The term 'lawful user' is not defined either in the original proposal or in the Database Directive. In the Software Directive, and in the original proposal for the Database Directive, the term 'a person having a right to use' was coupled with the term 'lawful acquirer', but that latter term does not appear in the Database Directive as adopted.

The concepts of a lawful acquirer and a lawful user appear to have been conflated in the Database Directive, so that a lawful acquirer of a copy of a database on a physical carrier, for example a CD-ROM, may be deemed to be a lawful user of that copy, unless a valid contractual obligation restricts his lawful use. Such contractual provisions are themselves subject to restrictions under the Database Directive[2].

Lawful user rights under copyright and the *sui generis* right are differently expressed in the Database Directive. Under copyright, a lawful user may perform any of the copyright restricted acts which are necessary for the purposes of access to the contents of a copyright protected database, and normal use of the contents of such a database by the user shall not require the authorisation of the author of the database. Presumably, this equally applies to the author's assignee or any other copyright rightholder, including for example the author's employer. In each case, the lawful user may be limited to the part or parts of the database which he is authorised to use[3].

Three points are to be noted:

(1) the lawful user of a copyright database needs no consent from the author or other copyright rightholder to access the contents of those parts of the database which the lawful user is authorised to use, even though such access may involve any of the copyright restricted acts;
(2) the lawful user may be restricted to part of the database; and
(3) other contractual provisions contrary to the lawful user right are void[4].

The lawful user exception under the *sui generis* right is differently expressed. The exception only applies to a database which has been made available to the public 'in any manner whatever'. The Database Directive contains no definition of either 'made available' or 'the public'. The exception prohibits the maker of a database which has been made available to the public from preventing the extraction and/or re-utilisation of insubstantial parts of the database's contents by a lawful user for any purposes whatsoever, but the right only attaches to the part or parts of the database which the lawful user is authorised to extract and/or re-utilise[5]. As for copyright, any other contractual restriction on the lawful user right is void[6].

There are three points to be noted:

---

1   Database Directive, Art 6(2)(d).
2   Database Directive, Art 15.
3   Database Directive, Art 6(1).
4   Database Directive, Art 15.
5   Database Directive, Art 8(1).
6   Database Directive, Art 15.

(1) in contrast to copyright, the *sui generis* lawful user right does not attach to a database unless it has been made available to the public;

(2) as for copyright, the right only attaches to parts of the database to which the lawful user has authorised access; and

(3) in contrast to copyright, the right is limited to extraction and/or re-utilisation of insubstantial parts of the contents of the database.

In the latter case, it is not clear whether intermediate temporary extraction of substantial parts of the database in order to search for and extract an insubstantial part is permitted. The Database Directive provides that 'the maker ... may not prevent ... a lawful user ... from extracting insubstantial parts ... for any purposes whatsoever'[1], so that perhaps, even if the lawful user right does not expressly extend to temporary extraction of substantial parts by searching to enable extraction of an insubstantial part, the maker may not exercise his *sui generis* right so as to prevent searching necessary to the extraction of an insubstantial part, unless the searching involves access to parts of the database to which the lawful user did not have authorised access.

In the case of copyright, the lawful user right is not to be interpreted or applied in a manner which unreasonably prejudices the rightholder's legitimate interests or which conflicts with normal exploitation of the protected work[2]. In the case of the *sui generis* right, the lawful user right is not to be exercised so as to cause prejudice to the holder of a copyright or a related right in respect of the works or subject matter contained in the database[3].

The optional exceptions which Member States may elect to provide for teaching and research are not to extend to commercial purposes, and copyright exceptions traditionally authorised under the national laws of Member States are similarly restricted. Accordingly, research which has a commercial purpose cannot be justified under the permitted exceptions, or in the UK under the fair dealing provisions of s 29 of the CDPA. This prohibition only applies to databases as defined: it does not, for example, apply to computer programs or to collections or compilations which do not fall within the Database Directive's definition of a database.

2.5   THE DATABASE DIRECTIVE AS ADOPTED

Directive 96/9/EC of the European Parliament and of the Council on the Legal Protection of Databases was adopted on 11 March 1996, and was published in the *Official Journal* on 27 March 1996. Its 60 Recitals and 16 Articles compare with the 40 Recitals and 14 Articles of the original proposal as presented by the Commission on 13 May 1992, and its provisions were both broadened and simplified from the terms of the original proposal.

Key changes reflected in the Database Directive as adopted, by comparison with the Commission's original proposal, include:

---

1   Database Directive, Art 8(1).
2   Database Directive, Art 6(3).
3   Database Directive, Art 7(5).

–   extension of the scope of the Database Directive to databases in any form, where the original proposal had been limited to electronic databases;

–   a significantly amended definition of the term 'database';

–   separation of the Database Directive's provisions relating to copyright and the *sui generis* right respectively into different chapters, followed by a chapter of common provisions applicable to both;

–   making copyright and the *sui generis* right more distinct and potentially more cumulative, so that a database as defined by the Database Directive may be protected by either, by both, or by neither depending on different criteria and independently of each other; and

–   removal of the original proposal's compulsory licensing provisions under the *sui generis* right.

Provisions of the original proposal which have been preserved and incorporated into the Database Directive include:

–   the copyright criterion of originality requiring a database to be its author's own intellectual creation, and a provision that no other criteria may be applied to determine a database's eligibility for that protection;

–   the concept of the *sui generis* right, with its own restricted acts of extraction and re-utilisation, protecting a maker's investment, and distinct from copyright protecting the author's creativity;

–   lawful user rights applying to both copyright and the *sui generis* right; and

–   application of the principle of Community exhaustion of the distribution right in a copy of a copyright database by the first sale in the Community of that copy with the consent of the copyright rightholder.

Some features in the Database Directive as adopted were either new or dealt with issues which had not been fully appreciated or reflected in earlier versions of the Commission's proposal.

Such features include the definition of a database, which was re-cast at a late stage to refer to 'a collection of independent works, data or other materials'. The requirement of independence was apparently to exclude from the definition works which comprise elements of content capable of standing alone as works in their own right and of being accessed, read or used independently of one another, but which in reality form part of the compiled complete work.

Recital 17 of the Database Directive states:

> 'Whereas the term "database" should be understood to … cover collections of independent works, data or other materials which are systematically or methodically arranged and can be individually accessed … [and] this means that a recording of an audiovisual, cinematographic, literary or musical work as such does not fall within the scope of this Directive.'

The example of single frames in a cinematographic film, each frame being capable of being used as a still picture, is clear. Equally, a symphony comprising movements each capable of being performed separately but each being dependent upon one another in the context of the symphony as a whole, is clear: in either of these cases the component works are not independent of one another in the context of their incorporation into the larger work, which accordingly is excluded from the definition of a 'database'. Less clear is the possibility of a collection of short stories, all by the same author and with similar characters in similar settings but not dependent upon one another as to detail, plot or sequence. Are these 'independent works' in the context of the book as a whole? Would their being set sequentially in time make them 'dependent', in that they together represent the growth of characters or development of an overriding scenario, so as to prevent the collection as a whole from being a database?

In the case of collections of data, other considerations may apply. A compilation of records of stock exchange transactions may range from being a record of transactions as they occur to a tabulation ordered by value, stocks, parties or other characteristics. At what stage will such a collection be or cease to be a collection of 'independent' data, so as to fall within or outside the definition of a database? If the collection is a database, it may qualify for protection under the *sui generis* right but cannot be protected by copyright unless it is its author's own intellectual creation: if it is not a database, it may still be protected by copyright under the national laws of one or more of the Member States notwithstanding its lack of human creativity, but it cannot be protected by the Community *sui generis* right.

A significant feature of the Database Directive as adopted, by comparison with earlier versions, is the addition at a late stage in the proposal's development of a provision allowing databases which were in existence and protected under copyright arrangements in a Member State on 27 March 1996, but which do not fulfil the originality criterion for copyright protection laid down by Art 3(1) of the Database Directive, to continue to enjoy copyright protection in that Member State for the remaining term of protection afforded to them under that Member State's arrangements[1]. Conversely, a database, as defined, created after 27 March 1996 which is not its author's own intellectual creation is required by the Database Directive to be excluded from copyright protection under the laws of each of the Member States as from 1 January 1998, the date by which Member States were required by the Database Directive to have complied with its terms.

As can be seen by comparison of the Database Directive as adopted with the original proposal, there has been considerable modification and elaboration of the initial concept borne out of the points raised in the Commission's 1988 Copyright Green Paper. Some points have emerged during the course of the Community legislative process, but have later been abandoned or reversed. Some of these have started as clear statements of principal but have later become de-emphasised: they remain as issues not fully resolved and are capable of re-emerging as major uncertainties.

One such uncertainty concerns the extent to which a computer program can be protected both by copyright under the Software Directive and by copyright and by the *sui generis* right under the Database Directive. The original proposal for the Database Directive defined a database as including 'the electronic materials necessary for the operation of [a] database (such as its thesaurus, index or system for obtaining or presenting information)', but as excluding 'any computer program used in the making

---

1   Database Directive, Art 14(2).

or operation of the database'[1]. The Database Directive as adopted has modified and transferred the inclusive words to a Recital as 'protection under this Directive may also apply to the materials necessary for the operation or consultation of certain databases such as thesaurus and indexation systems'[2], but has retained within its Article on the scope of the Database Directive an express exclusion of computer programs used in the making or operation of databases accessible by electronic means[3].

In the absence of any definition of the term 'computer program', it is unclear in what circumstances a collection of independent works, data or other materials which is, or may be, a computer program can be included within the definition of a database, and so protectable either under the Software Directive or the Database Directive or both.

An article-by-article comparison of the original proposal and the Database Directive as adopted is possible but is not attempted in this chapter. The full text of the Database Directive as adopted appears in Appendix 1, with a commentary, and now stands as the relevant Community legislation on the legal protection of databases. Uncertainties of interpretation of the Database Directive are likely to arise. This chapter has attempted to draw out of the changes made during the Community legislative process indications of where policy has identified issues and has moved to resolve them. Many more unresolved issues, beyond those indicated in this chapter and those identified during the legislative process, no doubt remain to be discovered and resolved, perhaps ultimately by the European Court of Justice in Luxembourg.

---

1   First Proposal, Art 1(1).
2   Database Directive, Recital 20.
3   Database Directive, Art 1(3).

Chapter 3

UK IMPLEMENTATION OF THE DATABASE DIRECTIVE: THE COPYRIGHT AND RIGHTS IN DATABASES REGULATIONS 1997, SI 1997/3032[1]

3.1 Legal effect of the Database Directive – 3.2 Interpretation of national legislation to comply with EC law, and the possibility of obtaining damages against the State for failure to implement – 3.3 The European Communities Act 1972 – 3.4 The structure and main content of the Database Regulations

3.1   LEGAL EFFECT OF THE DATABASE DIRECTIVE

The Database Directive, like all directives adopted under the EC Treaty, required implementation in national law in order to enter into effect. A directive is a form of legislation adopted under the EC Treaty, in this case by the European Parliament and the Council. It is addressed to the Member States, and requires them to ensure that the legal provisions of national law are in conformity with its provisions by a certain date. The EC Treaty provides that directives are 'binding as to the end to be achieved' on each Member State to which they are addressed while leaving 'the choice of form and methods' open to the Member State[2].

Member States must ensure that they adopt all necessary measures to implement a directive, in accordance with the objective it pursues. While this usually means the adoption of laws, regulations or administrative provisions to give effect to the requirements of a directive, that is not always the case. The adoption of new legal Acts is clearly not necessary, for example, where there are existing legal provisions which are sufficient[3], and in exceptional cases, general principles of constitutional or administrative law may be adequate[4]. However, where it is proposed to rely on such general principles, then the legal position arising from those principles must be sufficiently precise and clear to those who are intended to acquire rights under the directive, and it must be assured that they are fully aware of their rights.

---

1   Hereafter referred to as 'the Database Regulations'.
2   Article 189(3) of the EC Treaty.
3   Case C-190/79, *Commission v Belgium* [1980] ECR 1473, para 11; Case C-360/87, *Commission v Italy* [1991] ECR 1–791, para 11.
4   Case 29/84, *Commission v Germany* [1985] ECR 1661, para 23.

While no specific legal form is required for implementation, it is not sufficient to rely on administrative practice, which can by its nature be changed by the authorities at will[1].

National legislation does not have to transpose the provisions of a directive verbatim[2], provided that the objective set out by the directive is achieved. For this reason, details of the legislation may vary in every Member State, although the same ends must be achieved in all Member States.

3.1.1 What can be done when a Member State fails properly to implement a directive?

A directive clearly involves an obligation on Member States to implement its requirements in a sufficient and appropriate manner, but what do the provisions of a directive mean for the individual person or company affected by its terms? What can such an individual person or company do when a Member State has either not implemented a directive at all, or has failed properly to implement some aspect of a directive?

The Commission has the primary role in ensuring that Member States properly implement directives. Where the Commission considers that a Member State has not complied with its obligations, it will first attempt to resolve the situation by informally contacting the Member State concerned to notify it of its alleged failure. This may be enough in itself to bring about a resolution of the case. If there is no satisfactory outcome at this stage, the Commission may use its powers under Art 169 of the EC Treaty to bring the Member State before the European Court of Justice. For these purposes, it must first send a letter of formal notice to the Member State outlining the grounds of objection and requesting a response. If the response from the Member State is still not adequate, then the Commission may continue to the next stage, in which it issues a 'reasoned opinion' to the relevant Member State explaining why it considers an infringement has occurred and requiring the Member State to remedy it within a certain period. If the infringement is not remedied within the time-limit, the Commission may commence proceedings in the European Court of Justice. The initial intervention of the Commission often starts because a complaint has been made by an individual person or company. However, the length of time taken for the procedure to run its course within the Commission and before the European Court of Justice often means that making a complaint may not be an appropriate option for a person or company needing a more immediate solution. On the other hand, many Member States decide to modify their laws to comply with the applicable directive in the required manner at an early stage of the process.

---

1   Case 339/87, *Commission v Netherlands* [1990] ECR I-851, para 25; Case C-131/88, *Commission v Germany* [1991] ECR I-825, para 8; Case C-361/88, *Commission v Germany* [1991] ECR I-2567, para 24; Case C-221/94, *Commission v Luxembourg* [1996] ECR I-5669, para 22.

2   Case 363/85, *Commission v Italy* [1987] ECR 1733, para 7; Case C-131/88, *Commission v Germany* [1991] ECR I-825, para 6.

3.1.2 Relying on a directive against other persons or companies

Can a person or company seek to enforce a directive by relying on its terms in a national court or, in the terms used in European law, does a directive have 'direct effect'? The solution developed by EC law is that a directive may, in certain cases, have direct effect against the State (so called 'vertical direct effect') but it may not be relied on against other companies or persons (so called 'horizontal direct effect').

The reasoning behind the European Court of Justice's refusal to accept that a directive can be relied on by a person or company against another person or company was outlined in the case of *Marshall v Southampton and South-West Hampshire Area Health Authority*[1]. It is that the binding nature of a directive is the only basis on which such a right could be based, and Art 189 of the EC Treaty indicates that a directive is binding on the Member States to which it is addressed as opposed to being binding on persons within those Member States. Consequently, according to the European Court of Justice, it follows that a directive may not, of itself, impose obligations on a person or company and that a provision of a directive may not be relied upon as such against such a person or company. There have been further attempts to persuade the European Court of Justice to change its mind on this issue since the *Marshall* case in 1996, but without success[2].

3.1.3 Relying on a directive against a Member State

While reliance on a directive against other persons or companies is not possible, it is in some circumstances possible to rely on the terms of a directive against a Member State, or 'emanations of the State'.

The original justification for the principle of vertical direct effect of directives developed by the European Court of Justice was that it would be incompatible with the binding effect of directives, and would reduce the effectiveness of directives if the possibility of direct effect of directives was excluded[3]. However, in more recent case-law, the reasoning has been that where a Member State has failed to enact legislation fully implementing a directive by the deadline set for its implementation, then it cannot rely on its own failure to adopt legislation as against persons or companies[4].

Direct effect of a directive as against a Member State cannot be claimed until the date for implementation of the directive has passed[5], but after that time, it can be claimed in

---

1   Case C-152/84, *Marshall v Southampton and South-West Hampshire Area Health Authority (Teaching)* [1986] ECR 723, at para 48.
2   Case 14/86, *Pretore di Salò v Persons unknown* [1987] ECR 2545, para 19; Case 80/86, *Kolpinghuis Nijmegen* [1987] ECR 3969, para 9; Case C-106/89, *Marleasing SA v La Comercial Internacional de Alimentación SA* [1990] ECR I-4135, para 6; Case C-192/94, *El Corte Inglés SA v Blázquez Rivero* [1996] ECR I 1281, para 18; Case C 168/95, *Arcaro* [1996] ECR I-4705, para 36; Cases C-74/95 and C-129/95, *Procura Della Repubblica v X* [1997] 1 CMLR 399, para 23. Case C-91/92, *Faccini Dori v Recreb Srl* [1994] ECR I-3325, para 24. See, however, Case C-472/93, *Spano v Fiat Geotech SpA* [1995] ECR I-4321, paras 17–18.
3   Case 41/74, *Van Duyn v Home Office* [1974] ECR 1337–1353.
4   Case 148/78, *Criminal Proceedings against Tullio Ratti* [1979] ECR 1629–1647; Case C-91/92, *Faccini Dori v Recreb Srl* [1994] ECR I-3325.
5   Case 148/78, *Criminal Proceedings against Tullio Ratti* [1979] ECR 1629–1647.

respect of a failure to comply fully with the terms of a directive even where the Member State purports to have implemented the directive[1].

It should be noted that the principle of direct effect does not give persons or companies the right to demand that a directive be implemented[2], but only provides that the State cannot rely, as against individuals or companies, on provisions of national law which are inconsistent with a directive.

The principle is not reciprocal, so that the State cannot rely on the unimplemented terms of a directive against individuals. Equally, terms of a directive cannot have the effect of determining or aggravating the liability in criminal law of persons who act in contravention of its provisions[3].

There are also further conditions which must apply before the provisions of a directive may be relied on by individuals or companies:

- the provisions of the directive must be intended to create rights for individuals;
- the provisions of the directive must be unconditional;
- the provisions of the directive must be sufficiently precise to be enforced against a Member State or a State entity.

The concept of 'State entity' has been widely defined by the European Court of Justice to include any body, 'whatever its legal form, which has been made responsible, pursuant to a measure adopted by the State, for providing a public service under the control of the State and has for that purpose special powers beyond those which result form the normal rules applicable in relations between individuals'[4]. The concept of State entity has been held to include, for example, local and municipal authorities, local health authorities, chief constables of the police and bodies entrusted with public service duties. Cases decided in the courts in the UK stress that both the elements of: (1) State control; and (2) of having a special power to provide a public service, are necessary[5]. However, it has been argued that the cases decided in the European Court of Justice only require that one of these elements be present. Notwithstanding the restrictive approach of the UK courts, the High Court has decided that a privatised water company came within the concept of a State entity for the purposes of direct effect[6].

The Database Directive stipulates that each Member State must introduce legislation based on the Database Directive by 1 January 1998. Since some Member States have not yet introduced such legislation, this raises the further issue of whether there is any other way, apart from the principle of direct effect, that an individual in such Member

---

1   Case 51/76, *Verbond van Nederlandse Ondernemingen v Inspecteur der Invoerrechten en Accijnzen* [1977] ECR 113–129.
2   Case C-168/95, *Arcaro* [1996] ECR I-4705 16.
3   Case 14/86, *Pretore di Salò v Persons unknown* [1987] ECR 2545, para 20; Case 80/86, *Kolpinghuis Nijmegen* [1987] ECR 3969, para 13; Case C-168/95, *Arcaro* [1996] ECR I-4705, para 37; Cases C-74/95 and C-129/95, *Procura Della Repubblica v X* [1997] 1 CMLR 399, para 24. See, however, Case C-373/90, *Complaint Against X* [1992] ECR I-131.
4   C-188/89, *Foster v British Gas* [1990] ECR I-3313.
5   *Doughty v Rolls-Royce plc* [1992] IRLR 126; *Fidge v Governing Body of St Mary's Church of England Aided School* (1994) *The Times*, 9 November; *Griffin v South West Water Co Ltd* [1995] IRLR 15.
6   *Griffin v South West Water Co Ltd* [1995] IRLR 15.

States can take action on the basis of the Database Directive. That question is dealt with in the following sections.

3.2 INTERPRETATION OF NATIONAL LEGISLATION TO COMPLY WITH EC LAW, AND THE POSSIBILITY OF OBTAINING DAMAGES AGAINST THE STATE FOR FAILURE TO IMPLEMENT

3.2.1   Interpreting national legislation to comply with EC law

While it is not possible for individuals or companies to rely directly on a directive in national courts, Art 5 of the EC Treaty requires that States should 'take all necessary measures' to ensure fulfilment of their Community obligations. This has been determined by the European Court of Justice to apply to all authorities of the State, including the national courts. Consequently, the national courts are obliged to interpret national law, so far as possible, to ensure that the objectives of a directive are fulfilled[1]. This has been applied by the House of Lords in the UK, in the *Lister* case[2]. This concerned the interpretation of UK regulations designed to implement an EC directive guaranteeing employees rights in the event of the transfer of the undertaking for which they work. The House of Lords was prepared to interpret the regulations in a way which was contrary to their prima facie meaning in order to comply with the relevant directive, on the basis that the regulations in question had been introduced in order to comply with that directive. The extent of the principle was taken a step further in the *Marleasing* case[3]. That case involved a reference to the European Court of Justice from a Spanish court. The facts were that an EC directive provided for an exhaustive list of the situations where the formation of a company could be found to be void. The Spanish court had to determine whether the fact that a company had been formed with the purpose of defrauding creditors meant that the formation of the company was void. Under Spanish law, it was argued that, by analogy with the general law applying to contracts, the formation of a company could be void for 'lack of cause' in the circumstances of the case. This was not one of the bases of nullity which was permitted by the relevant EC directive. However, in contrast to the *Lister* case considered above, the EC directive had not been implemented in Spain at the relevant time. The European Court of Justice's judgment was that the obligation to interpret national law in the light of the requirements and purposes of the directive in order to achieve the result pursued by the directive applied whether the national provisions in question were adopted before or after the directive. The European Court of Justice ruled, without qualification, that national courts were required to interpret domestic law in such a way as to ensure that the objectives of the directive were achieved. This appeared to be a far-reaching obligation on national courts, which were effectively bound to read the obligations of the directive into the existing law in all circumstances. Later cases have, however, limited the scope of this obligation. In

---

1   Case 14/83, *Sabine von Colson and Elisabeth Kamann v Land Nordrhein-Westfalen* [1984] ECR 1891–1911; Case 79/83, *Dorit Harz v Deutsche Tradax GmbH* [1984] ECR 1921–1944.
2   *Lister v Forth Dry Dock and Engineering Co Ltd* [1990] 1 AC 546.
3   Case C-106/89, *Marleasing SA v La Comercial Internacional de Alimentación SA* [1990] ECR I-4135, para 6.

particular, the European Court of Justice has recognised that while courts should presume that compliance with the objectives of a directive is intended, sometimes the provisions of domestic legislation cannot be interpreted in such a way as to achieve the result intended by a directive[1]. Consequently, the doctrine reaches its limit where the provisions of national law clearly contradict the provisions of the directive. This appears to have been recognised in cases which have come before the courts in the UK since *Marleasing*[2].

3.2.2 Actions for damages against Member States for failure to implement a directive

Where it is not possible to benefit from the doctrine of direct effect of a directive because the other party to an action is a person or company, and where it is not possible to construe legislation to comply with a directive, it may still be possible to recover damages from the relevant Member State where damage has been suffered as a result of a Member State's failure to enact national legislation implementing the directive. The basic principles for such action were laid down in the *Francovich* case of 1991[3]. That case concerned a directive aimed at protecting workers in the event of insolvency of their employers, by requiring Member States to establish a guarantee fund to ensure payment of arrears of wages in such a situation. Italy had failed to set up such a guarantee fund. Two employees, Francovich and Bonifaci, made a claim against the State. They were not able to claim that the directive was directly effective, because the provisions were not sufficiently clear, precise and unconditional. However, it was found by the European Court of Justice that they would have a claim against the State in damages, since, although the details of the fund allowed a discretion as to the appointment of the guarantee institution, which was sufficient to negate the directive's direct effect, the intended class of beneficiaries and the content of the right were clear.

Three basic conditions for Member State liability in damages have been developed through this and subsequent cases[4]:

(1) the relevant provision of the directive must have been intended to confer rights on individuals;
(2) the breach must be sufficiently serious;
(3) there must be a direct causal link between the breach of the obligation resting on the State and the damage sustained by the injured parties.

The requirement that there should be a sufficiently serious breach of Community law means that the institution of the State concerned must have manifestly and gravely exceeded the limits of its discretion. For these purposes the following factors are

---

1   Case C-334/92, *Teodoro Wagner Miret v Fondo de Garantía Salarial* [1993] ECR I-6911.
2   *Webb v EMO (Air Cargo) (UK) Ltd* [1993] 1 WLR 102, [1992] 4 All ER 929, [1993] ICR 175, HL, Lord Keith of Kinkel obiter; *R v British Coal Corporation, ex parte Vardy* [1993] ICR 720.
3   Joined Cases C-6/90 and C-9/90, *Andrea Francovich and Danila Bonifaci and others v Italian Republic* [1991] ECR I-5357.
4   Joined Cases C-6/90 and C-9/90, *Andrea Francovich and Danila Bonifaci and others v Italian Republic* [1991] ECR I-5357; Joined Cases C-46/93 and C-48/93, *Brasserie du Pêcheur SA v Bundesrepublik Deutschland* and *The Queen v Secretary of State for Transport, ex parte Factortame Ltd and others* [1996] ECR I-1029.

relevant: the clarity and precision of the rule breached; the measure of discretion left by that rule to the relevant authorities; whether the infringement and the damage caused was intentional or voluntary; whether any error of law was excusable or inexcusable; and the fact that the position taken by a Community institution may have contributed to the breach[1]. It is not necessary to prove fault or intention on the part of the Member State, but merely that the breach is sufficiently serious.

Where a Member State fails to take any measure to transpose a directive within the deadline, this constitutes *per se* a serious breach of EC law[2]. As regards the question of whether or not the obligation set out in a directive is sufficiently precise, the Court of Justice found in the case of *R v HM Treasury, ex parte British Telecommunications plc* that an error in interpreting the relevant directive was not a sufficiently serious breach where the relevant article was imprecisely worded, and was reasonably capable of bearing the interpretation given to it by the UK in good faith, where there were substantial arguments for that interpretation, and where the interpretation was also shared by other Member States[3]. However, it may be different where there is existing jurisprudential indication as to the correct interpretation of the provision in question or where the Commission has offered interpretative indications at the time the rules were adopted.

The European Court of Justice has held that in the absence of EC harmonisation in damages, it is for the law of the Member State concerned to fix the type and amount of damages available, but such national law must not fix conditions which are less favourable than those which concern similar claims brought under national law, nor should they make it practically impossible or excessively difficult to obtain damages[4].

3.3 THE EUROPEAN COMMUNITIES ACT 1972[5]

The EC Act provides that Community law shall prevail over UK law, including Acts of Parliament both past and future, in any case of conflict. The EC Act empowers the Crown, by order in Council, and any designated Minister or Department, by Regulations, to make any alteration to UK law necessary for the purpose of implementing Community obligations or exercising Community rights or related matters. These powers are subject to a list of exceptions set out in the EC Act[6].

The scope of Community law is itself limited by the European Treaties, for example by Titles V and VI of the Treaty on European Union (the Maastricht Treaty), and by

---

1 Joined Cases C-46/93 and C-48/93, *Brasserie du Pêcheur SA v Bundesrepublik Deutschland and The Queen v Secretary of State for Transport, ex parte Factortame Ltd and others* [1996] ECR I-1029.

2 Case C-6/90 and C-9/90, *Francovich*, 19.11.91 and in Joined Cases C-178/94, C-179/84, C-188/94 and C-190/94, *Erich Dillenkofer and others v Bundesrepublik Deutschland* [1996] ECR I- 4845.

3 Case C-392/93, *R v HM Treasury, ex parte British Telecommunications plc* [1996] QB 615 and Case C-283/94, *Denkavit International BV v Bundesamt fur Finanzen* [1996] STC 1445.

4 Cases C-46/93 and C-48/93, *Brasserie du pecheur SA v Bundesrepublik Deutschland* [1996] ECR I-1029.

5 Hereafter referred to as the 'EC Act'.

6 EC Act, s 2(2) as amended by s 1 of the European Economic Area Act 1993.

the principle of subsidiarity. Precise definition of the limits of Community law is difficult, and issues have arisen from the resulting uncertainty: for example, the extent to which rights of intellectual property under national laws are within the scope of Community law. Further examination of these fundamental issues on Community law is not attempted here.

Aside from these uncertainties, the basic principles under which the EC Act is to be applied are as follows:

–   within the scope of Community law, the UK is obliged by EC Treaty obligations to give precedence to Community law;
–   Community law now extends to the whole of the EEA, by virtue of the European Economic Area Agreement ('EEA Agreement'[1]). The EC Act was amended by s 1 of the European Economic Area Act 1993 (the 'EEA Act') so as to enable regulations to be made under s 2(2) of the EC Act to implement obligations of the UK arising under the EEA Agreement;
–   the EC Act, as so amended, empowers Ministers designated for the purpose of s 2(2) of the EC Act, as amended, in exercise of powers conferred by s 2(2) and (4) of the EC Act to make regulations to give effect to Community directives to the extent that such directives are within the scope of Community law and to the extent that the regulations made are necessary for compliance with such directives;
–   although regulations made under the EC Act can amend or repeal Acts of Parliament in force at the time such regulations are made, it is arguable that the regulations will be *ultra vires* if they purport to amend UK law in any respect either:
    (1)   outside the scope of Community law; or
    (2)   otherwise than as necessary to secure compliance with a Community obligation.

The Community obligation to conform to a directive, and the powers given to Ministers to comply with directives by means of subordinate legislation, are themselves subject to Community law and to proper application of its scope.

It follows that, where a Community obligation requires a change in UK law which will render other aspects of UK law outside the scope of Community law inappropriate, there is neither power for Community institutions to compel changes to UK law which are outside the scope of Community law, nor is there power under the EC Act for Ministers to make such changes without primary legislation.

In such cases, the government must choose between either implementing Community obligations by subordinate legislation in a way which will leave other aspects of UK law in an inconsistent or otherwise unsatisfactory condition, or promoting primary legislation which can change UK law in order to secure compliance with Community law and at the same time make appropriate changes to those other elements of UK law which are outside the scope of Community competence.

---

1   Signed at Oporto on 2 May 1992, as adjusted by the Protocol signed at Brussels on 17 March 1993.

The net result may be, in some circumstances, that Community obligations can require changes to UK law within the scope of Community competence which will render unworkable other, related, aspects of UK law which are outside the scope of Community competence. Although the Community has no power to require the UK to change its law in areas outside the scope of Community competence, the Community's power to compel changes within the scope of Community law may thus in practice compel a change in other areas when, without such change, UK domestic law will become unworkable.

The Database Directive required the Member States of the EEA to bring into force the laws, regulations and administrative provisions necessary to comply with the Database Directive before 1 January 1998[1]. In December 1997, the Secretary of State laid draft Regulations before Parliament for approval by each House under s 2 of and Sch 2, para 2(2) to the EC Act. The draft Regulations were duly approved, were made on 18 December 1997 and came into force on 1 January 1998 as the Copyright and Rights in Databases Regulations 1997 (the 'Database Regulations').

These steps having been taken, UK law has been amended so as to comply, it is hoped, with the Database Directive and, it is also hoped, in terms which are not in excess of the powers delegated by Parliament to the Secretary of State under the EC Act. To the extent, if any, that compliance with the Database Directive has not been effectively achieved, the Database Regulations may be challenged before the UK courts and on reference to the European Court of Justice; to the extent that the Database Regulations may have exceeded the Secretary of State's delegated powers, the Database Regulations may again be challenged before the UK courts but on different grounds, namely that either one or more provisions of the Database Regulations were not necessary to secure compliance with the Database Directive, or, alternatively, that the Database Regulations have purported to make changes to UK law in areas which are beyond the scope of Community competence.

3.4 THE STRUCTURE AND MAIN CONTENT OF THE DATABASE REGULATIONS

The full text of the Database Regulations appears, with commentary, in Appendix 4 and other aspects of the Database Regulations are considered in detail in other chapters. The purpose of this section of this chapter is to give an overview of the structure of the Database Regulations, and the way the Secretary of State has sought to give effect, by means of the Database Regulations, to the obligation to comply with the Database Directive within the scope of Community law and within the limitations imposed by the nature of the Database Regulations as secondary legislation under the EC Act. This section does not attempt to give detailed interpretation or evaluation of particular provisions of the Database Regulations, as to which see later chapters in this book.

The Database Regulations are arranged in four parts and have two Schedules, as follows:

---

1   Database Directive, Art 16(1).

The original structure of the CDPA has already been amended several times by other Regulations implementing Community directives under the EC Act, notably the Software Regulations which implemented the Software Directive. The Database Regulations have followed the same technique as was adopted under the Software Regulations by inserting amendments directly into the text of the CDPA. Although Part II of the Database Regulations is in consequence difficult to read, once interpolation of its provisions has been made into the CDPA, that Act stands as a coherent statement of those aspects of UK statute law which apply to the new concept of copyright in a database, as defined by the Database Directive.

The amendments made to the CDPA by Part II of the Database Regulations are restricted to aspects of the Database Directive and of the Database Regulations dealing with copyright in databases. Part II of the Database Regulations does not deal with the *sui generis* right, referred to by the Database Regulations as 'database right', and where a change to the CDPA effected by Part II of the Database Regulations has an effect on database right that change is not expressed as referring to database right either in Part II of the Database Regulations or in the CDPA as amended.

For example, reg 6 in Part II of the Database Regulations inserts into the CDPA a new s 3A which defines 'database' in almost exactly the same terms as the Database Directive[1]. This latter definition is relevant to the *sui generis* right, since it determines what collections may qualify as databases under the Database Directive and so may be capable of qualifying for protection under the *sui generis* right. The definition of a database as imported into the CDPA makes no reference to database right: the connection between the new definition in s 3A(1) inserted by the Database Regulations into the CDPA and database right is left to be covered by Part III of the Database Regulations[2].

In addition to importing into the CDPA a new definition of database conforming to the Database Directive's definition, reg 6 of the Database Regulations provides a statutory criterion of originality for literary works which consist of databases, as so defined. The CDPA contains no other criterion of originality in relation to literary works, the skill and labour criterion as applied by the UK courts being judge-made. The skill and labour criterion is overridden, as the Database Directive requires, by the new s 3A(2) of the CDPA, but only in relation to a literary work which consists of a database as defined. Other literary works, notably tables and compilations which do not consist of databases as newly defined, are not referred to by the Database Regulations and so may continue to enjoy the UK's skill and labour criterion. There is, as yet, no Community obligation on the UK to change its criterion of originality for literary works other than databases, as defined by the Database Directive, and

1   Article 1(2).
2   Regulation 12(1).

computer programs, and to effect such a change would require primary legislation[1]. The technique of restricting amendment to the CDPA under Part II of the Database Regulations to amendments necessary to implementation of those provisions of the Database Directive which relate to copyright has enabled Part II of the Database Regulations to be economically drafted, and to be contained in five tautly constructed Regulations. Each of the Part II Regulations has effect only to amend the CDPA: once these changes have been transposed, Part II of the Database Regulations is exhausted.

Part III of and Schs 1 and 2 to the Database Regulations deal exclusively and comprehensively with database right. Database right is a new creation in UK law and Part III of the Database Regulations is the only current domestic legislation which refers to database right. However, the supremacy given by the European Treaties to Community obligations ensures that the provisions of the Database Directive and the EC Act have effect in determining the validity and completeness of Part III of the Database Regulations.

Although Part III of the Database Regulations comprehensively states the new UK law on database right, subject to the ultimate supremacy of the Database Directive, Part III incorporates by reference a limited number of provisions of the CDPA, including the new definition of database established under Part II, reg 6 and the new s 3A(1) of the CDPA. It follows that, to the extent that other provisions of the CDPA might logically have been expected to apply in relation to database right to collections qualifying as databases under the new s 3A(1) of the CDPA, those provisions will not so apply unless they are expressly incorporated by reference into Part III of the Database Regulations. Such incorporation occurs under reg 23 of the Database Regulations in relation to certain copyright provisions of the CDPA so as to apply them to database right[2]. A notable exception from incorporation into database right is s 56 of the CDPA, which applies when a copy of a work in electronic form has been purchased on terms which, expressly or impliedly or by virtue of any rule of law, allow the purchaser to copy the work or to adapt it or make copies of an adaptation, in connection with his use of it. Although s 56 of the CDPA will continue to apply to the copyright protection of databases which are protectable by copyright and to other literary works including computer programs and including compilations which do not qualify as databases, it does not appear to apply to database right. When a copy of a database in electronic form and protected by database right is sold the lawful user rights applicable to database right will apply without regard to the provisions of s 56 of the CDPA.

Part III of the Database Regulations also incorporates Chapter VIII of Part I of the CDPA (copyright tribunal)[3] and refers to certain of the Regulations in Part IV (saving

---

1   There is no mention of computer programs either in reg 6 or in the new s 3A of the CDPA. The Software Directive requires that a computer program shall be protected by copyright only if it is the author's own intellectual creation. This requirement was not reflected in the implementing Software Regulations and so does not appear in the CDPA as amended by those Regulations. It is an open question whether supremacy of the Software Directive will be seen to require intellectual creativity to be substituted for the skill and labour criterion for computer programs, including programs which are generated by computer.

2   Sections 90 to 93 (dealing with rights in copyright works); ss 96 to 98 (rights and remedies of copyright owner); and ss 101 and 102 (rights and remedies of exclusive licensee).

3   Regulation 25(2).

and transitional provisions)[1] and to Schs 1 and 2 to the Database Regulations. These Schedules deal with exceptions to database right for public administration and licensing of database right respectively, and so apply exclusively to database right and not to copyright.

Since the Software Regulations had effect exclusively to incorporate amendments into the CDPA, those regulations need not now be referred to in applying the provisions of the CDPA to copyright in computer programs. The Database Regulations are not so exhausted: they contain the sole statutory statement of UK law relating to database right. They are therefore likely to be with us for some time to come.

---

1   For example, the reference in reg 17(4) in Part III to reg 30 in Part IV.

Chapter 4

COPYRIGHT IN DATABASES AND OTHER COMPILATIONS

4.1 The law as at 31 December 1997 – 4.2 The US law on protection of compilations – 4.3 The Database Directive's copyright requirements – 4.4 The Database Directive's definition of 'database' – 4.5 Copyright protection of tables, compilations and databases after 1 January 1998 – 4.6 The copyright restricted acts – 4.7 Limitations and exceptions – 4.8 Conclusions

4.1   THE LAW AS AT 31 DECEMBER 1997

Since the early nineteenth century, UK law has recognised collections, in the form of tables or compilations, as capable of protection by copyright as literary works. This principle protects anthologies, dictionaries and other literary works which comprise collections of works or other materials provided by different authors or derived from different sources. Copyright in the compilation as such is distinct from copyright in the contents of the collection.

Tables and compilations, like other works, are required to achieve the criterion of originality before they may qualify for protection by copyright. In the UK, this means that sufficient skill, labour or experience must have been applied in the production of the work, and that the work must not have been copied from another work. Mere random collections of information are not protected, nor is 'a selection or arrangement of scraps of information' not involving any real exercise of labour, judgement or skill[1]. However, telegraph codes[2], football pool betting coupons[3], railway timetables[4], street directories and electrical circuit diagrams[5] have all been protected as literary works which are compilations.

What is protected is the author's contribution in finding, choosing and arranging the contents of the compiled collection, such protection being distinct from and additional to the copyright (if any) available to the items of content within the collection which may, or may not, belong to the same author but which is more likely to belong to another person or other persons as being the creator or creators of the separate items of content.

---

1   *GA Cramp and Sons Limited v Frank Smythson Limited* [1944] AC 329.
2   *DP Anderson & Co Ltd v Lieber Code Co* [1917] 2 KB 469.
3   *Ladbroke (Football) Limited v William Hill Football Limited* [1964] 1 WLR (HL).
4   *Leslie v Young and Sons* [1894] AC 335.
5   *Anacon Corporation Ltd v Environmental Research Technology Ltd* [1994] FSR 659. And see *Autospin (Oil Seals) Ltd v Beehive Spinning* [1995] RPC 683.

As at 31 December 1997, the UK's copyright protection for compilations was expressed in the CDPA[1] as follows:

> '1(1) Copyright is a property work which subsists in accordance with this Part in the following descriptions of work—
>   (a) original literary, dramatic, musical or artistic works, ...
> 3(1) "... literary work" means any work, other than a dramatic or musical work, which is written, spoken or sung and accordingly includes—
>   (a) a table or compilation, ...'

This formulation showed tables and compilations to be protected as literary works, without further elaboration or definition of the nature of protectable collections or of the elements which may be comprised within a protected table or compilation. The classification of literary works expressly excludes dramatic or musical works, and a literary work must be written, spoken or sung. 'Writing' includes any form of notation or code, whether by hand or otherwise and regardless of the method by which, or the medium in or on which, it is recorded, and 'written' is to be construed accordingly[2]. It follows that a dramatic or musical work, and any work that is not written, spoken or sung, cannot be a literary work.

Since tables and compilations are sub-classifications of literary works, collections which are not themselves literary works cannot be classified as compilations and protected as literary works.

The word 'collection' is not used in this part of the CDPA, and 'compilation' is not apt to describe collections of three-dimensional or physical materials. A collection as such is not in any event written. 'Compilation' is, however, apt to describe collections of written representations of all forms of works including other literary works, sound recordings, films, photographs, artistic works, works of architecture and works of artistic craftsmanship. It is possible to record by notation, and so 'in writing', digital representations of images, colours, sounds and three-dimensional objects: therefore written digital representations of, for example, the contents of art galleries and of statues and buildings are also possible. Could such collections of written digital representations of works, data or other materials which are not in themselves literary works qualify as compilations?

In *Anacon Corporation Ltd v Environmental Research Technology Ltd*[3], Jacob J held that, in addition to being artistic works, circuit diagrams were literary works, on the basis that they were written down and contained information which could be read, as opposed to merely appreciated by the human eye. Making a list of the components described in the diagrams was held to have been a reproduction of the information which was the literary work contained in the diagrams, and to have infringed them.

In *Autospin (Oil Seals) Ltd v Beehive Spinning*[4], Laddie J considered the nature of literary compilation copyright as covering such diverse works as telegraph codes, football coupons, railway timetables, street directories, novels, electrical circuit

---

1   CDPA, ss 1(1) and 3(1).
2   CDPA, s 178.
3   [1994] FSR 659.
4   [1995] RPC 683.

diagrams and poetry. Infringement required the reproduction, in any form, of the compiler's skill and labour.

Taking the above factors into account, the following may be a reasonable response to the question whether a compilation of written digital representations is to be protected by compilation copyright:

- a copyright work of any protectable class is capable of protection by copyright in accordance with the provisions applicable to works of that class;
- a digital record or representation of a work, or of a three-dimensional item which may or may not be a work, may itself be a work which is written, and so may be protectable as a literary work in accordance with the provisions applicable to literary works;
- a collection of such digital representations which, as a compilation, meets the criterion of originality is capable of protection as a compilation and so as a literary work in its own right, whether or not any or all of such representations are themselves protected by copyright; but
- a physical collection of three-dimensional items (photographs, paintings, statues) is not 'written', so cannot be a literary work, and so is not capable of protection as a compilation which is a form of literary work[1]; and
- a collection of dramatic or musical works, such works being expressly excluded by CDPA, s 3(1) from the classification of literary works is not capable of being a literary work in the form of a compilation, which is a sub-classification of literary works[2]; but
- a compilation of titles of musical and dramatic works is capable of being a literary work.

To be protected by copyright as a literary work under UK law as at 31 December 1997, a compilation must have met the UK's criterion of originality: that is to say, the compilation must not have been copied from another work and must have been the product of its author's exercise of skill, labour and/or judgement.

The scope for exercise of skill, labour and judgement in the making of a compilation will be restricted if the compiled collection is comprehensive (so that no selection for inclusion or exclusion of a particular item is possible) and if the collection is arranged automatically by a computer using a program not written by the compiler of the collection (so not allowing the compiler of the collection any opportunity for the exercise of skill, labour or judgement in the arrangement of the collection). In such a case, originality may arguably be justified by the skill and labour applied in making the compilation comprehensive.

A compilation may be a work which is generated by computer in circumstances such that there is no human author of the work[3], and so may be a computer-generated

---

1   CDPA, s 3(1). See also *Creation Records Ltd v News Group Newspapers Ltd* [1997] EMLR 444
     (arrangement of objects not a work of artistic craftsmanship).
2   See Jacob J in *Anacon Corporation Ltd v Environmental Research Technology Ltd* [1994] FSR
     659, at p 663.
3   CDPA, s 178.

literary work. Its author will then be deemed to be the person by whom the arrangements necessary for the creation of the work were undertaken[1].

Copyright protection for computer-generated works was first introduced under the CDPA. These provisions enable identification of the author of a computer-generated work for copyright purposes: but identification of the author of a work may not in itself be sufficient to qualify the work for copyright protection. In other circumstances, UK law requires that a work shall meet the criterion of originality by demonstrating that the work is the product of its author's exercise of skill, labour and/or judgement. A computer-generated work may meet this criterion: but if the work has been generated by computer in circumstances that there is no human author of the work, as the definition of 'computer-generated' requires[2], a deemed author who undertakes the arrangements necessary for the creation of the work may have no scope for the exercise of skill, labour or judgement in the process. If he has such scope, and exercises skill, labour and judgement, he will be the work's author in his own right, using the computer as a tool with which to create the work: in that case, the work will not qualify as a computer-generated work[3].

As yet, there has been no reported decision of a UK court on the application of the criterion of originality to computer-generated works. If, as may be the case, computer-generated works must still meet the usual criterion of originality it may be that no truly computer-generated compilation is capable of protection by copyright. An alternative view is that the unexpressed intention of the computer-generated provisions of the CDPA was to excuse computer-generated works from the obligation to meet the usual criterion of originality, and it is sufficient that the process of computer-generation should have performed tasks which, had they been performed by a human author, would have involved the exercise of skill and labour. In that case, computer-generated compilations may have a lower criterion of originality applied to them than was to be applied to other compilations prior to 31 December 1997.

4.2   THE US LAW ON PROTECTION OF COMPILATIONS

Before going on to look at the way that the Database Directive dealt with the matter, it will be instructive for us to pause for a moment to glance at the way that the US courts had protected compilations, and more particularly to describe the very important 'Feist' decision, which sent shock waves through publishing houses around the world during the early 1990s because of the threat it appeared to hold to the investment they had made in certain of their compilations.

Until the Supreme Court's 1991 decision in *Feist Publications Inc v Rural Telephone Co Inc*[4], it had been assumed that 'sweat of the brow' in the creation of a copyright work was sufficient to meet the US Copyright Act's criterion of originality. This decision concerned a claimed copyright in the white pages listing of a telephone directory and held that under US copyright law originality, not sweat of the brow, is

---

1   CDPA, s 9(3).
2   CDPA, s 178.
3   *Express Newspapers v Liverpool Daily Post* [1981] 3 All ER 241.
4   111 S Ct 1282 (1991).

the touchstone of copyright protection in directories and other fact-based works. Any reward for 'industrious collection' was held to be beyond the scope of existing US copyright law, which required originality. Accordingly, a compilation is copyrightable in the US only to the extent that it features an original selection, coordination or arrangement of its contents. This contrasts with the law in some other countries, notably the Scandinavian catalogue rule and the Netherlands Copyright Act, which protects non-original writings. In August 1997 this Act was applied by the Court of Appeal of Amsterdam to protect the 'White Pages' telephone directories of the Dutch PTT[1].

The *Feist* judgment referred to the definition of 'compilation' in s 101 of the US Copyright Act 1976 as 'a work formed by the collection and assembly of pre-existing materials or of data that are selected, co-ordinated or arranged in such a way that the resulting work as a whole constitutes an original work of authorship'. This definition is to be contrasted with the CDPA's bare reference to a literary work as including 'a table or compilation'.

The Supreme Court read the US Copyright Act's definition of a compilation as emphasising that collections of fact are not copyrightable *per se*: the US Statute requires, said the Supreme Court, three distinct elements to be present to enable a compilation to qualify for copyrightable compilation, namely:

(1) the collection and assembly of pre-existing material, facts, or data;
(2) the selection, coordination, or arrangement of those materials; and
(3) the creation, by virtue of the particular selection, coordination or arrangement, or an 'original work of authorship'.

This tripartite conjunctive structure, said the Supreme Court, was self-evident and should be assumed accurately to express the legislative purpose.

The *Feist* decision might have opened the floodgates to a spate of litigation alleging that different kinds of telephone directories and other factual listings were not copyrightable, but in *BellSouth Advertising and Publishing Corp v Donnelly Information Publishing Inc* the US Eleventh Circuit Court of Appeals, in June 1991[2], held that a 'Yellow Pages' telephone directory was sufficiently original in format to merit copyright protection as a compilation. The publisher of the directory had exercised selection in setting geographic boundaries, a directory close date, and business classifications. The publisher had also coordinated listings with various categories. These activities were held to be sufficiently creative for the publisher's format of its directory to be copyrightable.

A subsidiary issue was raised in the *BellSouth* case, namely that the publisher in seeking to enforce its copyright was exercising a monopoly power over information and misusing copyright in its format. This, it was said, was anti-competitive conduct and contrary to the Sherman Act. The abuse of copyright claim was analogous to an antitrust misuse defence to an allegation of patent infringement. A patentee who comes to court to enforce his patent will not succeed if he is guilty of abusing his

1   *Denda International v KPN*, 5 August 1997, Court of Appeal of Amsterdam.
2   933 F 2d 952 (11th Cir 1991).

patent rights. In *Lasercomb America Inc v Reynolds*[1], an allegation of misuse of copyright had been held to be inherent in the law of copyright just as a misuse of patent defence is inherent in patent law. The *BellSouth* court held that, although the patent misuse defence closely fits the copyright law situation and may some day be extended to discipline those who abuse their copyrights, the extension should not be allowed where, as in the *BellSouth* case, there was no antitrust violation. It was held that BellSouth as publisher had not attempted to block the use of information, but had sought only to maintain its copyright format.

4.3 THE DATABASE DIRECTIVE'S COPYRIGHT REQUIREMENTS

The Database Directive[2] required Member States to bring into force the laws, regulations and administrative provisions necessary to comply with the Directive before 1 January 1998.

The Database Directive's structure is as follows:

Recitals	(1) to (60)	
Chapter I	(Arts 1 and 2)	Scope
Chapter II	(Arts 3 to 6)	Copyright
Chapter III	(Arts 7 to 11)	The *sui generis* right
Chapter IV	(Arts 12 to 17)	Common provisions

The broad purpose of the Database Directive is to harmonise the laws of the Member States of the European Economic Area in relation to the protection by copyright of creativity in databases, and to create a new *sui generis* right[3] to protect investment in databases.

These two classes of right apply only to databases as defined by the Database Directive[4], are distinct, and are potentially cumulative so that a database as defined may be protected by either copyright or the *sui generis* right or both. In each case, protection is without prejudice to copyright and other rights subsisting in the contents of a protected database[5].

The Database Directive's principal requirements for the protection of databases by copyright are skeletally expressed in the Directive. They are that Member States should:

– protect by copyright databases, as defined, which constitute their authors' own intellectual creations. No other criteria are to be applied to determine eligibility for copyright protection of a database;

---

1   911 F 2d 970 (4th Cir 1990).
2   Directive 96/9/EC.
3   See Chapter 5 below.
4   Article 1(2). See **4.4** below.
5   Articles 3(1), 7(4) and 13.

- designate as author of a database the natural person, or group of natural persons, who created the base, or a legal person designated as rightholder by national legislation[1];
- recognise the copyright restricted acts set out in the Database Directive[2]; and
- recognise the copyright limitations and exceptions set out in the Database Directive[3], with further optional restrictions[4].

The Directive's requirement that Member States protect by copyright databases, as defined, is not limited to databases which are literary works and does not exclude databases which are, or are collections of, dramatic or musical works. It is possible, therefore, that the UK's implementation of this aspect of the Directive is incomplete. The Database Regulations[5] define 'database' in the same terms as the Directive, but classify databases as literary works[6]. It is arguable, therefore, that they fail to provide copyright protection for databases which are not literary works or which are excluded from that classification because they are, or comprise, dramatic or musical works.

The Database Directive is expressed[7] to be without prejudice to Community provisions relating to:

- the legal protection of computer programs[8]; and
- rental right, lending right and 'certain rights related to copyright in the field of intellectual property'[9].

Subject to these mandatory provisions, Member States are left to develop or apply their own national copyright laws to databases as defined, and to other non-database compilations.

Although there is no express reference in the Database Directive to the Berne Convention, those Member States which are members of the Berne Union are required in their copyright laws to reflect Berne's provisions in relation to the protection by copyright of literary works, and Art 2(5) of Berne which states:

'Collections of literary or artistic works such as encyclopaedias and anthologies which, by reason of the selection and arrangement of their contents, constitute intellectual creations shall be protected as such, without prejudice to the copyright in each of the works forming part of such collections.'

The need for harmonisation was accordingly reduced by Member States' prior acceptance of the principle that collections should be protected by copyright.

---

1   Article 4(1).
2   Article 5. See **4.6** below.
3   Article 6(1). See **4.7** below.
4   Article 6(2).
5   Regulation 6.
6   Regulation 5.
7   Article 2.
8   Directive 91/250/EEC on the legal protection of computer programs.
9   These rights are not further identified by the Database Directive.

4.4   THE DATABASE DIRECTIVE'S DEFINITION OF 'DATABASE'

The term 'database' is relatively new. To give uniform application of the Directive's provisions across the European Economic Area it was necessary to state clearly what kinds of collection were to be included within the term. The Database Directive accordingly provides:

— for the purposes of this Directive, 'database' shall mean a collection of independent works, data or other materials arranged in a systematic or methodical way and individually accessible by electronic or other means[1].

This definition does not classify databases as literary works, and needs careful analysis, for which some guidance is given by some of the Directive's Recitals:

'(17) whereas the term "database" should be understood to include literary, artistic, musical or other collections of works or collections of other materials such as texts, sound, images, numbers, facts and data;

whereas it should cover collections of independent works, data or other materials which are systematically or methodically arranged and can be individually accessed;

whereas this means that a recording or an audio-visual, cinematographic, literary or musical work as such does not fall within the scope of this Directive;

...

(19) whereas, as a rule, the compilation of several recordings of musical performances on a CD does not come within the scope of this Directive, both because, as a compilation, it does not meet the conditions for copyright protection and because it does not represent a substantial enough investment to be eligible under the *sui generis* right;

(20) whereas protection under this Directive may also apply to the materials necessary for the operation or consultation of certain databases such as thesaurus and indexation systems.'

The word 'independent' in the definition of 'database' was transposed to its present position in the definition at a late stage in the development of the proposal for a directive. It is, presumably, to be read in conjunction with the reference to 'independent' in Recital (17). The intention, apparently, was to prevent the recording of a succession of still photographic frames so as to create a series of moving images, as in a cinematographic film, from qualifying for protection as a database.

The principle is well illustrated by this example, but may be more difficult to apply to other collections of works, data or other materials. The Database Directive does not further explain or define the quality of independence which must exist as between the items of content in a collection to enable the collection to qualify as a database. The point is likely to be important since a collection of works, data or other materials which are not independent cannot qualify as a database. Such collections may be protected under national copyright laws, which may be at variance with the provisions of the Database Directive, but cannot qualify for protection under the *sui generis* right.

---

1   Article 1(2).

A further issue arising from the Directive's definition of the term 'database' concerns the nature of the materials which may be comprised in a database. Recital (17), quoted above, refers to 'collections of other materials such as texts, sounds, images, numbers, facts and data'. This list is wider than the CDPA's classification of literary works as meaning:

'... any work, other than a dramatic or musical work, which is written, spoken or sung and accordingly includes—

(a)   a table or compilation,
(b)   a computer program, and
(c)   preparatory design material for a computer program.'

Although the list in Recital (17) of materials which may be included in a database includes sounds, images, facts and data there is no reference here or elsewhere in the Database Directive to dramatic or musical works as such or to three-dimensional items, as for example sculptures or other works of artistic craftsmanship. While this suggests that a collection of three-dimensional materials may not qualify as a database, there seems to be no reason why a database should not include written or digitised representations of such materials.

On this basis, there seems no reason in principle why any of the following should be excluded from the Directive's definition of a database:

–   an anthology of poems;
–   a collection of dramatic or musical works or of recorded dramatic or musical performances[1];
–   a collection of circuit diagrams[2];
–   a library catalogue;
–   a telephone or street directory;
–   an inventory of a warehouse;
–   a multimedia collection of digital representations of texts, sounds and images;
–   a collection of digital representations of three-dimensional items; and
–   a tabulated record of Stock Exchange transactions.

4.5   COPYRIGHT PROTECTION OF TABLES, COMPILATIONS AND DATABASES AFTER 1 JANUARY 1998

A principal effect of the Database Directive's definition of 'database' is to create parallel but different copyright regimes for those literary work compilations which do, and those compilations which do not, fall within the definition.

As from 1 January 1998, and subject to transitional provisions[3], a collection within the definition of 'database' may only be protected by copyright if, by reason of the

---

1   But see Recitals 17 and 19 of the Database Directive, quoted above, and the express exclusion of dramatic and musical works from the CDPA's definition of 'literary work'.
2   *Anacon Corporation Ltd v Environmental Research Technology Ltd* [1994] FSR 659.
3   See Chapter 11 below.

selection or arrangement of its contents, it constitutes its author's own intellectual creation[1]. Since no other criterion may be applied to determine their eligibility for copyright protection, databases which would otherwise have qualified under the UK's skill and labour criterion are not permitted by the Directive, nor now by the CDPA, to be protected by copyright. This does not, however, prevent such a database from being protected by the Database Directive's *sui generis* right, the new database right under the Database Regulations, provided sufficiently substantial investment in the obtaining, verification or presentation of the database's contents can be demonstrated[2]: as to database right, see Chapter 5 below.

By contrast, a collection which does not conform to the Directive's definition of 'database' but which is a literary work and a compilation meeting the UK's skill and labour criterion of originality may not be protected by the *sui generis* right but may continue to qualify for copyright protection[3], even though it is not its author's own intellectual creation. Such a collection may have been generated by computer in circumstances where there is no human author of the work, and so will be within the CDPA's definition of 'computer-generated'[4].

There remain difficulties in reconciling the Database Directive's definition of a database with the new definition of that term, imported into the CDPA by the Database Regulations[5].

As already mentioned above, unlike the CDPA as amended the Database Directive does not classify a database as a literary work. The CDPA, as amended, also expressly excludes dramatic and musical works from the literary work classification[6]. The Database Directive makes no such exclusion.

This may lead to uncertainty as to:

–   the protection by copyright of collections comprising dramatic and musical works, either as databases or as non-database compilations; and
–   the application of the appropriate criterion of originality to such databases or compilations as such.

4.6   THE COPYRIGHT RESTRICTED ACTS

The parallel copyright regimes for non-database compilations which qualify for copyright protection as literary works on the one hand, and databases which are their authors' own intellectual creations on the other hand, are broadly similar but not identical.

---

1   Article 3(1) and reg 6 inserting a new s 3A into the CDPA.
2   Article 7 and reg 13(1).
3   CDPA, ss 1(1) and 3(1).
4   CDPA, s 178. See **4.1** above for a discussion of the effect of the computer-generated work provisions of the CDPA on the criterion of originality.
5   Regulation 6, amending CDPA, s 3, and see **4.4** above.
6   CDPA, s 3(1).

For non-database compilations, the copyright restricted acts are prescribed by the CDPA[1] as:

- copying the work[2];
- issuing copies of the work for the public[3];
- renting or lending the work to the public[4];
- performing, showing or playing the work in public[5];
- broadcasting the work or including it in a cable programme service[6]; and
- making an adaptation of the work, or doing any of the above in relation to an adaptation[7].

The CDPA also provides that copyright in a work is infringed by a person who, without the licence of the copyright owner, does or authorises another to do any of the acts restricted by copyright[8].

For databases, the copyright restricted acts prescribed by the Database Directive[9] are:

- temporary or permanent reproduction by any means and in any form, in whole or in part;
- translation, adaptation, arrangement and any other alteration;
- any form of distribution to the public of the database or of copies thereof, this right being exhausted in relation to a copy of the database on the first sale of that copy within the EEA by the rightholder or with the rightholder's consent;
- any communication, display or performance to the public; and
- any reproduction, distribution, communication, display or performance to the public of the results of any translation, adaptation, arrangement or any other alteration of the database.

Taken literally, there are divergences between these two regimes.

References in the CDPA to the doing of an act restricted by copyright in a work are to the doing of that act in relation to the work as a whole, or any substantial part of it[10]. The Database Directive's express reference to reproduction of a database 'in whole or in part' contrasts with this provision and is not inadvertent. The Database Directive refers, in relation to the *sui generis* right, to restriction of extraction and re-utilisation of the contents of a database 'in whole or in substantial part'[11], and elsewhere to 'extraction and re-utilisation of insubstantial parts' of a database[12]. Reproduction 'in whole or in part', as restricted for copyright by the Database Directive, and 'as a whole or any substantial part', as restricted by the CDPA, set different standards. The

---

1   CDPA, s 16.
2   CDPA, s 17.
3   CDPA, s 18.
4   CDPA, s 18A.
5   CDPA, s 19.
6   CDPA, s 20.
7   CDPA, s 21.
8   CDPA, s 16(2).
9   Article 5.
10   CDPA, s 16(3)(a).
11   Article 7(1).
12   Article 7(5).

Database Directive's standard is not reflected in the Database Regulations, and so is not imported in the CDPA.

For copyright infringement of a non-database compilation, clearly the CDPA's 'whole of any substantial part' applies, but it is unclear whether the supremacy of the Database Directive over the CDPA will allow such a provision to apply to a database in place of the Database Directive's 'in whole or in part'[1].

In other respects, the Database Directive's copyright restricted acts differ from the CDPA's copyright restricted acts, so creating divergent regimes for databases and non-database compilations. For example:

–   'adaptation', in the Database Directive, includes 'arrangement and any other alteration' of a Database. This provision is specifically applied by the Database Regulations[2], which amend CDPA, s 21 in relation to databases, but not in relation to non-database compilations; and
–   'communication to the public' under the Database Directive is applicable to databases but not to non-database compilations, and has no direct parallel in the CDPA's copyright restricted acts or in the Database Regulations.

4.7   LIMITATIONS AND EXCEPTIONS

For non-database compilations, the CDPA's normal limitations and exceptions apply. These include the fair dealing provisions for research and private study which are generally applicable to literary, dramatic, musical and artistic works[3].

For databases, the Database Directive provides a lawful user copyright exception[4] and allows Member States the option of providing for limitations of the copyright restricted acts[5] in the following cases:

–   reproduction for private purposes of a non-electronic database;
–   where there is use for the sole purpose of illustration for teaching or scientific research, as long as the source is indicated and to the extent justified by the non-commercial purpose to be achieved;
–   where there is use for the purposes of public security or for the purposes of an administrative or judicial procedure; and
–   where other exceptions to copyright which are traditionally authorised under national law are involved, without prejudice to the above permitted exceptions.

The Database Directive reflects the Berne Convention[6] by requiring that none of these exceptions may be interpreted in such a way as to allow their application to be used in a manner which unreasonably prejudices the rightholder's legitimate interests or conflicts with normal exploitation of the database.

---

1   *Marleasing SA v La Comercial Internacionale de Alimentacion SA*, Case C-106/89 [1990] ECR 1–4135.
2   Regulation 7.
3   CDPA, s 29.
4   Article 6(1).
5   Article 6(2).
6   Berne Convention, Art 9(2).

The copyright lawful user exception of the Database Directive is reflected in the Database Regulations[1], which allow a person who has a right to use a database or any part of a database (whether under a licence to do any of the acts restricted by the copyright in the database or otherwise) to do, in the exercise of that right, anything which is necessary for the purposes of access to and use of the contents of the database, or of that part of the database which the user has a right to use. This exception does not apply to non-database compilations.

For non-database compilations, the fair dealing provisions of s 29 stand unamended, and accordingly the use, including reproduction and other copyright restricted acts, of a non-database compilation for research for a commercial purpose is not specifically barred by the CDPA as amended by the Regulations. Any such use must still be 'fair dealing'. Research in commerce, industry or government may be fair dealing in a non-database compilation, but whether or not it is so is to be assessed on the particular facts.

This contrasts with the Regulations' absolute prohibition of use of a database for the purposes of commercial research, which is not fair dealing[2]. Again, the imprecision of the dividing line between compilations which are databases and compilations which are not, depending as it does upon the extent to which the materials comprised in the compilation are 'independent', may lead to uncertainty in the application of these different rules affecting commercial research.

4.8 CONCLUSIONS

Before 1 January 1998, the copyright protection under UK law of tables and compilations, as literary works, was a single code. A table or compilation which was a literary work was the product of its author's skill, labour and exercise of judgement, and which was not copied from another work, was protectable by copyright restricted acts and was subject to the fair dealing provisions and other exceptions of the CDPA[3].

On the coming into force on 1 January 1998 of the Database Regulations implementing the Database Directive[4] this single regime was amended, subject to transitional provisions[5], so as to:

– create a new sub-class of literary work, a 'database', which is a form of compilation but having a restricted meaning;
– define a 'database' in terms which may be difficult to apply to many collections, particularly as to the requirement of 'independence' which must exist as between the items of content in a database but which may not exist as between the items of content of many collections. The definition may also fail adequately to transpose the Database Directive's provisions into UK law, since it restricts databases

---

1   Regulation 9, inserting a new s 50D into the CDPA.
2   Database Regulations, reg 8, amending s 29 of the CDPA.
3   Sections 29 to 50C of the CDPA.
4   Copyright and Rights in Databases Regulations 1997, SI 1997/3032. See Appendix 4 below.
5   Database Regulations, Part IV.

under the CDPA to collections which are literary works: no such restriction is
applied by the Database Directive;
— establish a copyright code for databases which is broadly similar to the CDPA's
  copyright code for other compilations which are protected as literary works, but
  which differs from it in some significant respects including:
  — requiring that a database, to be protectable by copyright, shall be its author's
    own intellectual creation;
  — having slightly, but significantly, different restricted acts particularly in
    relation to adaptation and communication to the public;
  — excluding use for commercial research from fair dealing in databases; and
  — establishing special 'lawful user' rights which do not apply to non-database
    compilations, and which may not be excluded by contract.

It remains to be seen whether any of these changes create any practical difficulties in
the interpretation and application of the new law.

Chapter 5

DATABASE RIGHT

5.1 Definition of the database right – 5.2 Protection of investment – 5.3 Ownership of database right – 5.4 Qualification for the database right – 5.5 Scope of the database right

5.1 DEFINITION OF THE DATABASE RIGHT

The database right is described in Part III of the Database Regulations where it occupies 14 of the 30 Regulations (47 per cent). This contrasts with the position under the Database Directive where the provisions relating to the database right occupy five out of 17 Articles (29 per cent). The greater emphasis placed on the elaboration of the database right under the Database Regulations is to be welcomed, but upon reaching the end of Part III one is left with the feeling that the Database Regulations have left as many issues unresolved as resolved. None the less, let us see what the legislation has to tell us.

Our consideration of the database right must start with a reminder that the database right only applies to the form of database defined by the new s 3A(1) of the CDPA inserted by reg 6[1]. In order to enjoy the protection of the new property right, a database must therefore be:

'A collection of independent works, data or other materials which—

(a)   are arranged in a systematic or methodical way, and
(b)   are individually accessible by electronic or other means.'

The new database right subsists in relation to all such databases, provided there has been a substantial qualitative or quantitative investment of financial, human or technical resources in obtaining, verifying or presenting the contents of the database concerned[2].

The fact that the database or any of its contents may, or may not, enjoy copyright protection is irrelevant for the purpose of determining whether database right exists[3]. Thus, a database may be protected by both copyright and database right. Equally, it may enjoy protection under database right but may lack the necessary quality of originality in respect of the selection or arrangement of its contents so as to fail to qualify as an original literary work, and so fall outside the protection of copyright[4].

---

1   Database Regulations, reg 12(1).
2   Database Regulations, reg 13(1).
3   Database Regulations, reg 13(2).
4   CDPA, s 3A(2), as inserted by reg 6 of the Database Regulations. The requirement of originality only applies to databases created after 27 March 1996. Before this date, the usual skill, labour or experience test will apply.

The third possibility is that a database lacks one of the qualities necessary to fall within the definition given in s 3A(1) of the CDPA. For example, the materials within it may not be independent of one another, or they may be randomly, as opposed to systematically or methodically, arranged. Finally, they may not be accessible individually. The absence of any of those characteristics would rule a collection of data out of the classification as a 'database' under the Database Regulations. It would then be impossible for that particular collection of data to enjoy the benefit of the database right.

However, it should be appreciated that such a collection of data (and we use this shorthand phrase to include a collection of works or other materials as specified by the Database Regulations[1]), although falling outside the definition and therefore the ambit of the database right, might yet be protected by copyright. This seems at first sight counter-intuitive as the scheme of the Database Regulations is to create a subsidiary right, a database right, to be a junior, and therefore lesser, right to copyright. How can it be that a collection of data could enjoy the senior right but not the junior?

The explanation of that conundrum lies in a consideration of the treatment of tables and compilations under English copyright law, which falls outside the scope of this particular chapter[2]. For present purposes it will be sufficient to record that such a possibility does exist, and should be carefully borne in mind when analysing what rights may apply to a particular collection of data.

For the sake of completeness, we should end our tour of the possibilities involved by mentioning those collections of data which will qualify for neither database right (because they fail the s 3A(1) of the CDPA definition test) nor copyright (because they pass the s 3A(1) test but fail the s 3A(2) test, or are outside the scope of s 3A(1) and fail the common law test for tables and compilations to enjoy copyright protection). Then there is the possibility that a database, as defined by the Database Directive, falling outside the s 3A(1) definition of a database may gain copyright protection not as a literary work but, for example, as a sound recording under s 5(1), or in the case of a collage as an artistic work under s 4(1). Interestingly, because of the way that the criterion of originality has been included into the CDPA by the Database Regulations by an amendment to the definition of a 'literary work' consisting of a database, the other categories of copyright work contain no such additional criterion. The result is that a database, as defined by the Database Directive, may gain protection under ss 4 and 5 of the CDPA without constituting the author's own intellectual creation. This is, of course, contrary to the position required by the Database Directive which makes clear in Article 3 that only databases which constitute the author's own intellectual creation shall be protected as such by copyright.

All of the above discussion pre-supposes that we are dealing with works created after 1 January 1998. For works created before that date, it would be necessary to refer to the transitional provisions set out in Database Regulations 26–30[3] in order to establish the correct categorisation.

---

1   Database Regulations, reg 6.
2   See Chapter 4 above.
3   See Chapter 11 below.

Perhaps at this point it will help to put the matter in the form of a simplified table of possibilities.

Collections of work, data or other materials
Possible protection under English law
for work created after 1 January 1998

	Copyright	Database right
1.	✓	✓
2.	✗	✓
3.	✓	✗
4.	✗	✗

It should be borne in mind that the above table is intended to illustrate the most likely possible outcomes. In some cases, where a given collection falls within the matrix, it will require exhaustive, and possibly exhausting, analysis. The reader is referred to the flow chart set out in Appendix 10 for a useful tool to assist in this labour.

5.2 PROTECTION OF INVESTMENT

One of the main drivers to the implementation of the Database Directive was the recognition that substantial, not to say massive, investment is being made in the creation of databases by businesses across the economic spectrum. This investment will be jeopardised unless there is a stable and uniform legal regime to protect the remuneration of the makers of databases[1]. Accordingly, the database right should be seen very much in this economic context. It is the economic property right designed to protect collections of work, data and other materials. It should therefore be seen in contrast to copyright, which will, in appropriate circumstances, continue to protect the intellectual creativity involved in the creation of such collections. This explains why the first element in the equation that must be looked at in assessing whether the database right will be awarded is the level of investment that the database maker has put in to the creation of the database. Regulation 13(1) of the Database Regulations states that the investment must have been substantial. How should we determine whether the investment put in has been substantial enough? In answer to this question we are given clues but no real guidance by the legislation.

Recital 40 of the Database Directive provides that the object of the *sui generis* right is to ensure protection of *any* investment (our emphasis) in obtaining, verifying or presenting the contents of a database. Article 7 of the Database Directive goes on to make it clear that the investment must have been substantial, and that this is to be measured either on a quantitative basis or a qualitative one, or by a combination of both qualitative *and* quantitative measures. This approach is repeated in the definition of 'substantial' in the Database Regulations[2]. In addition, the Regulations provide the

---

1   Recitals 12 and 45 of the Database Directive.
2   Database Regulations, reg 12(1).

gloss that the investment can take the form of financial, human or technical resources. These are merely illustrative categories, as the Regulations repeat the words of Recital 40 of the Database Directive in referring to 'any investment'.

In concrete terms, it is clear that the advancing of capital to fund the making or renewal of a database would meet the test (financial resources), as would hiring staff or contractors or making them available for the work on the database (human resources), as also would the provision of computing capacity or know-how (technical resources). Bear in mind that this investment can be made either at the inception of a database project (obtaining its contents) or during the life of a database (verifying or presenting its contents). This leads to the conclusion that the owner of a database[1] would be well advised to take great care in formulating a marketing strategy for his database before granting a licence to anyone to modify or adapt his database.

The reason for this is that, once the database is licensed in this way, the owner runs the risk that his licensee will dedicate a level of resource to the modification and adaptation which makes it sufficient to qualify as being a 'substantial investment' in accordance with the above criteria. The consequence would then be that the licensee has acquired (subject to the satisfaction of the qualifying criteria set out in reg 18 of the Database Regulations) its own database right in its particular modification or adaptation of the database concerned. If the licensee then wishes to exploit its new or 'secondary' database it will have to seek the consent (that is to say the licence) of the owner of the original database to the exploitation of the secondary database, containing as it will, substantial elements of the original database. The owner of the original database has two options at this stage, neither of which is attractive. First, he could grant a licence to allow exploitation of the secondary database. The disadvantage of this is that he will thereby be admitting onto the market a new and potentially better version of his original work. This may not be directly competitive at first, but in fast moving product cycles there is no telling when the secondary database may turn out to be competing in the same market sector as the original database. It is rarely good business to provide the means of launching competitive product offerings.

The second alternative open to our original database owner is to sit on his hands and refuse to license the exploitation of the secondary database. Presumably, this will be more likely to be the stance taken by a database proprietor who sees that the rival database is already a potential competitor in some part of its sphere of activities. The problem with this approach is that it will be open to the owner of the secondary database to run a *Magill*-type argument based on its right to exploit the secondary database in a secondary or complementary market[2]. If the stakes are high enough (that is to say if considerable sums have been invested by both the original owner and his licensee in the creation of the original and the secondary databases) then this argument may well be worth running by the licensee, with all the attendant anxiety and uncertainty for the owner of the original database. It is for these reasons that we recommend that an exercise of carefully thinking through the marketing and licensing

---

1   We shall consider who this is in **5.3** below.

2   In August 1997, in *Denda International v KPN*, the Court of Appeal of Amsterdam in the Netherlands held that a refusal by the Dutch PTT to license its 'White Pages' telephone directories for re-publication on CD-ROM would be an abuse of a dominant position. See Chapter 9 for further discussion of this.

strategy for a database should be undertaken by the original owner whilst the original database is being created.

Such a competing product would not fall foul of Art 7(5) of the Database Directive which provides that acts which conflict with 'a normal exploitation of that database or which unreasonably prejudice the legitimate interests of the maker of the database' are not to be permitted. In the first place the Database Regulations do not import the same language regarding 'unreasonable prejudice' and 'legitimate interests' as these terms are more apt for the civil law jurisprudence and do not fit in so happily with the common law traditions. Secondly, the prohibition in Art 7(5) of the Database Directive only applies where the legitimate interests of the maker of a database are affected. It is submitted that the interests of a maker cease to be legitimate once he has granted a licence to carry out modifications to his database. The database maker's protection is to think through his strategy from the start, and if he decides to allow adaptations of his database to be further exploited he must make sure that he charges a sufficiently large licence fee for the grant of the modification right so as to ensure that the risk of rival products emerging from the exercise of the licence is taken into account.

5.3   OWNERSHIP OF DATABASE RIGHT

We mentioned above that we would explain who would be the owner of the database right. Regulation 15 of the Database Regulations states that the first owner of a database right in a database is the 'maker' of that database. That is straightforward enough. It then falls to consider who will be the maker of a database, and this is set out in reg 14 of the Database Regulations. It is the person who takes the initiative in obtaining, verifying or presenting the contents of a database *and* (our emphasis) assumes the risk of investing in that obtaining, verification or presentation[1].

The use of the term 'maker' in the Database Regulations is consistent and helpful. It assists us to keep a distinction between the 'authoring' (which requires intellectual creativity) of a copyright work and the 'making' (a more mechanical process) of a 'mere' database. Of course, bear in mind that a work can be both a database and a copyright work where the criteria of ss 3(A)(1) and 3(A)(2) of the CDPA are satisfied, but as we are dealing in this chapter just with the database right we shall focus on how the Database Regulations view ownership of that right rather than ownership of the copyright in a database (if any exists).

The draftsman of the Database Regulations is to be congratulated on the rigour with which he has pursued the distinction between author and maker in the drafting of the regulations. There is no mention of the term 'author' in the whole of the Database Regulations except in reg 6, where the word has to be used in order to refer to the inclusion of the intellectual creativity criterion in the existing scheme of copyright in an English literary (author's) work. Thereafter, ownership of the database right is quite properly only referred to in the context of the 'maker' of the database, never its author. This is in contrast to the approach in the Database Directive where the drafting

---

1   Database Regulations, reg 14(1).

gets into something of a muddle by dealing with the question of ownership under Art 4 which is entitled 'database authorship' and states that the author of a database shall be the natural person or group of natural persons who created the base[1]. This deals, after a fashion, with the position of a database entitled to copyright. When it comes to the ownership of the database right the Articles of the Database Directive are strangely silent. They do not employ the words of Recital 41 which are taken up by reg 14 of the Database Regulations that 'the maker of a database is the person who takes the initiative in obtaining . . . the contents of a database and assumes the risk of investing in that obtaining . . .'.

Not that the question of ownership is left entirely free from doubt under the Database Regulations. Whilst the use of the term 'maker' is helpful conceptually, its implementation under reg 14(1) of the Database Regulations leaves open the possibility that someone may have taken the initiative to obtain the contents of a database, and someone else will have assumed the risk involved in that obtaining. This is clearly intended to be covered by reg 14(5) which provides that in these circumstances the database is considered to have been made jointly. However, it is possible to conceive of circumstances where two people act in collaboration to obtain the contents of a database such that neither assumes the risk of so doing, for example, as two members of a three-party joint venture where the third party assumes all the risk. In this latter circumstance, the third party would itself fall within the definition of reg 14(5) and qualify as a joint maker with the first two. However, if the relationship between the parties is not that of joint-venturers or partners, but rather that of contractor and sub-contractor then Recital 41 of the Database Directive makes it clear that the sub-contractor is not to be treated as a maker.

The position regarding the ownership of an employee's work which is carried out in the course of his employment is that it is regarded as being owned by his employer[2] unless varied by agreement. This is a similar position to that which applies in respect of copyright[3].

5.4   QUALIFICATION FOR THE DATABASE RIGHT

It is important to realise that the database right is very much a creation of the European Commission. It has even been suggested that the motivation for the promulgation of the Database Directive lay in the somewhat high-handed manner in which the US administration imposed the need for the semi-conductor chip legislation on unsuspecting European Member States in 1987. The terms of the US Regulations were such that, in order to continue trading with the US for these vital building blocks of computer processing, it became necessary for the EU Member States hurriedly to pass their own legislation to give satisfactory protection to the design topographies of such chips.

---

1   This is the only time this rather odd term is found in either the Directive or the Regulations. It is
     presumed to be an oversight.
2   Database Regulations, reg 14(2).
3   Cf CDPA, s 11(2).

As such, it is only to be expected that there should be an element of nationalism, or perhaps more accurately, regionalism, in the qualifying criteria for the database right. These are set out in reg 18.

Regulation 18(1) of the Database Regulations states that, in order for the database right to exist, the maker of the database must be a national of one of the States comprised in the EEA[1] or habitually resident within the EEA at the time the database is made. If the making extends over a period of time then it will be sufficient if this consideration is satisfied for a substantial part of that period[2].

If the maker is a company or some form of unincorporated body then it will enjoy database right provided it was formed under the law of an EEA State and had either its principal place of business or its registered office[3] within the EEA at the time of creation of the database.

The possibility of there being joint makers of the database alleviates some of the severity of the above provision. This is because the qualification criteria of reg 18 are satisfied if *just one* of a number of joint makers passes the relevant tests. This looks suspiciously like a piece of self-serving legislation designed to encourage non-European, and one suspects especially US-based, companies, to move some of their database development work from wherever they might have placed it up to now to somewhere within the EEA, putting it under the corporate umbrella of a newly established EEA-based body. We have seen evidence of a number of US companies already having done exactly this and we would expect this to be a continuing and quickening trend as the database sector (which is really just a sub-set of the overall Information Market as we explained in Chapter 1) expands in importance in the coming years.

The alternative avenue open to non-European database developers wishing to protect their position regarding their ownership of database right would be to form a data-collection or risk-assumption collaboration with an EEA-based entity in order to develop the database. So long as the relationship is a true collaboration this arrangement should bring the EEA-based entity within reg 14(1) and so qualify it as a joint maker.

Once this had been done the database qualifies for database right under reg 18(1). However, great care must be taken in the drafting of the collaboration agreement between the EEA-based entity and the 'non-European' entity so as to ensure that the relationship does not subside into the category of contractor and sub-contractor. If that were to happen then Recital 41 of the Database Directive would, as we have seen,

---

1   The EEA comprises the Member States of the EU (Austria, Belgium, Denmark, Finland, France, Germany, Greece, Ireland, Italy, Luxembourg, Netherlands, Portugal, Spain, Sweden, UK) and EFTA (Norway, Iceland and Liechtenstein).

2   Unlike the other references to 'substantial' in regs 13(1) and 16(1) of the Database Regulations, there is no guidance given as to the meaning of substantial in this context.

3   Regulation 18(2)(b) of the Database Regulations also requires that in order for the registered office test to be satisfied it is necessary that the body's operations are linked on an ongoing basis with a Member State of the EEA. This is a form of anti-avoidance provision that is more familiar in tax regulations, but it shows how detailed Information Law statutes are likely to become in the future.

debar the sub-contractor from any claim to being a maker, thereby disqualifying any entitlement to database right under reg 18(1).

It has been objected that the net effect of the qualification criteria of reg 18 seems to amount to a rather cynical attempt to boost the European information technology market at the expense of the rest of the world. We would not quarrel with such an apparently harsh judgment. We are here dealing in the realms of Big Money and High Politics. The Commission, having cottoned on to the economic importance of databases[1], was not about to let the opportunity pass of digging another section of the trench around Fortress Europe and labelling it database right.

5.5   SCOPE OF THE DATABASE RIGHT

5.5.1   Extraction and re-utilisation

The database right will be infringed if a person does either of the acts specified by reg 16(1) of the Database Regulations during the period when the right subsists in accordance with reg 17[2]. The restricted acts are the extraction or re-utilisation of all or a substantial part of the contents of the database.

'Extraction' is defined in reg 12(1) as the permanent or temporary transfer of the contents of a database to another medium by any means or in any form. This definition is designed to ensure that the temporary holding of database contents within any processor so as to take the information content out of a database (ie searching the database) will amount to an infringing act. A similar provision[3] has been of great assistance in countering the mischief of software copyright infringement.

Re-utilisation means, according to reg 12(1), making the contents of a database available to the public by any means. It is therefore akin to an infringement of a publication right which the database owner, as the person who has taken the initiative and risk in creating a significant economic asset should, in all fairness, have the sole right to exercise.

In practice we suspect that extraction and re-utilisation may be hard to define precisely, but they will be pretty recognisable in most cases of alleged infringement. However, reg 16(2) gives some guidance on one particular point. It makes plain that repeated and systematic extraction or re-utilisation of insubstantial parts of the contents of a database may amount to the extraction or re-utilisation of a substantial[4] part of the database, and therefore an infringement of the database right. This must be right; very often the value in electronic databases resides in their ability to provide what may be tiny fragments of information but almost instantaneously. It would be iniquitous if the unauthorised, systematic user of such a database could raise a

---

1   Database Directive, Recitals 9–12.
2   By and large, this is 15 years from the end of the calendar year in which the database was completed, but see Chapter 11, Traditional Provisions, for more detailed treatment regarding databases existing at the commencement of the Database Regulations.
3   CPDA, s 17(6).
4   Substantial in this context means substantial in terms of quantity or quality or a combination of both: Database Regulations, reg 12(1).

spurious defence related to the tiny proportion of data he was 'borrowing' relative to the totality of the database. Support for this approach can be gained from Recital 42 of the Database Directive, which makes clear that the right to prohibit extraction and/or re-utilisation relates 'not only to the manufacture of a parasitical competing product but also to any user who, through his acts, causes significant detriment, evaluated qualitatively or quantitively to the investment'. Article 7(5) puts the matter beyond doubt when it specifies that the right will be infringed by acts which 'unreasonably prejudice the legitimate interests of the maker of the database'. This should allow considerable scope for creative judicial interpretation in appropriate circumstances in the years to come.

5.5.2   Dealings in the database right

Regulation 23 of the Database Regulations tells us that ss 90 to 93 of the CDPA shall apply in relation to database right in the same way as these sections apply to copyright works. Thus, a database right may be assigned[1] either in whole or in part[2]. To be effective, this assignment must be in writing signed by or on behalf of the assignor[3]. The owner of a database right is entitled to grant licences in and over a database[4]. This includes the right to grant exclusive licences[5]. The database right proprietor may enter into agreements in relation to prospective future ownership of database right[6]. This grant of rights will be binding on every successor in title to the original owner's interest in the database *except* a purchaser in good faith who acquires the right for valuable consideration without notice (actual or constructive) of the assignment or the licence[7]. Finally, both future generations and the Inland Revenue Capital Transfer Office should note that the database right may pass under a will[8].

5.5.3   Remedies for infringement

As is the case for a copyright holder, the owner of a database right acquires an actionable right for infringement by virtue of the provisions under ss 96 to 98 of the CDPA[9] and is entitled to claim relief 'by way of damages, injunctions, accounts or otherwise'[10] in the same way as for an infringement of any other property right. Further, at the court's discretion additional damages may be awarded[11] or the defendant may be required to take a licence of the database right which the defendant is found to have infringed[12]. The same rights and remedies are also accorded, except against the database right owner, to an exclusive licensee of database right[13].

---

1   Section 90(1) of the CDPA.
2   Section 90(2) of the CDPA.
3   Section 90(3) of the CDPA.
4   Section 90(4) of the CDPA.
5   Section 92 of the CDPA.
6   Section 91(1) of the CDPA.
7   Sections 90(4) and 91(3) of the CDPA.
8   Section 93 of the CDPA.
9   Applicable to database right by virtue of the Database Regulations, reg 23.
10   Section 96 of the CDPA.
11   Section 97(2) of the CDPA.
12   Section 98(1) of the CDPA.
13   Sections 101 and 102 of the CDPA.

5.5.4   Duration and renewal

The 15-year period that the owner of the database right enjoys looks on the paltry side relative to the newly extended period of 70 years enjoyed by copyright owners. However, it may be that the tortoise will outrun the hare in many cases as database right is capable of indefinite renewal provided a degree of investment is maintained in the database. Regulation 17(3) of the Database Regulations makes clear that any substantial[1] change to the contents of the database will qualify the database resulting from the change for its own new 15-year term of protection. The nature of databases is such that it is highly likely that their content will justify the sort of regular overhaul[2] and therefore investment that reg 17(3) envisages. They will thereby gain a further period of protection.

Thus, much like good trade marks, which can be renewed provided they remain in use, good databases will carry on indefinitely, requiring substantial investment to retain their value as do trade marks. Every now and again, the database will require a complete make-over, much as famous trade marks periodically adjust their format or style, but the database owners will be more than prepared to bear these costs, indeed, they will be essential to the justification for the new period of database right being granted – reg 17(3) requires there to have been a 'substantial new investment'). These costs are analogous to the advertising costs that have to be put behind any successful trade mark.

Yet, here is an interesting comparison: brand managers will often tell you that half of their advertising budget is simply wasted. The problem is they do not know which half. The money put into the renewal and improvement of a database by contrast is 100 per cent targeted not only to the functional goal of improving a particular product or service, and thereby producing more revenue for the database owner, but also to the growth in value of that asset itself (or the database property represented by it). How many other assets could be said to enjoy the characteristics of going up in value in direct proportion to the money spent on conserving them and becoming more valuable as they get older? Old Dutch Masters and fine French wines perhaps. And now databases. Not bad company for a young upstart Euro-right to be enjoying[3].

---

1   Substantial here meaning substantial in terms of quantity or quality or both: Database Regulations, reg 12(1) .

2   For example, as a rule of thumb it is said that one-third of the details in a customer database will become incorrect in some respect every year, thereby degrading the value of the entire database over time unless steps are taken to 'repair' the defective data.

3   Note that Recital 55 of the Database Directive provides that new investment may include the costs of substantial verification of contents. This will help the owners of mature databases where change in the contents is unlikely – as in the case of static and complete lists. It also allows us to add more force to our analogy by equating the investment in the verification of data to the gallery and cellarage costs incurred by the owners of the paintings and wine. There are certain costs which have to be incurred by virtue of the nature of the asset owned. In the case of a database these are the costs of the continuing intellectual effort needed to validate the database's contents.

Chapter 6

LIMITATIONS AND EXCEPTIONS

6.1 Lawful user rights under the Software Directive and the Software Regulations –
6.2 Section 56 of the CDPA – 6.3 Copyright lawful users of databases – 6.4 Database right
lawful users – 6.5 Lawful users of non-database compilations – 6.6 Lawful use, fair dealing
and s 29 of the CDPA in relation to non-database compilations – 6.7 Commercial use of
computer programs, non-database compilations and databases

6.1 LAWFUL USER RIGHTS UNDER THE SOFTWARE DIRECTIVE AND THE SOFTWARE REGULATIONS

The concept of a 'lawful user' of a computer program was first introduced into English law through the concept of 'lawful acquirer' in the Software Directive, adopted by the Council of Ministers on 14 May 1991. This was brought into UK law on 1 January 1993, when the Copyright (Computer Programs) Regulations 1992 (the 'Software Regulations') amended the CDPA to bring it into line with the Software Directive. There was no definition of a 'lawful acquirer' in the Software Directive, which also somewhat indiscriminately uses the terms 'licensee' and 'person having a right to use'. It could be that there would be a right in some circumstances to use a program without personally having acquired it – as for example in the context of group licences for commercial users, or where copies are rented or publicly loaned. The rights obtained by these different categories of user differ in some ways but the Software Regulations at reg 8 roll both of these into 'lawful user' and define a person as a 'lawful user' of a computer program if (whether under a licence to do any acts restricted by the copyright in the program or otherwise) he has a right to use the program, even though the right to use it may be limited to certain aspects only, of a limited duration.

The Software Directive set out to unify the protection granted to computer software throughout Europe. In its basic proposition, set out in Art 1, that computer software should be protected by copyright as a literary work, it did little to change the stance taken by English law from the days when the Copyright Act 1956 (as amended by the Copyright (Computer Software) Amendment Act 1985) was in effect.

6.1.1 Restricted Acts

Article 4 of the Software Directive specified the following restricted acts that could only be carried out with the authority of the copyright owner. To do these acts without the authority of the copyright owner would be an infringement.

Article 4

'Subject to the provisions of Articles 5 and 6, the exclusive rights of the rightholder within the meaning of Article 2, shall include the right to do or to authorize:

(a) the permanent or temporary reproduction of a computer program by any means and in any form, in part or in whole. Insofar as loading, displaying, running, transmission or storage of the computer program necessitate such reproduction, such acts shall be subject to authorization by the rightholder;

(b) the translation, adaptation, arrangement and any other alteration of a computer program and the reproduction of the results thereof, without prejudice to the rights of the person who alters the program;

(c) any form of distribution to the public, including the rental of the original computer program or of copies thereof. The first sale in the Community of a copy of a program by the rightholder or with his consent shall exhaust the distribution right within the Community of that copy, with the exception of the right to control further rental of the program or a copy thereof.'

The CDPA already offered this protection to computer programs as literary works; there was no need for any amendment to the CDPA specifically in order to protect software.

Instead, the innovative reforms were those relating to 'reverse engineering' and to software maintenance which, in particular circumstances, allowed 'lawful users' of software to do acts in relation to that software which hitherto would have constituted an infringement. 'Reverse engineering' is the term given to any process whereby, starting from a finished product, a black box as it were, one deduces how the product works or was made.

Broadly, the Software Directive was intended to ensure that software houses should not be able to use copyright to establish and maintain a long-term monopoly under which software users would be forever tied to the software and maintenance services of that particular supplier. To achieve this, it is necessary that:

–   programs should be able to work with programs produced by other software houses (that is, should be 'interoperable');
–   programs should be able to work with other hardware, either directly or through another's operating system or driver;
–   programs should be capable of transferring information and data between one computer system and another;
–   it should be possible to study the program in order to determine the underlying ideas and principles.

Reverse engineering may in some cases be essential for software maintenance, particularly if information concerning the program is no longer available from the software supplier – either wilfully, or because they have gone out of business or ceased supporting that particular product. Thus, the right to reverse engineer software products, without risk of infringing copyright, was intended to be a core measure both for this purpose and in achieving interoperability between the products of different manufacturers.

For anybody trying to reverse engineer a software product, the established method would normally be an infringement of copyright in that there would be an unauthorised permanent or temporary reproduction of the program code. To examine the operation of a program would involve the use of an in-circuit emulator ('ICE') which is a device which simulates the microprocessor that would usually be controlled by the software. The operation of the ICE can be controlled so that individual steps in the program's operation can be studied one by one if necessary. Even a temporary reproduction of the code in the ICE could therefore constitute infringement. An alternative method for studying the program would be to decompile the machine code in an attempt to reproduce as near as possible the original source code that was originally compiled to run on the computer. This would give a printed listing of the code which is a prima facie infringement of copyright.

Thus, in order to enable reverse engineering either for maintenance or for studying the program to write interoperable programs, Art 5 of the Software Directive sets out exceptions to the restricted acts.

6.1.2   Exceptions to the restricted acts

The exceptions comprise the following limited range of otherwise infringing acts which can, without express authorisation from the copyright owner, be performed by an authorised user (or licensee) of the software.

Article 5

'1. In the absence of specific contractual provisions, the acts referred to in Article 4(a) and (b) shall not require authorization by the rightholder where they are necessary for the use of the computer program by the lawful acquirer in accordance with its intended purpose, including for error correction.

2. The making of a back-up copy by a person having a right to use the computer program may not be prevented by contract insofar as it is necessary for that use.

3. The person having a right to use a copy of a computer program shall be entitled, without the authorization of the rightholder, to observe, study or test the functioning of the program in order to determine the ideas and principles which underlie any element of the program if he does so while performing any of the acts of loading, displaying, running, transmitting or storing the program which he is entitled to do.'

It should be noted that the rights of the lawful acquirer under Art 5(1) apply only insofar as they are not excluded by specific contractual provisions in the licence and are necessary for use of the program in accordance with its (undefined) intended purpose. By contrast, the Database Directive notably contains no equivalent 'let out' for right owners to exclude any of the lawful users' rights through specific contractual provision.

Article 5(3) of the Software Directive allows a person to observe, study or test the functioning of a program in order to determine the ideas and principles which underlie any element of the program provided this is done while he is performing any of the acts of loading, displaying, running, transmitting or storing the program *which the person is entitled to do*. This suggests more than merely running the program and watching the screen and would seem to permit one to use the software in conjunction with an ICE to observe how the program is working. Otherwise it is difficult to imagine how one could observe the operation of a program.

This provision is not without its difficulties, however. The right to observe, study or test the functioning of the program in order to determine the underlying ideas or principles is permitted where the user is performing acts that he is entitled to do. What the user is entitled to do will be wholly determined by the software licence save that the making of a back-up copy and the right to observe functioning cannot be excluded. Whilst Art 9(1) of the Software Directive is intended to make unlawful any contractual term that seeks to exclude the effects of Art 5(3), Recital 19 suggests that the acts done by the user must not be an infringement of copyright. There then arises a circular argument over whether a restriction in a licence for, say, a financial analysis program that states 'not authorised for use except in the ordinary course of business' is a legitimate marker establishing the extent of the copyright licence – thereby excluding operation of the software for test purposes – or whether it should be a provision which is disallowed by Art 9(1). Further, the Software Directive gives no clues as to what may or may not be done with the information so obtained, which may arguably still retain the status of trade secrets (although this must depend upon the facts in each case, since if every lawful user is entitled to observe the same information it could become too widely known to retain continued trade secret status).

6.1.3   Decompilation

Article 6 of the Software Directive introduced the right to decompile. Normally, this would, of course, constitute a reproduction and/or a translation of the code contrary to Art 4 of the Software Directive.

Article 6

'1.   The authorization of the rightholder shall not be required where reproduction of the code and translation of its form within the meaning of Article 4(a) and (b) are indispensable to obtain the information necessary to achieve the interoperability of an independently created computer program with other programs, provided that the following conditions are met:

(a)   these acts are performed by the licensee or by another person having a right to use a copy of a program, or on their behalf by a person authorized to do so;

(b)   the information necessary to achieve interoperability has not previously been readily available to the persons referred to in subparagraph (a); and

(c)   these acts are confined to the parts of the original program which are necessary to achieve interoperability.

2.   The provisions of paragraph 1 shall not permit the information obtained through its application:

(a)   to be used for goals other than to achieve the interoperability of the independently created computer program;

(b)   to be given to others, except when necessary for the interoperability of the independently created computer program; or

(c)   to be used for the development, production or marketing of a computer program substantially similar in its expression, or for any other act which infringes copyright.

3.   In accordance with the provisions of the Berne Convention for the protection of Literary and Artistic Works, the provisions of this Article may not be interpreted in such a way as to allow its application to be used in a manner which unreasonably prejudices the rightholder's legitimate interests or conflicts with a normal exploitation of the computer program.'

Even though they expressly permit decompilation, these provisions allow it only where the person decompiling has the right to use the program, and only in circumstances where the information necessary to achieve interoperability has not previously been readily available to that authorised user. This leaves the copyright owner the power to restrict the application of these rights through terms in any licence, for example. The acts of decompilation are also limited to decompiling only those parts of the program strictly necessary to obtain the information necessary to achieve interoperability.

At first sight, these rights seem very helpful to the third-party developer. Art 5(3) together with Art 6 of the Software Directive have the potential to allow the observer (as long as they are a licensee or other person having a right to use for the purposes of Art 6(1)) to study the operation of algorithms, functions and procedures incorporated in the software, and also to study the transfer, manipulation and formats of the data that the software uses. The information learned can then be used to develop an independently created computer program which is interoperable with another program or item of computer hardware, provided that the newly created program does not infringe copyright by using or adapting the code in the original program under study. Put simply, you can learn how to do something by reverse engineering, but you must write your own code in order to achieve what must be done and your use of the information derived from observation must not go beyond what is necessary for interoperability nor be inconsistent with the terms of any licence.

The potential uses for these privileges are as follows. One could determine:

- how operating system software or a device driver interacts with hardware; at low level, or in an embedded system. This could allow one to study memory management or how the software actually interacts with the microprocessor or microcontroller in an embedded system. This privilege is not restricted to software stored on disk and applies to software stored in ROM. Potentially, it could even allow one to study the microcodes in a semiconductor chip;
- how application software interacts with an operating system or device driver;
- how network protocols, packets and frames are constructed;
- how data formats in databases are organised, thereby enabling one manufacturer's application software to access files in another manufacturer's format.

Last, and possibly more controversially, it may be possible to use these provisions for legitimate study of other people's encryption or security systems. Given that the Software Directive intends to achieve interoperability between systems that have been produced by different manufacturers, it seems to follow that one can study the operation of encryption or security software with a view to producing one's own compatible software.

These are all potentially very attractive facilities, providing that achieving them does not involve breach of the provisions of Art 6 of the Software Directive.

Nevertheless, Art 6 of the Software Directive suffers from similar problems as to ambiguity as does Art 5(3). In Art 6(1), decompilation will be permitted only where it is *indispensable* to obtain the information necessary to achieve the interoperability of the independently created program. Whilst Art 6(1)(b) makes the reasonable requirement that the information required from decompiling should not be already readily available to the person contemplating the decompilation exercise, it is difficult to assess what is meant by 'readily available'. One can imagine many grey areas. For instance, the information that is required to achieve interoperability may not be published. Because the decompilation must be *indispensable*, does this mean that the party should first write to the copyright owner asking for the information? What if the copyright owner is willing to make the information available only for a fee? What if that fee is uneconomic – do these this constitute circumstances where decompilation becomes an indispensable activity?

Article 6(2)(a) of the Software Directive limits the use to which information obtained from decompilation may be put. Article 6(2)(c) and (3) raises a further practical problem. Article 6(2)(c) prohibits use of the information obtained to develop a program that is substantially similar in its expression to the program that has been decompiled, or for any other act which infringes copyright. Article 6(3) prohibits operation in a way that unreasonably prejudices the copyright holder's legitimate interests or that conflicts with a normal exploitation of the computer program. In a nutshell, if as a result of decompilation the lawful user establishes that interoperability with their own software cannot be achieved unless they reproduce part of the original program's code, they will be at risk of infringing copyright.

Despite all the potential advantages offered by the Software Directive, what effect has this legislation had in practice? The answer is probably 'far less than was thought'. Manufacturers have come to realise that commercial success generally rests on making their systems accessible to all. There would seem to be more money to be made from encouraging your product to become the industry standard than there is from retaining exclusivity.

Another area which the legislators were afraid could be subject to cartels and monopolies was in networking between computers. Again, the market seems to have taken care of that problem, in that a networking system which cannot be adapted for expansion or linking with other networks is most unlikely to appeal to any customer.

Finally, it should be remembered that s 29 of the CDPA is a general fair dealing provision. Prior to the introduction of the Software Directive, s 29(1) of the CDPA stated: 'fair dealing with a literary, dramatic, musical or artistic work for the purposes of research or private study does not infringe any copyright in the work or, in the case of a published edition, in the typographical arrangement'.

In implementing the Software Directive, Parliament rather enthusiastically added the following subsection:

'(4)   It is not fair dealing—

(a)   to convert a computer program expressed in a low level language into a version expressed in a higher level language, or

(b)   incidentally in the course of so converting the program, to copy it,

(these acts being permitted if done in accordance with section 50B (decompilation)).'

In fact, it is questionable whether the whole effect of s 29 of the CDPA has been taken away, because the Software Directive allows Member States to make fair dealing provisions in accordance with the Berne Convention, and s 29 of the CDPA would certainly be covered by this. It can therefore be argued that s 29 of the CDPA still applies in respect of all acts other than the two specified, which would avoid some of the complexities introduced by the Software Directive – although the number of programmers happy to work in machine code without conversion is likely to be limited.

6.2   SECTION 56 OF THE CDPA

Section 56 of the CDPA is of general application to copyright works of all classifications. It applies when a copy of a work in electronic form is purchased on terms which, expressly or impliedly or by virtue of any rule of law, allow the purchaser to copy the work, or to adapt it or make copies of an adaptation, in connection with his use of it.

If there are no express terms prohibiting transfer by the purchaser of the copy of the work, imposing obligations which continue after a transfer, prohibiting assignment of any licence, or terminating any licence on a transfer, anything which the original purchaser was allowed to do may also be done without infringement of copyright by a subsequent transferee, or successive subsequent transferees. A transferor must then delete and otherwise cease to use all copies, including backup copies, of the work which he may have made in the course his own use of the work before transferring the originally purchased copy on to a transferee.

A principal purpose of this provision is to deal with the problem of authorised copies of works, for example computer programs, which are bought on disks or other electronic carriers. Such copies are often provided under so-called 'shrink-wrapped' or 'click-wrapped' licences which grant permission to use the copyright work but impose conditions intended to restrict the uses which may be made of it and reserve the right of the licensor to terminate the licence for breach of its terms. There is uncertainty about the extent to which shrink-wrapped licences are enforceable against purchasers of electronic copies of works, although recent decisions in the US and in Scotland suggest that judicial opinion may be coming to treat them as enforceable[1].

Whether or not such shrink-wrap licences are enforceable against the original purchaser of an electronic copy of a work, the problems of enforceability are increased if that copy is transferred, whether by sale or gift, to another user who may not be aware of the terms of the original licence and who is not a party to it. Section 56 of the CDPA in part deals with this problem in copyright terms. It may be said that a transferee of such a copy, who will be aware of the need for a copyright licence, is on notice that the licence granted to his transferor may be available to him as transferee. Such licence must be taken in its entirety, including any enforceable restrictions which the licence may contain: a transferee of a contract cannot take parts of the contract selectively, ignoring those parts of it which do not suit him. Perhaps,

---

1   See *Step-Saver Data Systems v Wyse* 939 F2d 91 (3rd Cir 1991); *Arizona Retail Systems Inc v The Software Link Inc* 4 CCH Comp Cas 46, 963, 27 July 1993 (shrink-wrap licences not enforceable); *ProCD v Zeidenberg* 1 EPLR 303 (1996); *Beta Computers (Europe) Ltd v Adobe Systems (Europe) Ltd* Court of Session (Lord Penrose) 14 December 1995 (shrink-wrap licence enforceable).

therefore, the transferee of an electronic copy who needs a copyright licence to use that copy will find himself obliged to choose between being an unlicensed user, and so an infringer, or being a licensed user on the terms of his transferor's licence, warts and all. Alternatively, he may be able to rely on statutory lawful user rights, or an implied licence.

If the electronic copy transferred is a database as defined by the Database Regulations, the copyright owner's ability to control use of the database through restrictive licence terms, and to control transfers of the electronic copy of the database, is limited by the Database Regulations, reg 9, which inserts a new s 50D(1) into the CDPA as follows:

> '50D(1)   It is not an infringement of copyright in a database for a person who has a right to use the database or any part of the database, (whether under a licence to do any of the things restricted by the copyright in the database or otherwise) to do, in the exercise of that right, anything which is necessary for the purposes of access to and use of the contents of the database or of that part of the database;'

and by reg 10, which inserts a new s 296B into the CDPA as follows:

> 's 296B   Where under an agreement a person has a right to use a database or part of a database, any term or condition in the agreement shall be void in so far as it purports to prohibit or restrict the performance of any act which would but for s 50D infringe the copyright in the database.'

In the case of an electronic copy of a database, therefore, it is impossible to impose on a person having a right to use the database, who is thus a lawful user, an enforceable licence term which purports to prohibit or restrict anything which is necessary for the purposes of access to and use of the contents of the database, or of that part of the database which the lawful user has a right to use. Further, the right to control any subsequent distribution, sale or other circulation (except by rental or lending) of a purchased copy of a database will be exhausted on its first issue to the public by sale to the original purchaser with the consent of the copyright owner[1], so that the copyright owner will no longer be able to prevent subsequent and successive transfers of that copy.

In the result, the combination of Database Regulations, regs 9 and 10 and CDPA, ss 18, 18A and 56 have the effect of:

– enabling first purchasers and subsequent transferees of disk copies of databases, as lawful users, to ignore licence terms included in shrink-wrapped licences imposed on them to the extent that such terms prohibit or restrict access to or use of the contents of such databases, such terms being made void by the new CDPA, s 296B;

– preventing the copyright owner from controlling further sales or other distribution of those copies; and

– enabling any subsequent transferee of the disk, as well as the original purchaser, to claim lawful user rights in that part of the database to which a right of access has been granted.

These provisions apply to copyright in databases, as defined by the Database Directive and by the Database Regulations, but:

---

1   CDPA, ss 18 and 18A.

–   they do not apply to database right, which has its own distinct lawful user rights and is not subject to ss 18, 18A or 56 of the CDPA; and

–   although ss 18, 18A and 56 of the CDPA apply to non-database compilations, neither the Database Regulations, regs 9 or 10 nor the new ss 50D and 296B of the CDPA apply to non-database compilations.

It follows that the copyright owner of a non-database compilation is able to impose on its licensees contractual restrictions on use of that compilation which would not be enforceable in relation to a database, and to apply s 56 of the CDPA to make such restrictions enforceable against the transferee of electronic copies of the compilation.

The latter freedom to impose restrictions on use may be important to some non-database compilation copyright owners: the inability to do so may be a serious disadvantage to database copyright owners who are prevented by s 296B of the CDPA from imposing certain such restrictions on use.

The meaning of 'use' in relation to information was considered by the House of Lords in a data protection context in *R v Brown*[1], when 'use' was widely interpreted. A similarly wide interpretation of 'use' in a database context will heighten the importance of the distinction between databases, the 'use' of which may not be contractually restricted, and non-database compilations to which the prohibition of restrictions on 'use' imposed by Database Regulations, regs 9 and 10 (CDPA, ss 50D and 296B) do not apply. While 'use' of information and 'use' of databases may be different concepts, databases are essentially compilations of information and so the distinction between the two may be more apparent than real.

6.3   COPYRIGHT LAWFUL USERS OF DATABASES

The Database Directive is somewhat more helpful with its definitions than was the Software Directive. A 'lawful user' is explained (in Recital 34 of the Database Directive) to be someone to whom the rightholder has chosen to make available a copy of the database (whether by on-line service or by other means of distribution). Under the Database Directive, the lawful user of a database is permitted to do any restricted act necessary for the purposes of access to the contents of the database and its normal use, a provision reminiscent of a similar one in the Software Directive. However, there is no definition of what constitutes 'normal use' of a database: it is likely in all cases to include accessing the database in order to view the information contained, but beyond that may be a matter for determination on a case-by-case basis. In particular, it is difficult to envisage a database in the course of normal use of which it might be necessary to communicate, display or perform the database to the public – but logically this is permitted to the lawful user. The term may have a wider meaning than the term 'intended purpose' used in a somewhat equivalent context in Art 5(1) of the Software Directive, in that 'normal use' would appear to be defined by the uses made of the database by users, whereas 'intended purpose' begs the question 'intended by whom?' to which one plausible answer must be 'the rightholder'.

---

1   [1996] 1 AC 543.

The Database Regulations echo the term 'lawful user', but define it slightly differently and in line instead with the definition of a lawful user under the Software Regulations: a 'lawful user' is someone who (whether under a licence to do any of the acts restricted by any database right in the database or otherwise) has a right to use the database. However, the difference from the definition in the Database Directive is unlikely to be material, in that it is if anything broader since it could be taken to encompass a right such as that given by s 56 of the CDPA as well as any implied licence, whereas the Database Directive's definition would not necessarily cover a right to use under a statutory provision.

Article 15 of the Database Directive renders any contractual provision contrary to this exception void. These provisions have, by regs 9 and 10 of the Database Regulations respectively, been incorporated as ss 50D and 296B of the CDPA.

Certain other exceptions to the restricted acts are permitted under the Database Directive, including those that are traditional for the Member State. Thus, the fair dealing provisions of s 29 of the CDPA are preserved (in contrast to their express exclusion in respect of the Software Directive's permitted acts), although by a somewhat clumsy mechanism in that databases are first 'carved out' of the general ambit of s 29(1) of the CDPA and then reinserted in a new subs 29(1A). Subsection 29(1A) of the CDPA permits fair dealing with a database for the purpose of research (which at first sight includes commercial research) or private study, as long as the source of the information is indicated – in other words, the use of the database is conditional on some form of acknowledgement. There is no attempt to include any qualitative assessment of the purpose of the research in question, in line with the existing fair dealing provisions. However, a new subs 29(5) of the CDPA, reflecting Art 6(2)(b) of the Database Directive, expressly excludes from the permission for fair dealing 'the doing of anything in relation to a database for the purpose of research for a commercial purpose'. This very broad wording effectively restricts the operation of the whole fair dealing provision to purely private, and non-commercial purposes. What is considered to be commercial may be construed strictly, given the requirements in Art 6(2)(b) of the Database Directive that illustration for teaching or scientific research be the 'sole purpose' of the permitted uses and that use be only to the extent justified by the non-commercial purpose in question, even though this is not expressly incorporated in s 29 of the CDPA. Thus, even if research is initially undertaken as part of a charitable organisation, any database cannot be exploited beyond the extent required for that research, and if the information from the database is indirectly used as part of any associated commercial activity, the later use is likely to infringe and not to be fair dealing. What is meant by 'illustration' is not defined, although in most cases this will be obvious on the facts – indeed, it could be said that most of teaching beyond the imparting of principles consists of illustration.

The other exceptions permitted under Art 6(2) of the Database Directive were reproduction of a non-electronic database for private purposes and use for purposes of public security or an administrative or judicial procedure. Although (as discussed below) the exception in respect of public administration and judicial proceedings has been implemented for the UK in respect of database right itself, this exception has not been incorporated in respect of the copyright aspects of a database. The first exception was not applicable to the UK: Recital 35 of the Database Directive makes it clear that it only applies to those Member States which have a blank media or reprographic levy aimed at compensating right owners, and the UK does not.

6.4   DATABASE RIGHT LAWFUL USERS

Article 8 of the Database Directive, implemented in reg 19 of the Database Regulations, provides the basic exceptions from the restricted acts in respect of database right for lawful users of databases which have been made available to the public in whatever manner, although these take a somewhat different form from the copyright exceptions. Thus, such users cannot, inter alia, be prevented from extracting and/or re-utilising insubstantial parts of the contents of a database for any purpose – subject to the qualification that where the lawful user is entitled to extract and/or re-utilise only a part of a database, this provision (and the other permitted exceptions) shall apply only to that part. What is 'insubstantial' may be evaluated either qualitatively or quantitatively – so that the extraction or re-utilisation of a very small quantity, which nevertheless encapsulates the most valuable aspect of the database, may not be permitted. This is consistent with the test for copyright infringement, which requires the copying to be of the whole or a substantial part – substantiality being evaluated qualitatively or quantitatively, so that copying a small part could equally infringe the copyright as the database right. The extraction of so-called 'meta-data' – for example that a particular item of information is *not* present – is not directly addressed by the Database Directive, but transient extraction of substantial parts of an electronic database while searching for meta-data may infringe database rights.

The lawful user right is subject to the qualification that the lawful user may not perform acts which conflict with the normal exploitation of the database or unreasonably prejudice the legitimate interests of its maker. For database right normal user rights to arise, the database must initially have been made available to the public by the maker or rightholder. Further, the lawful user may not cause prejudice to the holder of a copyright or related right in respect of the works or services contained in the database. These qualifications are in broad terms and are not defined further; they presumably relate to Art 9(2) of the Berne Convention, which states that the countries of the EU may 'permit the reproduction of [copyright] works in certain special cases, provided that such reproduction does not conflict with a normal exploitation of the work and does not unreasonably prejudice the legitimate interests of the author'.

The lawful user rights may not be restricted or excluded by contract – any contractual provisions purporting to do so will be null and void (Database Directive, Art 8, implemented in reg 19(2) of the Database Regulations) – although their impact can be minimised by careful drafting of licences such that the user becomes a lawful user only in respect of limited parts of the database and with limited forms of permitted use.

In addition, Art 9 of the Database Directive permits Member States to provide for some 'fair dealing' type exceptions from the database right. These include, in parallel to the equivalent copyright exceptions, extraction of items from a non-electronic database for private purposes and extraction and/or re-utilisation for purposes of public security or an administrative or judicial procedure. The UK implementation again (as for the copyright lawful users) ignores the first of these, but Sch 1 to the Database Regulations sets out in exhaustive detail permitted uses of databases which will not infringe database right. They include: any use whatsoever for the purposes of, or of reporting, Parliamentary or judicial proceedings or the proceedings of a Royal Commission; extraction (but not re-utilisation) of information from public registers as long as this is done with the authorisation of the appropriate person; use by the Crown of databases the contents of which have been communicated to it in the course of public business; and the doing of acts specifically authorised by Act of Parliament. The remaining exceptions – illustration for teaching or scientific research – are very similar to their equivalents in respect of copyright protection for databases, and similarly apply only to the extent justified for the non-commercial purpose concerned. However, in the case of database right there is no 'sole purpose' test in the Database Directive itself, so the interpretation of what is commercial may be very slightly less stringent (insofar as any infringement of database right is not simultaneously an infringement of copyright).

Finally, the database right in a particular copy of a product embodying the database can be exhausted by the first sale of that copy, in the same way as other intellectual property rights. This provision is designed to avoid any potential clash with Art 30 of the EC Treaty, which is intended to ensure free movement of goods among the Member States and thereby encourage the development of a truly common market. Thus, once a CD-ROM or other product containing a copy of a database has been sold, the owner of the database right will not be able to prevent re-sale of that CD-ROM or other product . Extraction or re-utilisation of insubstantial parts of the database from that CD-ROM or other product by a legitimate second or later purchaser will be protected from infringing the database right by the lawful user right for those purchasers in the same way as they were protected for the first purchaser. Whether restrictions on a first purchaser's rights to the product, such as retention of title clauses, would be workable in practice on this sort of commodity, remains to be seen.

Where, however, the database is not embodied in physical products but is only accessed on-line, there will be no such exhaustion since the database itself will never be sold, merely access rights to it. These can be controlled by contract.

6.5   LAWFUL USERS OF NON-DATABASE COMPILATIONS

Where a compilation does not fall within the definition of a database for the purposes of the Database Directive, then the concept of a 'lawful user' is undefined. As 'lawful user' is a concept introduced from Europe in both the Software and Database Directives, there is no equivalent definition in the CDPA as a whole. Thus, although there will be those who are entitled to use a non-database compilation, either of right or under the terms of a licence of some form, they will not be 'lawful users' as such and there are no specific statutory exceptions to any protection the compilation may enjoy (principally, copyright), which may be invoked save for the transfer of rights under s 56 of the CDPA, discussed above.

6.6 LAWFUL USE, FAIR DEALING AND S 29 OF THE CDPA IN RELATION TO NON-DATABASE COMPILATIONS

Under s 29 of the CDPA, 'fair dealing' with a literary work for the purposes of research (including commercial research) or private study does not infringe copyright. 'Dealing' in this context may include any act such as copying or adapting, which would otherwise infringe the copyright or database right. It may equally be fair dealing, under s 30 of the CDPA, to copy for the purpose of criticism or review, or in the course of reporting current events (as long as a sufficient acknowledgement is made as to the source of the material copied).

The test for what is 'fair' is a matter of degree and the impression the court forms of the defendant's conduct – but any dealing which may have an impact on the copyright owner's ability to exploit the work is very unlikely to be considered 'fair'. Similarly, if the material has been published in breach of confidence, then it is unlikely to be considered fair – although leaking information which it is in the public interest to reveal may survive this hurdle. Thus, the copier's motive may be relevant to what is or is not 'fair'. Copying of a complete work, with the addition only of marginal notes, is unlikely to qualify as fair dealing for the purpose of criticism; but a long passage with detailed commentary may.

In the United States and, arguably, to some extent in Europe also, the copyright holder's motive may have become relevant to the courts' interpretation of what may or may not be permitted, whether under the rubric of 'fair dealing' or otherwise. For example, in the *Magill* case[1] the European Court of Justice held that reliance on copyright to prevent a competitor from publishing a competing product may in exceptional circumstances constitute an abuse of a dominant position by the right owners contrary to Art 86 of the EC Treaty, and required them to license the relevant information. One of the key factors in the decision was that the right owners, by their conduct, had reserved to themselves the secondary market of weekly television guides, excluding all competition in that market by denying access to the basic information which was the indispensable raw material for a weekly guide. This principle could equally be applied to copyright over databases and non-database compilations – although by definition the information contained in a compilation must be available from other sources and therefore the copyright owner is unlikely to be in quite the same kind of dominant position as the television stations in *Magill*.

6.7 COMMERCIAL USE OF COMPUTER PROGRAMS, NON-DATABASE COMPILATIONS AND DATABASES

It is arguable that computer programs – and in fact electronics systems generally – are treated differently from other technologies in that an infringement with a view to developing a commercial product is specifically permitted and condoned. This attitude is reflected not only in the Software Regulations, but also in the Design Right (Semiconductor Topographies) Regulations 1989, which state that it is not an infringement of design right in a semiconductor topography to reproduce the design

---

1   Case T-69/89.

for the purpose of analysing or evaluating the design or analysing, evaluating or teaching the concepts, processes, systems or techniques embodied in it. Compare this with s 60(5)(a) and (b) of the Patents Act 1977 which state that there will be no infringement of a patent if the act is done privately and for purposes *which are not commercial*, or for experimental purposes relating to the subject matter of the invention. There is no equivalent encouragement here for, say, a pharmaceutical company to work on another's patented product with a view to producing a commercial rival or accessory. Whether this generosity by the legislators is based on the belief that the operation of electronic systems is fundamental to the passing of information and that intellectual property rights should therefore be less restrictive, or whether it was prompted by the belief that Europe had some catching up to do against the rest of the world in developing its electronics, computer and software is a matter of conjecture.

The same generosity has not been extended to databases: commercial use is more strictly constrained than private or other non-commercial use. Non-database compilations fall in an intermediate position, in that, as discussed at **6.6** above, the applicable fair dealing provisions do not necessarily exclude a limited degree of commercial use.

Chapter 7

CHANGES TO THE COPYRIGHT, DESIGNS AND PATENTS ACT 1988

7.1 Under the Software Regulations – 7.2 Under the Database Regulations – 7.3 Effect on provisions relating to computer-generated works (ss 9(3) and 178 of the CDPA) – 7.4 Effect on originality in computer programs and non-database tables and compilations – 7.5 Effect on originality of databases

7.1 UNDER THE SOFTWARE REGULATIONS

The Software Regulations amended the definition of a 'literary work' in s 3(1) of the CDPA to include a new subs (c), bringing preparatory design material for a computer program (such as a flowchart) into protection as a literary work. Software design material would previously have been protected under UK copyright law – even if it was a flow chart which might otherwise be thought of as an artistic work – but defining it as a literary work made no significant difference and was not controversial. The Software Directive had provided that 'the term "computer programs" shall include their preparatory design materials'[1]: this provision was not fully reflected in the Software Regulations.

Section 18 of the CDPA, which deals with infringement of copyright by issuing copies to the public, was amended to specify that issuing copies in respect of a computer program is an infringement only upon the first sale of a particular copy and not in respect of any later dealings in that copy. This is the exhaustion provision, which is also mirrored in the Database Directive. The definition of 'infringing copy' in s 27 of the CDPA was amended accordingly, so that a copy which has once legitimately been sold anywhere in the European Union is not an infringing copy if imported into and resold in the UK.

Section 21 of the CDPA, which deals with infringement by making of adaptations, was amended by insertion of a new subs 21(3)(ab) to specify that an adaptation of a computer program means an arrangement or altered version of that program. Subsection 21(4) of the CDPA had formerly excluded from the meaning of 'translation' translations of computer programs into different languages or codes (for example, from source to object code) incidentally in the course of running the program; this provision was dropped.

Section 17 of the CDPA already provides that copying in relation to any description of work (thus including computer programs and databases) includes the making of copies which are transient or are incidental to some other use of the work.

---

1   Software Directive, Art 1(1).

The most significant change was the introduction of the rights of decompilation, to make back-up copies, and for lawful users to make copies or adaptations for certain restricted purposes. Terms in contracts which purport to exclude these rights are made null and void by the insertion of s 296A of the CDPA to that effect. As these rights have been treated in detail in Chapter 6 (at **6.1**) above, they will not be further discussed here.

Finally, reg 10 of the Software Regulations tailored the level of protection available against dealers in devices designed to circumvent copy-protection – that is, technical copying devices which could overcome the in-built anti-copy protection many manufacturers had introduced. This provision appears in s 296 of the CDPA. A person who issues copies of a copyright work to the public has the same rights against such dealers as the copyright owner. In respect of devices designed to circumvent copy-protection for computer programs, however, their rights were limited to being enforceable where the dealing in such devices is carried out in the course of a business.

7.2   UNDER THE DATABASE REGULATIONS

The changes made by the Database Regulations to existing UK copyright law look on their face to be small but they reflect a major change in approach. Thus, in relation to the existing copyright law one of the main issues raised by implementation of the Database Directive is that of subsistence, as to which it is recognised that the implementation of the Database Directive may deprive databases that would otherwise have secured copyright protection in the UK from such protection. However, there is a provision making it clear that copyright will continue to subsist in databases made on or before 27 March 1996, when the Database Directive was published, until the end of their copyright term, whether or not they would be eligible for copyright protection under the Database Directive. The relevant provisions of the CDPA in the UK as to subsistence are ss 1 and 3. The former, providing that 'copyright ... subsists in, [inter alia], original literary, dramatic, [or] musical works' remains unchanged but the expressions that it employs are themselves defined in s 3, which has already been amended once, in response to the Software Directive. In relation to literary works, this section now (showing successive amendments) states:

'**3.   Literary, dramatic and musical works**

(1)   In this Part—
        "literary work" means any work, other than a dramatic or musical work, which is written, spoken or sung, and accordingly includes—

        (a)   a table or compilation, ~~and~~ *other than a database*
        (b)   a computer program, ~~*and*~~
        (c)   *preparatory design material for a computer program, and*
        (d)   *a database ...*'

Previous amendments are in italics and in crossed-through ordinary text. This is now amended further, by the addition of the words which are both in italics and are underlined. Section 3 of the CDPA clarifies that a 'table or compilation' can amount to a literary work. Works which meet the new definition of a database are now excluded from this and treated as separate literary works in their own right. A definition of database is added as a new s 3A:

> '*3A. Databases*
>
> *(1) In this Part "database" means a collection of independent works, data or other materials which—*
>
> > *(a) are arranged in a systematic or methodical way, and*
> > *(b) are individually accessible by electronic or other means.*
>
> *(2) For the purposes of this Part a literary work consisting of a database is original if, and only if, by reason of the selection or arrangement of the contents of the database the database constitutes the author's own intellectual creation.*'

Section 3A(1) of the CDPA effectively adopts the language of Art 1(2) of the Database Directive, and s 3A(2) that of Art 3(1). However, the approach adopted in relation to Art 3 of the Database Directive differs radically from that adopted in the UK implementation of the Software Directive. There was no definition of the term 'computer program' either in the Software Directive or in the CDPA and it was not felt necessary to introduce one into the CDPA when the Software Directive was implemented in the UK.

Finally, the definition of the restricted act of 'adaptation' in s 21 of the CDPA is further amended, paralleling the changes introduced in response to the Software Directive and reflecting Art 5(b) of the Database Directive. A new subs 21(3)(ac) of the CDPA is added, stating that adaptation, in relation to a database, means an arrangement or altered version of the database or a translation of it.

7.3   EFFECT ON PROVISIONS RELATING TO COMPUTER-GENERATED WORKS (SS 9(3) AND 178 OF THE CDPA)

A computer-generated work is defined in s 178 of the CDPA as one which is generated by a computer in circumstances such that there is no human author of it. This does not relate to works produced using computers as tools – for example, for word-processing or as the support platform for a computer-aided design package. Rather, it is concerned with works produced by a computer, presumably applying software previously written, to a problem set by a human operator – for example, calculating the optimum configuration of electrical components in a circuit to minimise the resistance of the connections between them.

In respect of such works, s 9(3) of the CDPA states that the author shall be taken to be the person who made the arrangements necessary for the work to be generated – the programmer or operator.

The test for originality in respect of computer-generated works is not well-defined – there have not been any cases in which this was a significant issue. One leading copyright text suggests that the test should be whether the work is objectively original, such that its creation by a human would have taken skill, labour or experience sufficient to confer copyright. If so, then the fact that it was generated by a computer (capable of carrying out much the same work with a trivial expenditure of time or effort) should not prejudice its qualification for copyright.

7.4   EFFECT ON ORIGINALITY IN COMPUTER PROGRAMS AND NON-DATABASE TABLES AND COMPILATIONS

The standard of originality for copyright protection of literary works is a difficult one to quantify. A copyright claimant needs to establish that the work he has produced arose neither from slavish copying, nor from an essentially mechanical process of arrangement such as, for example, putting a list of words into alphabetical order. The production of the work must have entailed skill, labour or experience – or all three – for the result to attract the protection of copyright. How much skill or labour is required to have been invested, in order to invoke copyright protection for the resulting work, is a matter of degree and depends upon the circumstances. It is broadly true, however, that the greater the skill and labour invested, the stronger the protection which will be afforded since the degree of originality, and the proportion of the total work which could be claimed to have originality, are likely to be accordingly greater.

Computer programs, consisting of a written text (albeit in a programming language rather than a human one), may have copyright both in their preparatory works such as flowcharts and in the source and object (machine executable) codes. There is no definition in the CDPA of what a 'program' is, but neither has there been any controversy as to what is or is not a program in practice. The changes introduced to the CDPA by the Software Regulations have had no impact upon the standard of originality which is required for a program to attract copyright.

Where the work is a table or compilation (other than one qualifying as a 'database'), the originality will lie in the author's skill and labour in collecting (not necessarily producing), selecting and arranging the individual items making up the whole. The result is that the parts themselves are not protected by the copyright in the compilation as such; they may or may not be copyright works in their own right, but the copyright protection of the compilation is limited to the specific selection and arrangement. A competitor who obtains a similar collection of material from either the same or another source, but makes his own selection and arrangement, may not infringe the first compiler's copyright even if there is significant overlap between the two resulting compilations. Where no selection or arrangement is involved, there may still be copyright based on the comprehensiveness of the collection, but this will need to be all the more striking in its own right.

Copyright subsistence in compilations has not often been put in issue in the UK. Subsistence was conceded in the UK's so-called 'directory' case[1] unlike the *Feist v Rural Telecom* case in the US. In the US case[2], Rural, a telephone service provider, published an alphabetical list of some 7700 subscriber names, towns and telephone numbers. Feist published a larger directory, covering a wider area, including some 1300 listings copied out of Rural's directory. The Supreme Court reversed two decisions in favour of the plaintiff in the lower courts, holding that the Rural directory

---

1   *Waterlow Directories Ltd v Reed Information Services Ltd* [1992] FSR 409.
2   *Feist Publications Inc v Rural Telephone Service Co*, 499 US 340.

did not have the requisite level of originality to qualify for copyright protection. Originality in the copyright sense, the Court held, meant independent creation plus some minimal degree of creativity, which may be very low but must none the less be present. It criticised the so-called 'sweat of the brow' test, characterising the courts which had applied this as having 'thereby eschewed the most fundamental axiom of copyright law – that no one may copyright facts or ideas'. There has not been any case which has considered electronic databases, whether on-line or on CD-ROM, which by their nature are rarely *selective* and where much of the arrangement is chosen by the person accessing them. Instead, much of the commercial value of such databases lies in their *comprehensive* nature and the freedom of the user to choose how to search.

This subject is apt to cause a degree of confusion and so, in order to keep the matter as clear-cut as possible, we would suggest that in considering the issue the reader should bear in mind two cardinal principles which have been adverted to elsewhere in this book:

(1)   methodical arrangement does not make a non-database compilation into a database; and

(2)   a compilation must be compared against the full definition of a database as set out in the Database Regulations to determine its classification as either a database or as a literary work non-database compilation.

The granting of database right protection in the first place recognises the potentially limited nature of copyright protection for electronic databases when the requirements for copyright to subsist are formulated in terms of originality. Indeed, it is quite hard to conceptualise what is meant in Art 5 of the Database Directive by the expression of the database which is protectable by copyright, although it is suggested in Recital 15 of the Database Directive that this covers 'the structure of the database', which is presumably what some database designers would refer to as the 'database schema'.

7.5   EFFECT ON ORIGINALITY OF DATABASES

As we have already seen, prior to the introduction of the Database Regulations databases were protected under UK copyright law as tables or compilations. Thus, the standard of originality required of them was the same as that which still applies for non-database tables and compilations: the expenditure of sufficient skill, labour or experience in the collection, selection or arrangement of the data.

The 'author's own intellectual creation' wording in the new s 3A of the CDPA in relation to databases has no counterpart anywhere else in UK law, and in particular does not appear in relation to computer software, despite its appearance in the Software Directive. It is a carry-over from the continental, civil law approach to copyright which confers protection on works only because of their status as the emanations of the author's creative genius. As such, UK law applies a lower standard and will protect a wider class of works. It is not apparent why it would not have been possible to implement the Database Directive by adopting only the 'selection or arrangement' wording, thereby leaving 'the author's own intellectual creation' implicit, as many had suggested, but the UK Government chose not to adopt this course. As a result, it is difficult to estimate the standard of originality which may be required to meet this criterion. The words taken literally do not give much help: a creation may be anything that is made, not copied, exactly as under the old copyright standard. The criterion that it be an 'intellectual' creation is almost tautologous, as it is difficult to see how a database within the definition could be created by purely mechanical means; this term probably does no more than exclude computer-generated databases, as discussed above. Thus, it remains to be seen, in light of future case-law, how this standard will be interpreted and applied by the courts.

The approach actually adopted may be a result of the criticism by the Commission of the omission of the 'author's own intellectual creation' wording, when the UK came to implement the Software Directive. The Copyright Directorate responded by arguing that this was implicit in the concept of originality under UK copyright law, but the new Database Regulations place this approach in doubt, by conceding that there are tables or compilations which are not the 'author's own intellectual creation' but which are sufficiently original under UK law to attract copyright. How then can the UK say that other works must be the 'author's own intellectual creation' for copyright to subsist? The approach adopted in the Database Regulations would, however, appear to have had the desired effect of appeasing the Commission, as is apparent from the most recent Commission Report on the implementation of Community legislation which states:

> 'All Member States have now notified the Commission of national measures implementing Directive 91/250/EEC on the legal protection of computer programs. The examination of the measures notified by the United Kingdom revealed problems of compatibility with Community legislation, the United Kingdom having chosen to retain certain concepts of copyright in the transposal of the Directive, instead of adapting its traditions in this area to the requirements of the Community regulations. After an Article 169 letter to the United Kingdom and a reply from the British authorities, it transpired that the issue could be resolved once and for all by transposing the other Directives on copyright into national law.'

Much UK criticism of the Database Directive during its passage was directed to the effect it was perceived that the measure would have of reducing the protection believed by many to have been enjoyed by databases under copyright in the UK. This may, however, be a myth, and the practical effect of the Regulations on copyright is less significant than some commentators may think, since (as mentioned above) the extent to which compilations such as databases do secure copyright under UK law has been rarely tested and, in those cases where it has been, the results have been somewhat equivocal.

Chapter 8

LICENSING AND ENFORCEMENT

*8.1 Introduction – 8.2 Licensing – 8.3 References to the Copyright Tribunal –
8.4 Enforcement and remedies*

8.1 INTRODUCTION

It will rarely be realistic or sensible to separate such copyright as may subsist in the 'selection or arrangement of the contents of a database' from the database right that also subsists in such database. The consequence of this in terms of licensing is that the two should be licensed in one and the same transaction and by means of the same document, and in terms of litigation that most actions will involve the assertion of the two rights together. The only exception in each case will arise where, for whatever reason, the respective rights are not held by the same person or company, a situation which should be remedied if at all possible by securing suitable assignments, but which is not farfetched given that the provisions relating to first ownership as between the two rights differ. In the case of copyright, first ownership vests in the 'author'; in the case of database right, the first ownership vests in the 'maker'[1], who need not be, and may well not be, the same person as the author. In both cases, of course, these provisions are subject to employment relationships or agreements to the contrary. This chapter deals with both licensing and litigation in relation to such rights, as well as the jurisdiction of the Copyright Tribunal in relation to the terms of licences of such rights.

8.2 LICENSING

8.2.1 Introduction

We have already emphasised the importance of licensing such copyright as may subsist in the 'selection or arrangement of the contents of a database' at the same time and in the same document as the database right that also subsists in such database. A licensee ought not to take a licence of only one right without also securing a licence under the other right from whoever is the appropriate owner. In any licence of such rights, consideration should also be given to any copyright or neighbouring rights that may subsist in the contents of the database, although in some cases the contents will be either: (1) so old that any copyright in them has expired; or (2) material in which copyright is not capable of subsisting. The following discussion concentrates on the copyright and database right in databases themselves and, after starting with the

---

1   Database Regulations, regs 14 and 15.

statutory framework governing licences granted under these rights, reviews the nature of the provisions typically to be found in most such licences.

8.2.2   Statutory framework affecting licensing

Other than those constraints which are imposed under competition law in relation to intellectual property rights in general, and which are discussed below, there are relatively few statutory or common law provisions of relevance to the licensing of rights in copyright works and of database right.

To the limited extent that statute makes specific provision for dealing with rights in copyright works and in database right such provisions are identical[1], and are as set out in ss 90 to 93 of the CDPA. These sections deal respectively with assignments and licences, prospective ownership, exclusive licences and the right to pass under a will with unpublished work. Of particular relevance from the point of view of licensing are s 90(4) of the CDPA, dealing with priorities in licences and s 92 of the CDPA, dealing with the position of exclusive licensees. These provide as follows:

'**90   Assignment and licences**

. . .

(4)   A licence granted by a copyright owner is binding on every successor in title to his interest in the copyright, except a purchaser in good faith for valuable consideration and without notice (actual or constructive) of the licence or a person deriving title from such a purchaser; and references in this Part to doing anything with, or without, the licence of the copyright owner shall be construed accordingly.

92   Exclusive licences

(1)   In this Part an "exclusive licence" means a licence in writing signed by or on behalf of the copyright owner authorising the licensee to the exclusion of all other persons, including the person granting the licence, to exercise a right which would otherwise be exercisable exclusively by the copyright owner.

(2)   The licensee under an exclusive licence has the same rights against a successor in title who is bound by the licence as he has against the person granting the licence.'

In addition, the Database Regulations, reflecting the Database Directive, introduce ss 50D and 296B into the CDPA[2] in relation to copyright, and reg 19 of the Database Regulations in relation to database right[3]. The effect of these measures is to make specific provision for the benefit of 'lawful users' of databases and to impose limitations on the scope for 'contracting out' from these benefits, whether by the use of licence terms or otherwise[4].

---

1   Regulation 23 of the Database Regulations provides that ss 90 to 93 of the CDPA 'apply in relation to database right and databases in which that right subsists as they apply in relation to copyright and copyright works'.
2   Implementing Arts 6(1) and 15 of the Database Directive which is set out in Appendix 3.
3   Implementing Arts 8 and 15 of the Database Directive which is set out in Appendix 3.
4   These are analogous to provisions relating to computer programs, as to which see ss 50A, 50B 50C and 296A of the CDPA, inserted by the Software Regulations, implementing the Software Directive.

'50D Databases: permitted acts

(1) It is not an infringement of copyright in a database for a person who has a right to use the database or any part of the database, (whether under a licence to do any of the acts restricted by the copyright in the database or otherwise) to do, in the exercise of that right, anything which is necessary for the purposes of access to and use of the contents of the database or of that part of the database.

(2) Where an act which would otherwise infringe copyright in a database is permitted under this section, it is irrelevant whether or not there exists any term or condition in any agreement which purports to prohibit or restrict the act (such terms being, by virtue of section 296B, void).'

'296B Databases

Where under an agreement a person has a right to use a database or part of a database, any term or condition in the agreement shall be void in so far as it purports to prohibit or restrict the performance of any act which would but for section 50D infringe the copyright in the database.'

'19 Avoidance of certain terms affecting lawful users

(1) A lawful user of a database which has been made available to the public in any manner shall be entitled to extract or re-utilise insubstantial parts of the contents of the database for any purpose.

(2) Where under an agreement a person has a right to use a database, or part of a database, which has been made available to the public in any manner, any term or condition in the agreement shall be void in so far as it purports to prevent that person from extracting or re-utilising insubstantial parts of the contents of the database, or of that part of the database, for any purpose.'

Such provisions, by limiting the scope for the owner of these rights to impose restrictions on the manner in which a lawful user can exploit a database, can be perceived as having a basis in competition law. However, it is convenient to discuss general competition law considerations, which apply to all intellectual property rights, separately.

8.2.3 Competition law considerations

Any exploitation of intellectual property rights can have competition consequences, and hence be subject to competition law constraints. In Europe, these may arise either under national law or under the Treaty of Rome. Control under the former arises in the UK under the Restrictive Trade Practices Act 1976 and the Resale Prices Act 1976. The Restrictive Trade Practices Act 1976 expressly excludes most copyright licences from its scope[1] and this and the Resale Prices Act 1976 are due shortly to be replaced by the Competition Bill, once it has completed its passage through Parliament and been brought into force. This will establish a national competition law regime which is much more similar to EC competition law. Control under EC competition law can arise either under Art 86 of the EC Treaty[2] or, in relation to agreements only, under Art 85 of the EC Treaty. The Commission has established a framework of block

---

1   Schedule 3, para 5A.
2   As in *RTE v EC Commission, Magill TV Guide Ltd intervening* [1989] ECR 1141, [1989] 4 CMLR 739. For further analysis of *Magill* and Art 86, see Chapter 2 at **2.2**.

exemptions which set out those provisions in intellectual property licences that either: (1) do not fall within the scope of Art 85 of the EC Treaty; or (2) which are permitted under it having regard to the benefits that they confer. However, there is no block exemption covering the licensing of copyright, even in relation to computer software, and there have been no decided cases as to the permissible scope of restrictions in copyright licences. Accordingly, one can only proceed by drawing analogies from those areas of intellectual property licensing which have been the subject of case-law under Art 85 of the EC Treaty, or have given rise to block exemptions, in particular patents and know-how.

The Technology Transfer Block Exemption[1] lists, in Art 3, several restrictions in patent and know-how licences that are specifically 'blacklisted'. If these restrictions are found in an agreement then the Block Exemption cannot apply, nor can a party take advantage of the accelerated notification (or so-called 'opposition') procedure. The 'blacklisted' restrictions are:

'(1)   one party is restricted in the determination of prices, components of prices or discounts for the licensed products;

(2)   one party is restricted from competing within the common market with the other party, with undertakings connected with the other party or with other undertakings in respect of research and development, production, use or distribution of competing products without prejudice to the provisions of Article 2(1)(17) and (18);

(3)   one or both of the parties are required without any objectively justified reason:

(a)   to refuse to meet orders from users or resellers in their respective territories within the common market;

(b)   to make it difficult for users or resellers to obtain the products from other resellers within the common market, and in particular to exercise intellectual property rights or take measures so as to prevent users or resellers from obtaining outside, or from putting on the market in the licensed territory products which have been lawfully put on the market within the common market by the licensor or with his consent;

or do so as a result of a concerted practice between them;

(4)   the parties were already competing manufacturers before the grant of the licence and one of them is restricted, within the same technical field of use or within the same product market, as to the customers he may serve, in particular by being prohibited from supplying certain classes of user, employing certain forms of distribution or, with the aim of sharing customers, using certain types of packaging for the products, save as provided in Article 9(1)(7) and Article 2(1)(13);

(5)   the quantity of the licensed products one party may manufacture or sell or the number of operations exploiting the licensed technology he may carry out are subject to limitations, save as provided in Article 2(1)(8) and Article 2(1)(13);

(6)   the licensee is obliged to assign in whole or in part to the licensor rights to improvements to or new applications of the licensed technology;

(7)   the licensor is required, albeit in separate agreements or through automatic prolongation of the initial duration of the agreement by the inclusion of any new improvements, for a period exceeding that referred to in Article 1(2) and (3) not to license other undertakings to exploit the licensed technology in the licensed territory, or a party is required for a period exceeding that referred to in Article 1(2)

---

1   Regulation 240/96/EC of 31 January 1996.

and (3) or Article 1(4) not to exploit the licensed technology in the territory of the other party or of other licensees.'

Where a licence contains any of the provisions listed below, then Art 4 of the Technology Transfer Block Exemption mandates the use of the 'opposition procedure'. Accordingly, these provisions can be seen as potentially anti-competitive, even if they are not as objectionable as 'blacklisted' provisions. The relevant provisions are:

> '(a) the licensee is obliged at the time the agreement is entered into to accept quality specifications or further licences or to procure goods or services which are not necessary for a technically satisfactory exploitation of the licensed technology or for ensuring that the production of the licensee conforms to the quality standards that are respected by the licensor and other licensees;
> (b) the licensee is prohibited from contesting the secrecy or the substantiality of the licensed know-how or from challenging the validity of patents licensed within the common market belonging to the licensor or undertakings connected with him.'

It would be wise not to impose conditions similar to the above in any licence of copyright or database right. If such conditions are imposed, then one should consider notifying the licence to the Commission, unless the Commission's Notice on Minor Agreements applies[1].

As with copyright, there is no block exemption which covers the licensing of database right. Accordingly, licences of database right will be subject to Art 85 of the EC Treaty in the same way as any licence of an intellectual property right (as discussed above). However, the treatment of database right under UK competition law differs from that of copyright: there is no express exception under the Restrictive Trade Practices Act 1976 which is applicable to database right, unlike copyright[2].

8.2.4   Licensing terms

Licences of copyright and database right in databases, as with any licence of intellectual property rights, can take a wide variety of forms. The form will vary depending on whether the licence is direct to end users (in which case it may be convenient to have it in 'shrink-wrap' form, subject to issues as to the enforceability of the terms of such licence) or to intermediate licensees who then commercialise the licensed rights themselves by means of sub-licences to end-users. Licences in the latter case will cover much more than licences in the former, and indeed it will usually be advisable for the rights holder licensing an intermediate licensee to specify precisely the nature of the terms on which the licensee is authorised to sub-license to end-users. The following discussion of licence terms focuses on the rights in the database itself, but the policy adopted as to such rights should always be consistent with the position adopted as to any rights in the contents of the database.

---

1   See Chapter 9 at **9.1.5** for key details of the Notice on Minor Agreements.
2   However, licences of database right should still fall outside the Restrictive Trade Practices Act 1976, by virtue of the *Ravenseft* doctrine. *Re Ravenseft Property Limited's Application* [1978] QB 52, [1977] 1 All ER 47 held that a licence of property rights was neither a 'good' nor a 'service' and, hence, outside the RTPA. The Office of Fair Trading has applied the same principle to intellectual property rights (see Annual Report of the Director General of Fair Trading 1976, p 36).

(a) Exclusivity

Is the licence exclusive[1], sole (precluding the grant of other licences in respect of the same right) or (as will always be the case in licences to end users) non-exclusive? In the absence of specific provision, the last alternative is likely to be implied.

(b) Territorial scope

Which territory or territories are covered by the licence? The point is of especial importance in licences to intermediate licensees. The Database Directive is a purely European measure. Although its copyright provisions reflect the WIPO Copyright Treaty of 1996[2], there is as yet no equivalent elsewhere in the world to the *sui generis* database right that the Database Directive mandates Community Member States to confer. It should also be borne in mind that splitting the licensed territory as between European countries, in the case of a sole or exclusive licence, increases the risk that European competition law will have some bearing on the licence, and no contractual provision can provide true territorial division given the scope for parallel imports within the EEA.

(c) Other aspects of scope

In the case of a licence to an intermediate licensee, provision should be made permitting sub-licensing, as in the absence of such a provision a right to sub-license is not implied under English law. If such a licensee is only permitted to make copies, or to distribute these, this should be stated; in the absence of so doing, no such limitation will be inferred. The product range which is the subject of the licence should be specified, and the licence should also identify the precise nature of the technology by which the licensee is permitted to exploit the right (such as hard copy, CD-ROM, DVD-ROM, the Internet or otherwise). In addition, if there is any specific associated software, such as a specific operating system or any particular field of use, such as education or business, this should be stated. Slicing up the rights licensed in this way is of considerable importance to the licensor, as limiting this aspect of the licence may enable it to secure a wider variety of licensees. In the case of a licence to an end-user, as great a limitation on scope as possible should be included, subject to s 296B of the CDPA[3].

(d) Term of licence

The commencement date of the licence should be specified, as should its duration in the absence of premature termination. It is important here to note that copyright and database right have different natural terms, the former being 15 years from the end of the year in which it was first made, or if made available to the public before the end of such period, 15 years from the end of the year in which such making available

---

1   As to which, see s 92 of the CDPA.
2   Article 5 of which provides:
     'Compilations of Data (Databases)
     Compilations of data or other material, in any form, which by reason of the selection or
     arrangement of their contents constitute intellectual creations, are protected as such. This
     protection does not extend to the data or the material itself and is without prejudice to any
     copyright subsisting in the data or material contained in the compilation.'
3   Section 296B of the CDPA and reg 19(2) of the Database Regulations provide that any attempt to
     prevent a 'lawful user' from exercising certain acts are void. See Chapter 6 at **6.2** and **6.3** for
     further comment.

occurred, and the latter 70 years after the end of the year in which the author died. However, new terms for both rights can subsist in an amended database, subject to this meeting the 'selection or arrangement' criteria for copyright, or the more permissive criteria for database right, which requires a 'substantial change' including one 'resulting from the accumulation of successive additions, deletions or alterations which would result in the database being considered to be a "substantial new investment"'. Licences to end-users will typically be for the life of the right, whereas those for intermediate licensees will typically be for a term of a couple of years, with provision for them to grant sub-licences that are longer but which provide for the intermediate licensee's rights to vest in the rights owner, or as it directs on termination of the licence, to such intermediate licensee.

(e) Royalties and fees

The consideration for the licence, such as a single fee, or an initial and recurrent fee and/or a running royalty based on sales turnover by value or by volume, should of course be specified, as should any minimum royalty obligations imposed on intermediate licensees. In addition, in licences to such intermediate licensees there will be the usual 'royalty boilerplate' dealing with matters such as deeming (for non-arm's length sales by licensee, products hired or leased, and products sold as part of a larger piece of equipment), taxation (for example, whereby the licensee bears the risk of withholding taxes and other deductions, and pays the grossed up figure, with the licensor crediting any payments that it receives from the revenue authorities), reporting (at least as to sales figures), timing (monthly, quarterly, half-yearly or yearly), payment procedure (destination, currency conversion, exchange controls) and the position on overdue payments (interest, exchange loss).

(f) Licensee's obligations

Typical obligations on the part of an intermediate licensee may include: to use its best endeavours to promote the licensed goods, to include specified copyright notices, to comply with quality specifications, to provide samples to the licensor, and to use the licensor's trade mark (entering into a suitable licence agreement for registration purposes in relation to such trade mark) and not to use any other trade mark.

(g) Restrictions on licensee

Restrictions on an intermediate licensee typically included in licences may relate to territorial protection (although care should be taken with these from a European competition law point of view), being engaged or interested in any business which deals in competing products, and against soliciting licensor's employees. Another typical restriction imposed on both intermediate licensees and end users is against amending the licensed product. A provision that, in the event that such amendment is made, all rights in this would vest in the licensor, so as not to fragment such rights, would be analogous to that blacklisted under Art 3(6) of the Technology Transfer Block Exemption, and so should be used with care. However, non-exclusive licences back are permitted under this Block Exemption.

(h) Licensor's warranties

The most important warranty on the part of the licensor relates to its title to the rights being licensed, and the fact that it has done nothing with such rights inconsistent with the current licence, such as assigning the rights to a third party or granting a sole or an exclusive licence of the same rights to a third party. Additional considerations of especial importance here may relate to the contents of the database, as to which there may also be express warranties as to these not being defamatory, untrue or otherwise actionable. Any limitations on such warranty and on liability should also be set out.

(i) Termination and its consequences

Most licences provide for early termination on the occurrence of certain eventualities. Licences to intermediate licensees will often provide for termination without cause after a certain time, and invariably for termination for specified cause. Such cause on the part of the licensor may be the licensee's failure to pay royalties when due, or to achieve minimum sales or royalties, or on a change of control of licensee. Licences to end users, as well as to intermediate licensees, will typically provide for termination on the part of either party on unspecified breach by the other (subject to remedy where remediable) or insolvency. The agreement may also specify the consequences of termination, such as survival of certain provisions, the cessation of the licensed rights, and what, in the case of licences to intermediate licensees, is to be done with unsold products, and with sub-licences previously granted to end users.

(j) Boilerplate

Licence agreements, especially those with intermediate licensees, may also include a certain amount of 'boilerplate' such as provisions: precluding the licensee (or perhaps even the licensor) from assigning; as to there being no partnership; what to do in the event that others infringe the licensed rights or if the operation of the licence is alleged to infringe third party rights; as to the licensee not purporting to act as the licensor's agent; confidentiality[1]; further assurance; force majeure; severance or renegotiation in the event of partial illegality; notices precluding indulgence from constituting waiver, providing that the licence represents the entire agreement between the parties; specifying the governing law, the courts that have jurisdiction, and, where arbitration is provided for, the rules of the arbitral institute chosen, the language of arbitration and so on.

8.3   REFERENCES TO THE COPYRIGHT TRIBUNAL

Regulation 24 of the Database Regulations, somewhat misleadingly entitled 'Licensing of Database Right', provides for Sch 2 to the Database Regulations 'to have effect with respect to the licensing of database right'. In fact, the provision is of relatively narrow application, in that it provides for the Copyright Tribunal (the successor to the Performing Rights Tribunal) to have jurisdiction over 'licensing schemes' and 'licensing bodies' in relation to database right in the same way as it has already under parts of Chapter 7 of the CDPA in relation to copyright, including of course the copyright in the selection or arrangement of the contents of the database.

---

1   In appropriate circumstances, an obligation of confidentiality may help a database rightholder to assert that a database has not been 'made available to the public', so avoiding the restrictions imposed by reg 19 of the Database Regulations on contractual limitation of lawful user rights.

Apart from para 15 of Sch 2 to the Database Regulations, which gives the Copyright Tribunal jurisdiction over the terms of a compulsory licence awarded consequential to a Monopolies and Mergers Commission Report and an Order under the Fair Trading Act 1973, Sch 2 is exclusively concerned with the activities of 'licensing bodies'. A 'licensing body' is defined at para 1(2) as 'a society or other organisation which has as its main object, or one of its main objects, the negotiation or granting, whether as owner or prospective owner of a database right or as agent for him, of database right licences, and whose objects include the granting of licences covering the databases of more than one maker'. There is as an equivalent definition, substituting 'copyright' for 'database right', 'work' for 'database', and 'author' for 'maker' in the CDPA[1]. Thus, 'licensing body' is in effect another term for 'collecting society' and so, apart from para 15, which by its nature will hardly ever be used, Sch 2 has no application to licences negotiated by a single licensor, or even on behalf of a single licensor by such licensing body, given that paras 2 and 9 limit these jurisdictions to 'licensing schemes' and to other licences 'relating to database right which cover databases of more than one maker'.

The function of the Copyright Tribunal is to review the licensing practices of (and in particular the royalty rates charged by) such 'licensing bodies'. Under paras 3 to 8 of Sch 2 (and for copyright under ss 118 to 123 of the CDPA), the Copyright Tribunal is given control over 'licensing schemes' operated by licensing bodies. Under paras 10 to 13 of Sch 2 (and for copyright under ss 125 to 128 of the CDPA) the Copyright Tribunal is given powers in relation to licences granted or proposed to be granted by such bodies for extraction or re-utilisation of all or a substantial portion of a database (and copying, renting, lending, performing, broadcasting or including in a cable programme service in relation to copyright), unless the licence is pursuant to a 'licensing scheme'.

8.4 ENFORCEMENT AND REMEDIES

8.4.1 Introduction

As already noted, actions to enforce copyright in the selection or arrangement of the contents of a database and actions to enforce database right will in general be brought at one and the same time and in the same proceedings. In contrast with licensing, where consideration needs also to be given to any copyright or neighbouring rights in the contents, it will be rare to include the rights in the contents in any such proceeding, because the owner of the copyright in the selection or arrangement of the contents of a database and the database right is unlikely also either to own, or to have an exclusive licence to, rights in the contents themselves. One should not forget that the person who owns the copyright in the contents which are included in the database may also have his own cause of action.

Copyright in the selection or arrangement of a database, as in the contents of the database, can be enforced in England in either the criminal courts[2] or the civil courts, although the database right can only be enforced in the civil courts. However, the subtle nature of copyright in a database, as opposed to copyright in its contents, is

---

1   Section 116(3) of the CDPA.
2   See s 107 of the CDPA, as well as s 107A (not yet in force) and ss 108 to 110.

unlikely to make it a suitable subject for criminal proceedings. The owners of database rights do not share the rights and remedies of copyright owners set out at ss 99, 100 and 111 of the CDPA. These provide respectively for the availability of an order for 'delivery up'[1], for the right, without a court order but subject to other safeguards, to seize infringing copies and other articles, and for the right to request the customs authorities to prohibit the import (from outside the EEA) of infringing published literary, dramatic or musical works. The more useful right (conferred by the Counterfeit and Pirated Goods Regulation[2]), to have the customs authorities seize (at a point of entry into the Community) material suspected of infringing copyright or neighbouring right does not appear to cover material which infringes only the database right, unless the term 'neighbouring right' in the definition of 'pirated goods' in the Counterfeit and Pirated Goods Regulations is broad enough to cover such right.

8.4.2   Statutory provisions common to copyright and database right

To a considerable extent the statutory provisions setting out the rights and remedies in civil proceedings of the owners (and exclusive licensees) of copyright and database right are identical[3]. These are set out in ss 96 and 97 of the CDPA[4], which deal respectively with infringement actionable by the copyright owner and provisions as to damages in infringement actions, and in ss 101 and 102 of the CDPA, which relate to the rights and remedies of exclusive licensees. Section 96 of the CDPA gives the rights owner, whether this be a copyright owner or the owner of database right, the right to bring an action for infringement seeking the usual remedies in intellectual property actions ('all such relief by way of damages, injunctions, accounts or otherwise . . . as is available in respect of the infringement of any other property right') and s 97 of the CDPA provides for a very limited defence of innocence and for additional damages:

'**97   Provisions as to damages in infringement action**

(1)   Where in an action for infringement of copyright it is shown that at the time of the infringement the defendant did not know, and had no reason to believe, that copyright subsisted in the work to which the action relates, the plaintiff is not entitled to damages against him, but without prejudice to any other remedy.

(2)   The court may in an action for infringement of copyright having regard to all the circumstances, and in particular to—

(a)   the flagrancy of the infringement, and
(b)   any benefit accruing to the defendant by reason of the infringement,

award such additional damages as the justice of the case may require.'

---

1   As to which, ss 113 and 114 of the CDPA also make provision.
2   Regulation 3295/94/EC of 22 December 1994 laying down measures to prohibit the release for free circulation, export, re-export or entry for a suspensive procedure of counterfeit and pirated goods.
3   Regulation 23 of the Database Regulations provides that ss 96 to 98, 101 and 102 of the CDPA 'apply in relation to database right and databases in which that right subsists as they apply in relation to copyright and copyright works'.
4   Section 98 of the CDPA also applies to both copyright and database right, but is of limited application as it permits a defendant, where a licence is available as of right in consequence of a Monopolies and Mergers Commission Report, to limit the remedies available against it in infringement proceedings by undertaking to take a licence of right.

Section 97(2) of the CDPA is a provision, rare in English law, whereby an award of damages (additional damages, or 'flagrant damages') can be made other than on a purely compensatory basis, but this can only be claimed where the plaintiff elects to seek damages rather than an account of profits[1]. Sections 101 and 102 of the CDPA go on to provide for an exclusive licensee of copyright, and an exclusive licensee of database right, to bring its own action for infringement:

'**101 Rights and remedies of exclusive licensee**

(1) An exclusive licensee has, except against the copyright owner, the same rights and remedies in respect of matters occurring after the grant of the licence as if the licence had been an assignment.

(2) His rights and remedies are concurrent with those of the copyright owner; and references in the relevant provisions of this Part to the copyright owner shall be construed accordingly.

(3) In an action brought by an exclusive licensee by virtue of this section a defendant may avail himself of any defence which would have been available to him if the action had been brought by the copyright owner.

102 Exercise of concurrent rights

(1) Where an action for infringement of copyright brought by the copyright owner or an exclusive licensee relates (wholly or partly) to an infringement in respect of which they have concurrent rights of action, the copyright owner or, as the case may be, the exclusive licensee may not, without the leave of the court, proceed with the action unless the other is either joined as a plaintiff or added as a defendant.

(2) A copyright owner or exclusive licensee who is added as a defendant in pursuance of subsection (1) is not liable for any costs in the action unless he takes part in the proceedings.

(3) The above provisions do not affect the granting of interlocutory relief on an application by a copyright owner or exclusive licensee alone.

(4) Where an action for infringement of copyright is brought which relates (wholly or partly) to an infringement in respect of which the copyright owner and an exclusive licensee have or had concurrent rights of action—

(a) the court shall in assessing damages take into account—
  (i) the terms of the licence, and
  (ii) any pecuniary remedy already awarded or available to either of them in respect of the infringement;

(b) no account of profits shall be directed if an award of damages has been made, or an account of profits has been directed, in favour of the other of them in respect of the infringement; and

(c) the court shall if an account of profits is directed apportion the profits between them as the court considers just, subject to any agreement between them;

and these provisions apply whether or not the copyright owner and the exclusive licensee are both parties to the action.

(5) The copyright owner shall notify any exclusive licensee having concurrent rights before applying for an order under section 99 (order for delivery up) or exercising the right conferred by section 100 (right of seizure); and the court may on the application of the licensee make such order under section 99 or, as the case may be, prohibiting or permitting the exercise by the copyright owner of the right conferred by section 100, as it thinks fit having regard to the terms of the licence.'

---

1 *Redrow Homes Ltd and another v Betts Bros plc and another* [1998] All ER 385.

8.4.3 What must the plaintiff prove?

As in a copyright action, to prevail in a database right action, the plaintiff has the onus of demonstrating that the right subsists, that the plaintiff has the legal title to it, that there is a prima facie case, that the alleged infringement derives from material which is the subject of the right and takes sufficient of that material to meet the requirements as to the taking being of a 'substantial part'[1].

Given that the first owner of copyright is the author, and the first owner of database right the maker, it is important to ensure before any action is brought either that the author and the maker are one and the same or that the appropriate assignment has been made from one to the other so that both rights are held together. Otherwise both must be plaintiffs. Certain presumptions as to title may also assist in such actions, particularly at an interlocutory stage. Those in relation to copyright are set out in s 104 of the CDPA[2] and those in relation to database right are set out in reg 22 of the Database Regulations. These provide:

'**104 Presumptions relevant to literary, dramatic, musical and artistic works**

(1) The following presumptions apply in proceedings brought by virtue of this Chapter with respect of a literary, dramatic, musical or artistic work.

(2) Where a name purporting to be that of the author appeared on copies of the work as published or on the work when it was made, the person whose name appeared shall be presumed, until the contrary is proved—

(a) to be the author of the work;
(b) to have made it in circumstances not falling within section 11(2), 163, 165 or 168 (works produced in course of employment, Crown copyright, Parliamentary copyright or copyright of certain international organisations).

(3) In the case of a work alleged to be a work of joint authorship, subsection (2) applies in relation to each person alleged to be one of the authors.

(4) Where no name purporting to be that of the author appeared as mentioned in subsection (2) but—

(a) the work qualifies for copyright protection by virtue of section 155 (qualification by references to country of first publication), and
(b) a name purporting to be that of the publisher appeared on copies of the work as first published,

the person whose name appeared shall be presumed, until the contrary is proved, to have been the owner of the copyright at the time of publication.

(5) If the author of the work is dead or the identity of the author cannot be ascertained by reasonable inquiry, it shall be presumed, in the absence of evidence to the contrary—

(a) that the work is an original work, and
(b) that the plaintiff's allegations as to what was the first publication of the work and as to the country of first publication are correct.'

---

1   Under the Database Directive, there appears to be a slight discrepancy between the requirements for proving infringement of copyright (where reproduction 'in whole or in part' (Art 5(a) is prohibited)) and database right (where 'whole or a substantial part' is required (Art 7(1)).

2   Other than those as to computer programs, and which are set out in s 105(3) of the CDPA, but which are not relevant to copyright in databases as such, because a 'database' as defined is different from a 'computer program' as is emphasised by Art 1(3) of the Database Directive.

'22   Presumptions relevant to database right

(1)   The following presumptions apply in proceedings brought by virtue of this Part of these Regulations with respect to a database.

(2)   Where a name purporting to be that of the maker appeared on copies of the database as published, or on the database when it was made, the person whose name appeared shall be presumed, until the contrary is proved—

   (a)   to be the maker of the database, and
   (b)   to have made it in circumstances not falling within Regulation 14(2) to (4).

(3)   Where copies of the database as published bear a label or a mark stating—

   (a)   that a named person was the maker of the database, or
   (b)   that the database was first published in a specified year,

   the label or mark shall be admissible as evidence of the facts stated and shall be presumed to be correct until the contrary is proved.

(4)   In the case of a database alleged to have been made jointly, paragraphs (2) and (3), so far as is applicable, apply in relation to each person alleged to be one of the makers.'

8.4.4   Procedure

(a) Jurisdiction

The same principles, in terms of the courts in which actions can be brought, will apply to actions for infringement of database right as apply to actions for the infringement of copyright. In England and Wales these are generally tried in the Chancery Division of the High Court. Such actions can be brought in county courts (although they would not normally be tried in county courts if the damages claim exceeds £25,000) or in the Patents County Court if the proceedings for copyright or database right infringement are ancillary to or arise out of the same subject matter as proceedings relating to patents or designs. Such actions can also be brought in District Registries of the High Court which have a Chancery jurisdiction. The jurisdiction of the High Court and of the Patents County Court extends throughout all of England and Wales whereas that of the normal county courts is local and determined by the location of the defendant. In Scotland, actions may be brought in the Court of Session, which has jurisdiction throughout Scotland, or in the Sheriff Courts, the jurisdiction of which, as with county courts in England and Wales, is local. The following summary of the formal steps in an action deals with High Court proceedings in England and Wales.

(b) Interlocutory injunction

In some cases the plaintiff may wish to secure an 'interlocutory injunction' as soon as possible against further allegedly infringing activity pending the full trial of the action. The plaintiff may be required to give a 'cross-undertaking in damages' – an undertaking to the court to pay to the defendant any damages it suffers should such an interlocutory injunction be determined at trial to have been wrongly granted. The evidence by the plaintiff in support of such an application, and by the defendant resisting it, is on affidavit. In deciding whether to grant an interlocutory injunction, the court will try to assess which side will suffer the greater potential damage, and whether either side can adequately be compensated financially at trial for what may ultimately transpire to have been an incorrect interlocutory decision – the plaintiff for the failure to grant an injunction which ought to have been granted, the defendant for the grant of an injunction which ought not to have been granted. Thus, if an injunction would effectively close the recipient's business until trial, then this factor will reduce the likelihood of an injunction being granted, since the damage may not be capable of being remedied. In extremely urgent cases the plaintiff may seek such relief without notice to the defendant, but then the plaintiff has an obligation to the court in its evidence to make clear any weaknesses in its own case. A further form of relief which may be appropriate if the plaintiff has a very strong prima facie case and there is a real risk of the defendant destroying or disposing of evidence is the *Anton Piller* Order, once again secured without notice to the defendant, and enabling the owner to track down, seize and preserve evidence such as unsold stocks of infringing material.

(c) Pleadings
Whether or not an interlocutory injunction has been sought or granted, the stages of the action leading to the final hearing on the merits are the same. The initial such stages involve the exchange of documents referred to as 'pleadings'. An action for infringement is commenced by the issue of a writ in the High Court, which is little more than a form giving the names and addresses of the plaintiff and defendants. It must be issued within six years of the infringing act. The document usually claims an injunction, which is an order that the defendant stops infringing the copyright and/or database right, in specified works, and asks for damages or an account of profits and costs. The writ is then served on the defendant, which must be done within four months of issue. Within 14 days of such service, the defendant must either satisfy the claim or acknowledge receipt of the writ. This acknowledgement is a formal document that merely gives notice of the intention to defend the action and prevents the plaintiff from entering judgment against the defendant by default. It is at this time that a defendant must also challenge the jurisdiction of the court if it wishes so to do.

Within 14 days of the last day for acknowledging service, the plaintiff must serve a statement of claim. This identifies the specific copyright or database right protected works on which reliance is placed if this was not done in the writ, although it is often served with, or may be incorporated in, the writ. It will also identify for each of the works which are said to have been infringed: the date of creation of each work; the author and/or maker; why the plaintiff says that copyright/database right subsists in it; and why it claims to own the copyright/database right. It must also set out fully the plaintiff's claim together with instances of infringement, giving, where possible, dates, places, facts and figures. If no plaintiff is resident within the EEA or Switzerland the defendant may ask for security for costs before proceeding to prepare a defence, in an amount determined by the court if not agreed. The defendant must serve a defence within 14 days of the receipt of the statement of claim or within a longer time period agreed by the parties or permitted by the court. In practice, the court will grant reasonable extensions of time if satisfied that the defendant is diligently proceeding with the preparation of the defence. The plaintiff has 14 days after receipt of the defence in which to serve a reply to the defence, should it wish to do so. Fourteen days after the last of these documents have been served, the pleadings are deemed 'closed'.

(d) Discovery
Within a further 14 days after pleadings are closed (although this is sometimes deferred until after hearing of the summons for directions, as to which see below) the

parties ought to exchange lists of documents listing all documents in their possession, custody or power relating to any matter in question in the action and permitting their inspection by the other party. The full extent of such 'discovery' varies from case to case depending on the matters raised by and not admitted in the pleadings. Only parties involved in the action must provide discovery. Documents which, although relevant, are 'privileged' (such as correspondence with legal advisers) are not disclosed to the other side but are described in general terms in the list. If the discovery given is considered inadequate then either party may apply to the court for an order for specific discovery of certain classes of documents. For example, one matter normally in issue in an action for infringement of copyright or of database right and as to which discovery should be given is that of the origins of the alleged copy if copying is denied, so the defendant should disclose to the plaintiff all documents showing how the alleged copy was arrived at, although if the defendant is an importer or distributor it is unlikely to have access to such documents. Documents disclosed on discovery can only be used for the purposes of the action for which discovery is given. However, this may be regarded by the parties as providing insufficient protection for confidential, technical or commercial information and the parties can agree, and the court can direct, that disclosure of certain types of documents be limited to, say, lawyers and independent experts.

(e) Summons for directions

Within one month after pleadings are closed the plaintiff should issue a summons for directions requiring the parties (represented by their lawyers) to attend court not less than 14 days later. At the hearing the court gives directions as to the future conduct of the case. Before attending the court on the summons for directions, each party usually undertakes a review of how the case is progressing, what is needed by way of evidence and (in the case of the plaintiff) how to counter any unexpected attacks by the defendant. The summons will generally deal with such matters as requests for further and better particulars of the pleadings, discovery (either if this has not yet been given or if that already given is regarded as inadequate), notices to admit facts, interrogatories, exchange of witness statements and the provision of expert evidence (see below). Often the parties are able to agree on these matters before the matter is referred to the court, in which case the court will generally make an order for directions in the form agreed by the parties. The order for directions may also set a trial date although normally it specifies when the trial may be 'set down', by which is meant that the case is put on a list of cases ready for trial.

(f) Notice to admit facts

Either party may serve on the other a notice requiring the admission of various facts or parts of the case as are specified in the notice. It is not unusual for each party to serve such a notice on the other parties prior to discovery, but the main purpose is to establish those parts of the case that need not be proved at trial. In an action for infringement of copyright or of database right, those issues often the subject of such notices are subsistence and ownership. The order for directions will generally provide for responses to be served within a specified time. A party is not obliged to make any admissions in response to a notice but a failure to make admissions that are properly sought, whether or not responses were ordered by the court, can be penalised in costs.

(g) Interrogatories

One party may by way of a document known as 'interrogatories' interrogate the other party on any matter in question in the case so long as this is necessary either for disposing of the case fairly or for saving costs, and is not oppressive. They need not be answered unless the court so directs. Interrogatories are generally served after discovery, and typically address various matters raised by the documents disclosed on discovery. There are limitations on the type of interrogatories which can be sought, but in practice they are rarely used.

(h) Evidence

The order for directions will provide for witness statements to be exchanged at a certain period (usually a couple of months) prior to the trial. Each party must ensure that all oral evidence as to fact which it intends to adduce at trial is set out in its witness statements. These statements are then exchanged with the other side on a set date. In addition, expert evidence may be required. The order for directions will generally limit the number of expert witnesses that each side may call at trial. The function of the experts is to give expert assistance to the court or to inform the court as to the state of public knowledge regarding the matters before it. Opinion evidence given by non-expert witnesses is likely to be inadmissible. Expert reports, similar to witness statements, are prepared and exchanged normally at the same time as witness statements.

(i) The trial

Unlike most ordinary actions, actions for infringement of copyright or of database right proceed by way of a 'split trial'. Evidence is only given with regard to liability and not as to damages, which are assessed in separate proceedings in the event that liability is established. The evidence (except certain limited factual evidence the subject of unopposed Civil Evidence Act Notices) is given by witnesses under oath. The court is not provided with detailed written statements setting out the arguments, although very shortly before trial 'skeleton arguments' (identifying the legal points in issue and the relevant references in the pleadings, discovery, statements and reports) are submitted to the court. Witnesses whose witness statements have been served and on whose evidence a party wishes to rely and which the other side seeks to challenge must be available to attend court to confirm their statements on oath and be cross-examined as to the content of their witness statements. Likewise, experts whose reports have been served and on which one wishes to rely must attend court.

Each witness (including expert witnesses) is first examined by counsel for the party relying on his evidence. The witness will usually confirm on oath the contents of his statement but generally not much more. The witness may be allowed to add orally to what he has said in his statement but only in certain restricted cases and only at the judge's discretion. The witness is then cross-examined by counsel for the other side. An opportunity to put further questions arising on the cross-examination ('re-examination') is given to counsel for the party relying on the witness. The normal 'running order' at the trial is for counsel for the plaintiff to open the case and call the plaintiff's witnesses for examination and cross-examination. Counsel for the defendant then calls his witnesses and, when the evidence is finished, makes his final speech to the court. Counsel for the plaintiff then makes his final speech. The defendant's counsel has no right of reply after this unless a new point of law has been introduced in closing, in which case the right of reply is restricted to dealing with the new point of law.

(j) Judgment

The judge may then give his judgment at once but he is more likely to reserve judgment. The time it takes before judgment is given tends to vary. It could be a few days and it is unlikely to be more than a couple of months. In his judgment the judge gives reasons for his conclusions on liability. Thereafter the precise form of order consequential on this (including provision as to costs) is often discussed between the judge and counsel and then drawn up and formally entered by the court.

If the plaintiff succeeds the normal order would be:

– a permanent injunction against the defendant preventing infringement but which will cease on expiry of the copyright or database right on which it is based (in special cases it may be possible to suspend this pending appeal);
– an order for an inquiry as to damages (this takes into account the six-year period up to issue of the writ);
– an order for delivery up (or destruction upon oath) of all infringing articles and any dies, tools or plates used for making such articles;
– costs in favour of the plaintiff.

If the plaintiff fails the normal order would be:

– costs in favour of the defendant;

and also, if an interlocutory injunction had been previously granted:

– discharge of the interlocutory injunction;
– an order for an inquiry on the cross-undertaking in damages given to the defendant by the plaintiff as a precondition for obtaining an interlocutory injunction (an unsuccessful plaintiff is not otherwise liable to a defendant in damages).

If an inquiry as to damages is ordered, the parties will often try to agree a figure. Failing agreement, the figure is determined in separate proceedings initiated after judgment. Unless the plaintiff has lost profits on manufacturing activities as a result of the infringement this will usually be by application of a notional royalty as if between a willing licensor and a willing licensee, although 'flagrant damages' may be available. The alternative, which is to ask for an account of the profits made by the defendant's contribution to the infringement, has been rarely used in the past, but may become more common now that the defendant can be required to give some discovery as to the level of profits before the plaintiff must elect as to whether to seek damages or an account.

The successful party will usually secure an order for costs in his favour. An order for payment of costs does not necessarily mean that the successful party can recoup all his out-of-pocket legal expenses. In practice, it tends to mean that he will only recover between one half and two-thirds of these legal costs. If these cannot be agreed between the parties, the successful party can apply to the court to determine the recovery, having scrutinised the costs incurred, the costs of this assessment being ultimately paid by the unsuccessful party. It is often found that the parties incur roughly the same costs. On this basis, the plaintiff is likely to be out of pocket (disregarding any sums payable as damages) to the extent of up to about one half of its costs if it wins and, if it loses, all of its own costs plus two-thirds of the other side's costs.

(k) Appeal

Appeal from the High Court or from the county court to the Court of Appeal is available as of right from final judgments, but leave from the lower court or from the Court of Appeal is required for appeal to the Court of Appeal against other types of order. The time allowed for appeal to the Court of Appeal is four weeks and runs from entry of the order and not from pronouncement of the judgment. Appeal from the Court of Appeal to the House of Lords requires leave from the Court of Appeal or from the House of Lords, and is rare. The Court of Appeal and House of Lords can also refer matters of interpretation of Community legislation (such as those arising under the Database Directive) to the European Court of Justice.

8.4.5   Pan European injunctions

It has been confirmed[1] that an English court can hear an action for breach of a Dutch copyright, and would therefore be in a position to grant a copyright injunction having pan European effect. This, of course, assumes that jurisdiction could be founded under the Brussels Convention against the defendant, for example because the defendant was domiciled in the UK (Art 2) or because the infringement took place in England (Art 5(3)). Because copyright is not a registered right, Art 16(4) of the Brussels Convention (reserving exclusive jurisdiction, in matters concerned with the validity of patents, trade marks or designs, to the courts of the country in which the right is registered) has no application to it, this provision having been held[2] to preclude the English courts from jurisdiction over patent (or trade mark) infringement elsewhere in Europe where (as would usually be the case) validity of the registered right sued on was in issue. In the same way as it would be able to hear an action for breach of Dutch copyright law, an English court would be able to hear an action for breach of database right in another European country, as the database right is not a registered right and so Art 16(4) does not present a problem. Likewise, those other European courts which are prepared to take jurisdiction over disputes in relation to foreign intellectual property rights and grant injunctions having pan European effect would also have no barrier to taking such jurisdiction and granting injunctions enforceable in the UK both in relation to copyright and to database right.

---

1   *Gareth Pearce v Ove Arup Partnership Limited and others* [1997] FSR 641.
2   *Coin Controls v Szuko* [1997] FSR 660 and (subject to a pending reference to the European Court of Justice) *Fort Dodge v Akzo* [1998] FSR 222.

Chapter 9

COMPETITION LAW AND DATABASES

SECTION A: EC LAW – 9.1 Article 85 of the EC Treaty – 9.2 The effect of falling within Article 85(1) of the EC Treaty – 9.3 Exemption from Article 85(1) of the EC Treaty – 9.4 Examples of database issues under Article 85 of the EC Treaty – 9.5 Article 86 of the EC Treaty – 9.6 Abuse – 9.7 The effect of falling within Article 86 of the EC Treaty – SECTION B: UK LAW – 9.8 The Restrictive Trade Practices Act 1976 – 9.9 General exclusions and exceptions under the RTPA – 9.10 Exceptions relating to licensing of intellectual property rights – 9.11 The Resale Prices Act 1976 – 9.12 The Competition Act 1980 – 9.13 The Competition Bill

SECTION A: EC LAW

9.1   ARTICLE 85 OF THE EC TREATY

Article 85(1) of the EC Treaty prohibits agreements between undertakings, decisions by associations of undertakings and concerted practices that, to an appreciable extent, affect trade between Member States and have as their object or effect the prevention, restriction or distortion of competition within the EU. As a result, in determining whether Art 85(1) of the EC Treaty applies it is necessary to consider whether:

– an agreement or concerted practice exists between undertakings;
– which prevents, distorts or restricts competition within the EU;
– which affects trade between Member States; and
– which has an appreciable effect.

9.1.1   Agreements and concerted practices

Most forms of competitive coordination between undertakings are covered by the terms 'agreement' and 'concerted practice'. It is sufficient to constitute a 'concerted practice' that undertakings coordinate their behaviour in a way that 'knowingly substitutes practical co-operation between them for the risks of competition'[1]. There is no requirement that a legally binding contract exist between the parties, or that there be any agreement in writing; a so-called 'gentlemen's agreement' is sufficient[2]. Similarly, several separate contracts may be found, together, to form a single agreement[3].

---

1   Case 48/69, *ICI Ltd v Commission* [1972] ECR 619, at para 64.
2   Cases 209/78 etc, *Van Landewyck v Commission* [1980] ECR 3125, paras 85–91.
3   *BP Kemi*, OJ No L 286/32, 1979.

9.1.2   Between undertakings

The term 'undertaking' is defined broadly and covers virtually any entity, regardless of its legal status, engaged in economic or commercial activity[1]. Limited companies, partnerships and individuals may all be undertakings. State-owned companies will also be covered by the term if they engage in commercial or economic activity[2]. The fact that an entity is non-profit making will not prevent it being an undertaking[3].

To be caught by Art 85(1) of the EC Treaty, an agreement or concerted practice must exist between at least two undertakings. A parent company and its wholly controlled subsidiaries are usually considered to form a 'single economic entity' and, as a result, are treated as a single undertaking for this purpose[4]. Consequently, many inter-group transactions will fall outside Art 85(1) of the EC Treaty.

9.1.3   Effect on trade between Member States

Again, the concept of effect on trade between Member States is broad. It is sufficient that an agreement 'may have an influence direct or indirect, actual or potential, on the pattern of trade between Member States, such as might prejudice the aim of a single market'[5]. In practice, an effect on trade will generally be found where an agreement includes terms which relate to imports or exports, extends to more than one Member State or covers the whole of the territory of a single Member State (since this may have the effect of partitioning that State from the rest of the EU market)[6]. For these purposes, most if not all economic activity will qualify as 'trade'.

9.1.4   Preventing, restricting or distorting competition in the EU

In principle, any agreement which may lead to reduced competition between the parties or restricts the ability of third parties to compete may be caught by Art 85(1) of the EC Treaty, and there is no particular significance in the distinction between preventing, restricting and distorting competition. Particular types of clause which may amount to a restriction of competition are described below.

Among the factors that will be considered in determining whether an agreement leads to a restriction of competition, the most important is likely to be the size of the parties' combined share of the relevant market (the concept of 'relevant market' is discussed below in the section dealing with Art 86 of the EC Treaty, see **9.5**).

9.1.5   Appreciable effect

The European Court of Justice has established that an agreement will not be caught by Art 85(1) of the EC Treaty if it has no appreciable effect on competition in the EU or

---

1   See, eg, EEC Competition Rules – Guide for Small and Medium Sized Enterprises (1983) European Documentation, at p 17.
2   Case 153/73 *Sacchi* [1974] ECR 409; *Aluminium Imports from Eastern Europe,* OJ No L 92/1, 1985, at p 37.
3   *GVL*, OJ No L 370/49, 1981.
4   Case C-73/95, *Viho Europe v Commission,* judgment of 24 October 1996.
5   Case 42/84, *Remia v Commission* [1985] ECR 2545, para 22.
6   Case 8/72, *Cementhandelaren v Commission* [1972] ECR 977.

on trade between Member States[1]. The scope of this exception has never been precisely defined by the European Court of Justice. The Commission has, however, issued a notice identifying several categories of agreement to which, in its view, Art 85(1) of the EC Treaty will not apply by reason of their limited impact. This notice states that:

(i) agreements between parties that compete or have equivalent activities in separate geographic markets ('horizontal agreements') will not be considered appreciable where the parties have a combined market share of 5 per cent or less on the relevant market[2];

(ii) agreements between parties that operate at different levels in the chain of supply or demand ('vertical agreements') will not be considered appreciable where the parties have a combined market share of 10 per cent or less on the relevant market[3]; and

(iii) agreements (whether horizontal or vertical) in which all the parties are small and medium-sized enterprises ('SMEs') will not be considered appreciable. To qualify as an SME, an undertaking must belong to a group that has less than 250 employees and either an annual turnover not exceeding ECU 40 million or an annual balance-sheet total not exceeding ECU 27 million. For these purposes, an undertaking's group includes all undertakings linked by a holding, in capital or voting rights, of 25 per cent or more[4].

However, the Commission states that, even if they meet the market share thresholds above, agreements that fix prices, limit production or sales, confer territorial protection or share markets or sources of supply may be considered to have an appreciable impact and therefore to be caught by Art 85(1) of the EC Treaty[5]. In addition, agreements falling within the SME threshold may, none the less, fall within Art 85(1) where they significantly impede competition in a substantial part of the relevant market[6]. Finally, Art 85 may apply to agreements meeting either the market share or the SME thresholds where competition in the relevant market is restricted as a result of the cumulative effect of parallel networks of similar agreements between different undertakings[7].

Agreements that do not have an appreciable effect on competition when entered into may none the less subsequently be caught by Art 85(1) if changes in the size or market positions of the parties (or other factors) bring them outside the scope of the exception. For this reason, and because proper identification of the relevant market may be complex (see below), care should be taken by undertakings seeking to rely on the appreciable effect exception.

---

1   See, eg, Case 5/69, *Volk v Vervaecke* [1969] ECR 295.
2   Commission notice on agreements of minor importance which do not fall within the meaning of Art 85(1) of the EC Treaty, OJ No 372/13, 1997, at para 9.
3   Ibid.
4   Ibid, at para 19; and the Annex to the Commission recommendation 96/280, OJ No L 107/4, 1996.
5   Commission notice on agreements of minor importance which do not fall within the meaning of Art 85(1) of the EC Treaty, OJ No C 372/13, 1997, at para 11.
6   Ibid, at para 20.
7   Ibid, at paras 18 and 20.

9.2   THE EFFECT OF FALLING WITHIN ARTICLE 85(1) OF THE EC TREATY

Several consequences may follow if an agreement falls within Art 85(1) of the EC Treaty, unless the agreement is notified to the Commission and receives an exemption under Art 85(3). First, under Art 85(2), the anti-competitive aspects of an agreement which falls within Art 85(1) are void and will not be enforced by national courts in the EU. This may, depending on the relevant national legal provisions, result in the whole of the agreement becoming unenforceable. Nor will EU courts enforce judgments of foreign courts based on aspects of an agreement which are contrary to Art 85(1). Secondly, the Commission has powers to impose fines of up to 10 per cent of turnover on undertakings involved in a breach of Art 85(1)[1]. Fines are, however, typically imposed only in the most serious cases. Thirdly, the Commission may, by decision, order infringing undertakings to take such action as is necessary to terminate the infringement[2]. Finally, it should be possible for third parties injured as a result of a breach of Art 85(1) to sue the offending undertakings for damages, although the circumstances under which such a remedy is available are governed by the relevant national law. Under English law, it seems that such damages are, in principle, available[3].

9.3   EXEMPTION FROM ARTICLE 85(1) OF THE EC TREATY

Exemption from Art 85(1) of the EC Treaty may be granted by the Commission under Art 85(3). Two routes are available to undertakings wishing to obtain an Art 85(3) exemption: (i) compliance with one of the Commission's so-called 'block exemption' regulations, in which case the exemption is automatic; and (ii) individual exemption, which requires a notification to the Commission.

Complying with a block exemption regulation ensures immunity from fines, legal enforceability of the agreement and protection from damages actions under Art 85. In the case of individual notification, it is the act of notification itself which ensures immunity from fines. However, it is the subsequent exemption which ensures that an agreement is legally enforceable and that the parties are protected from damages actions.

9.3.1   Block exemption regulations

The Commission has enacted block exemption regulations in relation to various categories of agreement. Such block exemptions typically indicate the types of agreement which they cover, the conditions for their application, and those agreements which are excluded, as well as which clauses are exempted, which clauses are not normally contrary to Art 85(1) but are exempted in case they do fall within Art 85(1), and which clauses are considered to exclude the application of the block exemption ('the black list'). Agreements which impose restrictions going beyond

---

1   Article 15(2) of Regulation 17/62, OJ 21.2.1962, p 204 (special edition 1959–62, p 87).
2   Article 3 of Regulation 17/62, above.
3   *Plessey v Siemens* [1988] ECR 384.

those permitted by the relevant regulation obtain no exemption and all restrictions in them, including those which would otherwise be covered by the block exemption, may fall under Art 85(1).

Existing block exemption regulations include the Technology Transfer Block Exemption (Regulation 240/96)[1] and the Exclusive Distribution Block Exemption (Regulation 1983/83)[2]. Ignoring the question of what clauses are exempted by these block exemptions, are there any agreements relating to databases that could fulfil the basic conditions for them to apply?

The Technology Transfer Block Exemption applies to patent licences, know-how licences, and combined patent and know-how licences. It also covers patent and know-how licences which include terms relating to additional intellectual property rights to the extent that such rights are licensed together with patents or know-how and subject to similar (or more limited) restrictions of competition. If a database is subject to patent rights which are being licensed under the agreement, then the block exemption may apply, provided that the agreement does not contain any of the black-listed clauses, or any other restrictions which are not expressly exempted under the block exemption, and that the application of the block exemption is not excluded for some other reason. However, assuming that there are no relevant patent rights, under what circumstances could a database licensing agreement fall within the block exemption on the basis that it contains know-how? Know-how is defined for the purposes of the block exemption as 'a body of technical information that is secret, substantial and identified'[3]. This means that for a database licence to come within the Technology Transfer Block Exemption, it must cover know-how which is:

(i)   technical, rather than commercial or marketing, information (eg not customer lists or market surveys);
(ii) secret, in the sense of not generally known or easily accessible, so that part of its value consists in the lead time which the licensee gains when the know-how is communicated to him (this may require that it is confidential and supplied under an obligation of confidentiality)[4];
(iii) substantial, in the sense that it includes information which can reasonably be expected at the date of the agreement to be capable of improving the competitive position of the licensee, for example by helping him enter a new market, or giving him an advantage in competition with others who do not have access to comparable information[5]; and
(iv) identified, in that the know-how must be described or recorded, either in the licence or at the time, or shortly after know-how is transferred, in a way which makes it possible to verify the fulfilment of the previous two criteria above.

Although some database licences may include a licence of know-how, the block exemption can only apply if the know-how qualifies under the above tests. A further limitation is that the Technology Transfer Block Exemption only applies where the licensee is actually manufacturing a product under the licence or having it

---

1   OJ No L 31/2, 1996.
2   OJ No L 73/1, 1983, corrigendum OJ No L 281/24, 1983.
3   Technology Transfer Regulation, Art 10(1).
4   Ibid, Art 10(2).
5   Ibid, Art 10(3).

manufactured on his account, or is providing the licensed service or having it provided on his account[1]. It does not apply to pure sales licences[2].

The Exclusive Distribution Block Exemption does not cover the supply of services and, in relation to goods, applies only when they are supplied 'for resale'[3]. This requirement means that the original supplier must 'dispose of' the goods to the distributor before the distributor sells them on[4]. In many cases, it is doubtful that the distribution of a database will constitute the sale of a good, and it may be more in the nature of the supply of a service. Further, even in the case of the distribution of a packaged product, if this involves licensing arrangements, and not merely the outright sale of a product, then the transaction between the distributor and the database user may not amount to resale for the purposes of the Exclusive Distribution Block Exemption. Since, in practice, most distribution of databases is likely to involve some form of licensing, it is unlikely, or at least questionable, that many exclusive distribution agreements relating to databases will be automatically exempt under the Exclusive Distribution Block Exemption.

9.3.2   Individual exemptions

If no block exemption applies, an agreement that risks falling within Art 85(1) of the EC Treaty may be notified to the Commission for an individual exemption[5]. To qualify for exemption, an agreement must improve production or distribution or promote technical or economic progress, while allowing consumers a fair share of the resulting benefit, and, at the same time, must not impose restrictions that are not indispensable to these objectives or eliminate competition in respect of a substantial portion of the relevant products[6].

There is no obligation to notify agreements falling within Art 85(1), and no time-limit for doing so. The downside is that in respect of the time during which the agreement is not notified, the parties are exposed to the risks outlined above and that any clearance ultimately obtained from the Commission may only be backdated to the date of notification. Notification must be made on the correct form, Form A/B, which requires a substantial amount of information to be supplied, including information about the notified agreement, the parties to it and the markets affected by it[7]. As a result, notification can be costly and time-consuming. Also, there is no time-limit within which the Commission must reach a decision on a notified agreement. However, notification gives the parties immunity from fines, pending a formal decision by the Commission, so that notified agreement may be implemented[8].

---

1   Technology Transfer Regulation, Recital 8.

2   Ibid, Art 5(1)(5).

3   Exclusive Distribution Block Exemption, Art 1.

4   See Commission notice on Regulations 1983/83 and 1984/83, OJ No C 101/2, 1984, at paras 9 and 11.

5   It should be noted that, in most cases, the Commission will close its file with regard to a notified agreement following the issuance of an administrative 'comfort letter' without granting a formal negative clearance or exemption. In principle, such comfort letters are without legal force.

6   Article 85(3) of the EC Treaty.

7   OJ No L 377/31, 1994.

8   Regulation 17/62, Art 15(5)(a).

It is also possible to apply to the Commission for a formal declaration that an agreement falls outside the scope of Art 85(1), a so-called 'negative clearance'. Where such an application is made, it is usually combined with a request for an individual exemption, since an application for negative clearance alone gives no immunity from fines[1].

9.4 EXAMPLES OF DATABASE ISSUES UNDER ARTICLE 85 OF THE EC TREATY

Article 85(1) of the EC Treaty applies to various forms of restrictive agreement. There are certain types of agreement between competitors which will, in nearly all cases, be contrary to Art 85(1) and are not only unlikely to receive an exemption but involve a considerable risk of fines. These include cartel-type situations where competitors agree to fix prices or other trading conditions, to limit the amount which they produce, or to divide markets, customers or territories amongst themselves. However, more standard types of agreement which are commonly used in respect of databases may also contain clauses which are contrary to Art 85. These types of clauses will be discussed in the following sections.

9.4.1 Exclusive acquisition of content

Agreements relating to the exclusive acquisition of content for databases may be contrary to Art 85 of the EC Treaty in some circumstances where this tends to exclude competitors from the market. Whether or not this will be the case depends on the quality and scope of the content acquired and the length of the agreement[2].

9.4.2 Contract for the development of a database

A company may hire a developer to develop the database on its behalf. It may want to require that the developer assign to it all the rights in the database or grant it an exclusive licence, to oblige the developer not to develop similar databases for competing companies, or to require the developer not to start competing in the market itself. Clauses attempting to achieve these objectives could potentially fall under Art 85 and advice should be sought from a lawyer in each case.

9.4.3 Distribution

A variety of different methods may be used for distribution of databases, most of which will involve licensing, and many of which may amount to the distribution of services rather than goods. Where a distributor is appointed to distribute a database, certain aspects of the agreement may fall under Art 85(1). For these purposes, a distributor of goods can be taken to mean any purchaser who is supplied for the purposes of resale on his own account, no matter what title is applied (eg dealer, importer, wholesaler). A distributor in respect of services may be slightly more

---

1   *John Deere*, OJ No L35/58, 1985.
2   *Film purchases by German television stations*, OJ No L 284/36, 1989; *FA/BBC/BSkyB*, Commission press release IP/93/614.

difficult to define for the purposes of Art 85, but essentially it means a purchaser who sells on the service without providing it himself or adding any significant value to it. There is very little case-law of the European Court or decisional practice of the Commission on the application of Art 85(1) to distribution agreements involving the supply of services or licensing. However, for many forms of distribution arrangement, especially those which are close to the distribution of goods, the principles which have been applied to the distribution of goods may apply by analogy. The principles which have been applied to the distribution of goods are the following:

(i) The appointment of an exclusive distributor in itself will often be contrary to Art 85(1), but will normally be exemptable under Art 85(3), as is the case under the Exclusive Distribution Block Exemption.

(ii) Restrictions on the distributor selling outside the territory will normally be contrary to Art 85(1). However, a distinction is made between a restriction on 'active sales' outside the territory and a restriction on 'passive sales'. A restriction on 'active sales' means a restriction on actively seeking customers by promoting and marketing the products outside the territory, and on setting up branches or distribution depots for these purposes. While contrary to Art 85(1), such a restriction is usually exemptable under Art 85(3) in the case of an exclusive distribution agreement (where exclusive means that no other distributor of any kind will be appointed in the territory). Where the distributor is not exclusive, there may be a question as to whether a restriction on active sales would be exempted or not. On the other hand, restrictions on 'passive sales' (meaning that the distributor is prohibited from responding to unsolicited requests from outside of the territory) are not usually exemptable and are regarded as serious restrictions which may result in a fine, regardless of whether the distributor is exclusive.

(iii) Any attempt to prevent parallel imports by restricting the distributor from selling to others who are likely to export the goods will be contrary to Art 85(1), will not normally be exemptable, and will usually be regarded as so serious that it is likely to result in a fine.

(iv) Requiring the distributor to restrict its sales to specific classes of customer or requiring him not to sell to specific customers will normally be contrary to Art 85(1) and not exemptable.

(v) Requiring the distributor not to supply or distribute competing goods is usually contrary to Art 85(1) but is exemptable in the case of an exclusive distributor.

(vi) Requiring a distributor to purchase exclusively from the supplier will often be contrary to Art 85(1) but may be exemptable.

These principles, which relate to the distribution of goods, may not in all cases be applied in an analogous way to alternative forms of distribution, but they do at least provide an indication of some clauses on which legal advice should be sought.

9.4.4 Selective distribution and authorised dealers

In some situations, the supplier or owner of a database may want to distribute it only through an authorised dealer network. Authorised dealers in such a network may be prohibited from selling to third parties who are not either authorised dealers or end-users. In such a case, it may be necessary to examine whether the selection criteria for authorised dealers meet the requirements of Art 85(1). These are that the application of selective conditions be justified by the nature of the product (commodity products do not need specialist resellers) and that the selection be based on justified qualitative conditions such as the technical competence of the distributor and its ability to provide support services (rather than, eg, simple restrictions on the number of distributors).

9.4.5 Licensing to developers and other forms of licensing not for resale purposes

Licensing of the intellectual property rights in databases to developers and others who intend to manufacture a product or provide a service which uses the licensed material or database are likely to be dealt with differently from distribution agreements. These cases may well be analysed more by analogy with the principles which have been developed under Art 85 in respect of the transfer of technology to a licensee to allow it to manufacture a product or provide a service. In this respect, the rules contained in the Technology Transfer Block Exemption may be applicable by analogy. This suggests the following analysis:

- The grant of a sole or exclusive licence will often be contrary to Art 85(1), but will be exemptable for a certain period of time. The Technology Transfer Block Exemption permits a restriction on the licensor exploiting patent and/or know-how rights or granting other licences in the terms of the licensee for the period of the licensed patents or, in the case of know-how, for ten years from the first marketing of a product within the common market by a licensee.

- Restrictions on the licensee selling outside its territory within the EU or the EEA into the territory of other licensees or the licensor will be contrary to Art 85(1), but will be exemptable for a certain period of time. Significantly, contrary to the principles relating to distribution agreements, restrictions on passive sales which prevent the licensee from responding to unsolicited requests from outside its territory are exempted under the Technology Transfer Block Exemption, although only for five years from the time when the product is first put on the market within the common market by a licensee. Restrictions on active sales are exempted under the block exemption for the longer periods set out in respect of territorial exclusivity above. However, in the case of pure patent licences, restrictions on either active or passive sales are exempted only as long as parallel patents remain applicable in all territories affected by the restriction.

    Requiring the licensee to accept quality specifications or further licences or to purchase goods or services will not normally be contrary to Art 85(1) where such an obligation is necessary for a technically satisfactory exploitation of the licensed technology or to ensure conformity with quality standards respected by the licensor and other licensees. In other cases they may be contrary to Art 85(1) but will sometimes be exemptable.

- Requiring the licensee to assign back rights to improvements or new applications of the licensed technology will be contrary to Art 85 and will not usually be exemptable under Art 85(3). On the other hand, a requirement to license back, as opposed to assign, rights relating to improvements or new applications may not be contrary to Art 85 provided that, if the improvements are severable from the licensed technology, the licence is non-exclusive and the licensor is obliged to license its own improvements to the licensee.

- Restrictions on the price which the licensee or the licensor can charge for its products or services will be contrary to Art 85, and will not normally be exemptable.
- A requirement on one party not to compete with the other (apart from the sole or exclusive licence and the territorial restrictions described above) will be contrary to Art 85 and will not normally be exemptable.
- Restrictions on either party selling to parallel importers (eg to resellers within their territory who are likely to export the product outside of the territory within the EEA) will be contrary to Art 85, will not be exemptable and may well result in a fine.
- Restrictions as to the customers which may be supplied by either party, other than genuine field of use restrictions applied to the licensee, will be contrary to Art 85(1), and are unlikely to be exemptable where the parties were already competing manufacturers or service providers before the licence. They may be exemptable in other cases.
- Restrictions on the quantity of products one party may manufacture or sell are contrary to Art 85(1) and not usually exemptable.

Once again, these principles may not apply to all cases, but they do give an indication of some of the risk areas in which advice should be sought.

9.4.6   Licences to end-users

Licences to end-users may in some cases fall within the application of Art 85, although the lack of guidance from the Commission or the European Court of Justice in respect of end-user copyright licences in general means that the rules in this area are to a great extent a matter of conjecture. Limitations restricting the use of a database to a particular physical site, or to a particular computer platform or CPU will arguably fall outside of Art 85 in many cases, as would other restrictions designed to control the number of users of a database. However, Art 85 might well apply to a restriction which merely limited the use of the database to a particular manufacturer's hardware platform (if, for example, the licensor was thereby attempting to tie the use of his own hardware to the use of the database, without an objective justification). Restrictions on copying or sub-licensing may also arguably fall outside of the scope of Art 85 in many cases. On the other hand, restrictions on the use of competing products, or on the user himself competing with the licensor, are likely to fall within the application of Art 85, and may be very difficult to justify under Art 85(3).

9.5   ARTICLE 86 OF THE EC TREATY

Article 86 of the EC Treaty prohibits any abuse by one or more undertakings of a dominant position within the EU or a substantial part of it that affects trade between Member States. To determine whether an abuse contrary to Art 86 has occurred, it is therefore necessary to consider whether an undertaking:

- holds a dominant position in a substantial part of the EU;
- has abused that dominant position; and
- has, as a result, affected trade between Member States.

9.5.1 Dominance

The European Court of Justice has defined dominance as: 'a position of economic strength enjoyed by an undertaking which enables it to hinder the maintenance of effective competition on the relevant market by allowing it to behave to an appreciable extent independently of its competitors and customers and ultimately of consumers'[1].

To determine whether an undertaking holds a dominant position, it is first necessary to identify the relevant market. This has two aspects: (i) the relevant product market, and (ii) the relevant geographic market.

9.5.2 The relevant product market

The relevant product market will include 'all those products and/or services which are regarded as interchangeable or substitutable by the consumer, by reason of the products' characteristics, their prices and their intended use'[2]. Non-substitutable products may also come within the relevant product market definition if their producers are able to switch to manufacturing substitutable products in the short term without significant additional costs or risk[3]. To date, the Commission's practice has tended to be to define product markets narrowly, restricting the definition to the relevant products and close substitutes.

In its most recent communication on the definition of relevant markets, the Commission suggests that products are sufficiently substitutable to be included within the relevant product market if sufficient customers would switch to them in response to a small permanent rise of between 5 per cent and 10 per cent in the price of the affected products to make such a price rise unprofitable[4]. In practice, however, it is unlikely to be possible to apply this test.

9.5.3 The relevant geographic market

The relevant geographic market has been defined as 'the area in which the undertakings concerned are involved in the supply and demand of products or services, in which the conditions of competition are sufficiently homogeneous and which can be distinguished from neighbouring areas because the conditions of competition are appreciably different in those areas'[5]. As with the relevant product market, the Commission's latest communication suggests that an area should be included within the relevant geographic market if sufficient customers would switch their purchases to it in response to a small permanent rise of between 5 per cent and 10 per cent in the price in the affected area to make such a price rise unprofitable[6]. Again, it is unlikely, in practice, to be possible to apply this test.

---

1   Case 322/81 *Michelin v Commission* [1983] ECR 3461 at 3503.
2   Commission notice on the definition of relevant market for the purposes of Community competition law, OJ No C 372/5, 1997, at para 7.
3   Ibid, at para 20.
4   Ibid, at para 17.
5   Ibid, para 8; see also Case 27/76, *United Brands v Commission* [1978] ECR 207.
6   Commission notice on the definition of relevant market for the purposes of Community competition law, OJ No C 372/5, 1997, at para 17.

Whether an area constitutes a substantial part of the EU market is a question of fact dependent on the economic significance of an area as well as its geographic scope. The ports of both Genoa and Holyhead have been found to be substantial parts of the EU due to their importance for shipping[1], and it seems that an area as small as Luxembourg (which represents less than 0.25 per cent of the population of the EU) may qualify[2].

9.5.4   Measuring economic strength on the relevant market

A firm will usually be regarded as having sufficient economic strength to be regarded as dominant where it controls a large share of the relevant market for a significant period, at least provided that other relevant factors point in the same direction. For example, the European Court of Justice has found that a market share in excess of 84 per cent held for three years was proof of dominance[3]. Similarly, a market share of around 50 per cent held for around three years was sufficient, in the absence of counter-indications, to raise a presumption of dominance[4]. Conversely, it is unlikely that an undertaking controlling less than 25 per cent of the relevant market would be considered dominant[5].

However, an undertaking's market share is not the only factor which determines dominance, and a high market share may not be conclusive of dominance where there are other factors which negate it. The other relevant factors include: the market shares of the other undertakings in the market, the evolution of market shares over time, control of key technology and other existing barriers to market entry.

9.5.5   The notion of an essential facility

A doctrine is currently developing under Art 86 in relation to 'essential facilities' without access to which competitors cannot provide services to their customers in a related market. It seems that those who control essential facilities are under special obligations and may be required to grant access to those facilities even if they would not be required to do so if they were merely dominant on the conventional assessment suggested above. In addition, they may be required to grant access on terms which are no less favourable than those they grant to themselves as participants in a related market. The principal case concerned a port authority which was operating a ferry service from the port, and which, in its capacity as port authority, was allegedly applying sailing schedules that disadvantaged other ferry operators[6]. The Commission reasoned that a dominant undertaking which both owns or controls and uses an essential facility and which refuses access to that facility or grants access to competitors on terms less favourable than it applies to its own services (thereby placing them at a competitive disadvantage) infringes Art 86 unless it has an objective justification for its actions. In another case concerning a port controller, the

---

1   Case C-179/90, *Port of Genoa* [1991] I ECR 5889 and *Sealink/B & I* [1992] 5 CMLR 255.
2   Advocate-General Warner in 77/77, *BP v Commission* [1978] ECR 1513.
3   Case 85/76, *Hoffman-La Roche v Commission* [1979] ECR 461.
4   Case C-62/86, *AKZO v Commission* [1991] I ECR 3359.
5   See Recital 15 of Regulation 4064/89, the 'Merger Regulation', OJ No L 257/13, 1990 (now amended by Regulation 1310/97, OJ No L 180/1, 1997).
6   *Sea Containers v Stena Sealink*, OJ No L 15/8 1994.

Commission decided that this principle would apply even if the dominant undertaking did not operate a ferry company and so was not active in the relevant market[1]. A refusal of the right to use the port without a valid reason could be an abuse even where the port controller had no economic interest in any of the ferry operators using the port.

The doctrine would be of little interest, however, if it applied only to ports. The Commission has claimed, in draft guidelines on the application of the competition rules to access agreements in the telecoms sector, that even the control (presumably by the incumbent telecoms operator) of basic information relating to the public voice telephony service (presumably of the type that would be incorporated in telephone directories) could amount to the control of an essential facility[2]. In addition, some decisions which were taken before the doctrine was expressly formulated by the Commission are now being recast as applications of the principle. One example of a case which is claimed to have been an application of the principle is the *London European–Sabena* case[3]. In that case, the Commission decided that the Belgian national airline, Sabena, had infringed Art 86 by refusing to grant another airline, London European, access to its computerised reservation system which would allow its flight schedules and fares to be quoted and reservations to be made.

Clearly, the essential facilities doctrine could have important consequences for database owners, especially in relation to possible obligations to grant rights to database content. However, the doctrine is still in the process of being developed, and many aspects of it are still unclear. In particular, it is not clear when something will amount to an essential facility. In one case, the Commission defined an essential facility as 'a facility or infrastructure which is essential for reaching customers and/or enabling competitors to carry on their business, and which cannot be replicated by any reasonable means'[4]. However, a much more detailed consideration of this question will be necessary before the issue is fully clarified.

9.6   ABUSE

The following sections list forms of behaviour and contractual requirements which may be considered to be abusive.

9.6.1   Obtaining exclusive rights to content

In certain circumstances, an operator which is dominant in the market for certain databases might be committing an abuse if it acquired such a degree of exclusivity regarding the content of such databases that competitors were excluded from the

---

1   *Irish Continental Group v CCI Morlaix* Commission press release IP/95/492, [1995] 5 CMLR 177.

2   *Communication from the Commission on the application of the competition rules to access agreements in the telecommunications sector*, OJ No C 76, 1997 at point 59.

3   *London European – Sabena*, OJ No L 317/47, 1988.

4   See the *Notice on the application of the competition rules to access agreements in the telecoms sector* at point 68.

market. Considerations of this type may well have been behind the *Nielsen* case[1]. This concerned retail tracking services (also known as sales or market tracking services), which involve information on product sales, prices and other market information being obtained electronically from retailers and aggregated, with the aggregated information then being supplied to manufacturers of the relevant products and others. AC Nielsen Company is the world's leading provider of these services. The second largest provider, IRI, complained to the Commission that the terms of Nielsen's contracts with retailers were preventing IRI from entering the market. The Commission issued a statement of objections alleging infringement of Art 86. The case never resulted in a formal decision, but was resolved by Nielsen giving undertakings to the Commission, one of which was that, in relation to the purchase of data from retailers, Nielsen would not conclude exclusive contracts or contracts including any restriction on the retailer's freedom to supply data to any other retail tracking services provider.

9.6.2   Excessive pricing

A dominant company which charges prices which are unfairly high in comparison to the 'economic value' of the products or services being supplied may be committing an abuse. Whether or not this is the case may be assessed by examining prices for comparable goods or services or the cost of producing the relevant goods or services[2]. However, there are considerable difficulties in determining when a price is so high that it constitutes an abuse, with the result that Art 86 has been applied in respect of excessive prices in very few cases. On the other hand, it may be that where excessive prices relate to an essential facility (see above) the Commission will be more keen to take action. Indeed, the recent case *ITT/Belgacom* may suggest that prices for access to an essential facility cannot exceed cost plus a reasonable rate of return[3]. The case concerned the prices charged by Belgacom, the incumbent Belgian telecoms operator, to ITT Promedia NV, a provider of alternative telephone directories, for lists of its telephone subscribers and other data (which the Commission may well have seen as an essential facility). ITT complained that the prices were excessive and discriminatory. The Commission closed its case after Belgacom agreed to reduce such prices to a level that would cover its costs in collecting, compiling and providing such data plus a reasonable profit margin. The new price constituted a reduction of 90 per cent over that originally charged by Belgacom.

9.6.3   Predatory pricing

Predatory pricing, meaning pricing below cost aimed at eliminating a competitor, may be abusive and contrary to Art 86. The European Court of Justice has held that pricing below average variable cost is an automatic abuse under Art 86 and that pricing below average total cost may be abusive if it forms part of a plan to eliminate a competitor[4].

---

1   See Commission press release IP/96/1117.
2   Case 27/76, *United Brands v Commission* [1978] ECR 207, at para 251 et seq (cost of
     production); Case 226/84 *British Leyland v Commission* [1986] ECR 3263 (comparisons with
     equivalent transactions).
3   *ITT/Belgacom*, Commission press release IP/97/292.
4   Case C-62/86 *AKZO v Commission* [1991] ECR I-3359.

9.6.4 Discriminatory pricing

Discriminatory pricing may be condemned as an abuse. Art 86 itself lists 'applying dissimilar conditions to equivalent transactions with other trading parties, thereby placing them at a competitive disadvantage' as an example of abuse[1]. Does this mean that companies in a dominant position cannot charge different prices for a product in different countries? One practice which has been condemned is where a dominant company charges distributors different prices for particular goods delivered to the same place, according to the country where the distributor is intending to resell them[2]. On the other hand, where the discrimination is less artificial, and there is some objective justification for the difference in price, a price difference may, in many cases, be permitted.

9.6.5 Tying

A typical form of abusive tie-in or tying occurs where, as a condition of purchasing one product or service in which an undertaking is dominant, a buyer is forced to purchase another product or service which it could otherwise have bought from a competing supplier, or which it could have self-provided[3]. However, this is not the only form of tying behaviour that may be considered abusive. If a dominant company gives a reduction in price when products or services are purchased together (as compared with the price of purchasing them separately), then that may also be abusive, especially where it forecloses the market because competitors which offer the products or services separately are unable to compete. On the other hand, if the difference in price reflects a reduction in the costs of supplying the bundled package, then it should be permitted. This is illustrated by a recent case involving the Digital Equipment Corporation ('DEC') which did not reach the stage of a formal decision, and which was resolved by DEC giving undertakings to the Commission[4]. DEC, which was alleged to be dominant in the supply of software and hardware maintenance services for its products, offered a combined package of software maintenance services and hardware maintenance services at a price lower than the combined prices for software and hardware maintenance services if purchased separately. To avoid action by the Commission under Art 86, DEC had to undertake that the discount in respect of software services which were bundled would not be greater than 10 per cent compared with the price for purchasing software maintenance services and hardware maintenance services separately. A greater discount would have made it uneconomic for competitors to offer hardware maintenance services alone. The Commission commented that the 10 per cent discount allowed cost savings and other benefits to be passed on to system users while ensuring the maintenance of effective competition in the supply of hardware services.

9.6.6 Exclusive purchasing requirements and loyalty bonuses

An obligation imposed by a dominant firm on its customers or distributors requiring them to purchase all or a percentage of their requirements from the dominant firm may

---

1   Article 86(c) of the EC Treaty.
2   Case 27/76, *United Brands v Commission* [1978] ECR 207.
3   Case C-53/92 P, *Hilti v Commission* [1994] ECR I-667.
4   See Commission press release IP/97/868.

be an abuse of a dominant position because it has a foreclosure effect on other suppliers. Pricing practices such as loyalty or fidelity discounts or rebates where a rebate or discount is conditional on a customer purchasing all or a proportion of its requirements from the undertaking offering the discount may also be abusive for the same reason. Even discounts or rebates which are based on the purchase of fixed amounts may be contrary to Art 86, where those fixed amounts are in fact calculated for each customer to cover all or a substantial amount of that customer's requirements.

9.6.7   Refusal to supply and refusal to license

Refusals to supply, in particular refusals to continue supplies to existing customers, may be abusive. For example, it has been held to be abusive for an undertaking which has previously supplied raw materials to a producer of finished goods to refuse to supply the raw materials to that customer because it wishes to break into the market for finished goods itself[1]. A refusal to supply an existing distributor because it starts to sell the products of a competitor, or starts to compete by itself providing competing products or services, could also be an abuse[2]. While refusal to supply a new customer may not in many cases be an abuse, there are some cases where refusal to supply a new customer has been held to be one. These cases are difficult to categorise, but factors involved have included the fact of having a legal monopoly over the service refused, as well as essential facilities considerations.

A special case of a refusal to supply is a refusal to license, an issue which will be of considerable relevance to holders of rights in databases. In certain circumstances, a refusal to grant a licence of intellectual property rights may be abusive. In the *Magill* case, which involved copyright material, the European Court of Justice held that, in exceptional circumstances, the owner of intellectual property rights may be obliged by Art 86 to grant licences to third parties[3]. *Magill* concerned a refusal by a number of television broadcasters in the UK and Ireland to license weekly programme schedules said to be covered by copyright to Magill for inclusion in a weekly television listings magazine. The following were some of the elements which the European Court of Justice identified as justifying an obligation to license in this case:

- the requested material was basic information concerning channel, day, time and title of the programme;
- each of the broadcasters was the only possible source of information on its programming schedule and, as a result, the refusal to license was preventing the emergence of a new product, namely a comprehensive television guide, for which there was 'specific, constant and regular' potential demand;
- by their conduct the broadcasters reserved to themselves the market for weekly television guides;
- there was no justification for such a refusal either in the activity of television broadcasting or in that of publishing television programmes.

---

1   Cases 6 and 7/73, *Commercial Solvents v Commission* [1974] ECR 223.
2   Case 27/76, *United Brands Co v Commission* [1978] ECR 207; *BBI/Boosey and Hawkes* OJ No L 286/36 1987.
3   Cases C-241/91 P and C-242/91, *RTE and ITP v Commission* [1995] ECR I-743.

The scope of the *Magill* judgment has now been interpreted in the later case, *Tiercé Ladbroke*[1]. This concerned the broadcasting of sound and pictures of French horse races, the rights to which were controlled by the French horse racing companies, or '*sociétés de courses*'. Ladbroke wanted a right to broadcast the French races in its booking shops in Belgium, but the French horse racing companies refused. The European Court of Justice in this case found that there was no obligation to license. The *Magill* case could not be relied on because, in contrast to *Magill*, in this case the applicant was not only present in but had the largest share of the main betting market in Belgium, on which the product in question would be offered to consumers, while the French horse racing companies were not present on the market. In the absence of exploitation by those companies of their intellectual property rights in Belgium, their refusal to supply could not be regarded as involving any restriction of competition. Even if the absence of the horse racing companies was not a decisive factor, the refusal to supply could not be contrary to Art 86, unless it concerned a product or service which was either essential for the exercise of the activity in question in that there was no real or potential substitute, or it concerned a new product whose introduction might be prevented, despite specific, constant and regular demand on the part of consumers. Sound and pictures were not necessary for taking bets, as shown by the Ladbrokes significant position in Belgium for taking bets on French races. Further, broadcasting was not indispensable, because it took place after bets were placed, and therefore did not prevent bookmakers from pursuing their business.

In the Netherlands, the Amsterdam Court of Appeal has held that a refusal by the Dutch PTT to licence its 'White Pages' telephone directories for re-publication on CD-COM would be an abuse of a dominant market position[2].

9.6.8 Effect on trade between Member States

The concept of effect on trade between Member States under Art 86 appears to be interpreted in much the same way as the equivalent concept under Art 85.

9.7 THE EFFECT OF FALLING WITHIN ARTICLE 86 OF THE EC TREATY

The Commission may impose fines on undertakings in breach of Art 86 of up to 10 per cent of their turnover[3]. In addition, it may, by decision, order infringing undertakings to take such action as is necessary to terminate the infringement[4]. Damages may also be available to third parties harmed as a result of an infringement of Art 86, although this may depend on the applicable national law. Under English law, damages are, in principle, available[5].

---

1   Case T-504/93, *Tiercé Ladbroke v Commission,* judgment of 12 June 1997.
2   *Denda International v KPN,* 5 August 1997, Court of Appeal of Amsterdam.
3   Article 15(2) of Regulation 17/62, OJ 21.2.1962, p 204 (special edition 1959–62, p 87).
4   Article 3 of Regulation 17/62, above.
5   *Garden Cottage Foods v Milk Marketing Board* [1984] 1 AC 130.

SECTION B: UK LAW

The most relevant provisions of UK law relating to database agreements are to be found in the Restrictive Trade Practices Act 1976, the Competition Act 1980 and, to a lesser extent, the Resale Prices Act 1976. However, the Competition Bill currently before Parliament will repeal the Restrictive Trade Practices Act 1976, the Resale Prices Act 1976 and the relevant parts of the Competition Act 1980 when it enters into force[1]. It is currently expected that the Competition Bill will be enacted in mid- to late-1998 and will enter into force a year later in mid- to late-1999.

9.8   THE RESTRICTIVE TRADE PRACTICES ACT 1976

An agreement between two or more parties that carry on a business in the UK is registrable under the Restrictive Trade Practices Act 1976 ('the RTPA') if: (i) two or more parties to it accept restrictions relating to the supply of goods; or (ii) two or more parties to it accept restrictions relating to the supply of services[2]. For the purposes of the RTPA, an agreement need not be legally enforceable[3], and several separate but related contracts may be considered to form a single agreement[4]. For the purposes of calculating whether there are two or more parties to an agreement, or whether two or more parties accept restrictions, companies that belong to the same corporate group are treated as a single party[5].

In practice, the most important aspect of the RTPA is that failure to notify a registrable agreement to the Office of Fair Trading within three months of the agreement being made will result in any relevant restrictions contained in the agreement being legally unenforceable[6]. In addition, third parties who have suffered loss as a result of the implementation of void relevant restrictions may have an action for damages[7].

If an agreement is notified to the Office of Fair Trading and found to be registrable, it is placed on a public register (with the exception of any aspects of it which qualify for confidential treatment, and for which such treatment has been requested)[8]. Agreements which have been registered may then be referred to the Restrictive Practices Court, although in the vast majority of cases no reference is made because the agreement is not found to represent a significant restriction of competition[9].

The following section looks at some of the exceptions and exclusions in the RTPA which may be relevant to agreements concerning databases, specifically with regard to the question of whether or not an agreement is registrable. It should be noted, however, that there are many other relevant exceptions and exclusions. The

---

1   Sections 1 and 17 of the Competition Bill.
2   Sections 6 and 7 (goods) and 11 and 12 (services) of the RTPA.
3   Section 43(1) of the RTPA.
4   RE Royal Institute of Chartered Surveyors' Application [1986] ICR 550, CA.
5   Section 43(2) of the RTPA.
6   Section 35(1) of the RTPA.
7   Section 35(2) of the RTPA.
8   Sections 1(2) and 23 of the RTPA.
9   Sections 1(2) and 21(2) of the RTPA.

application of the RTPA is highly technical and a lawyer should always be consulted as to the registrability of any particular agreement.

9.9 GENERAL EXCLUSIONS AND EXCEPTIONS UNDER THE RTPA

The RTPA will not apply where the aggregate group turnover in the UK of all the relevant parties is less than £50 million at the time of the agreement, provided the agreement does not involve price fixing[1].

Restrictions relating exclusively to goods supplied pursuant to the agreement are to be ignored for the purposes of determining registrability under the RTPA[2], but this does not apply where the relevant restrictions are accepted by two or more persons by whom, or two or more persons to whom, goods are to be supplied in pursuance of the agreement[3]. Similar provisions apply to the supply of services[4].

The general exception in Sch 3, para 2 to the RTPA (in combination with the exception for restrictions relating exclusively to goods supplied pursuant to the agreement) means that distribution agreements relating to goods, including exclusive distribution agreements, are often not registrable under the RTPA. Schedule 3, para 2 provides that the RTPA does not apply in agreements for the supply of goods to which there are only two parties in which the only restrictions accepted are: (i) restrictions on the party supplying the goods in respect of the supply of goods of the same description to third parties; and/or (ii) restrictions on the party acquiring the goods in respect of the sale or purchase of goods of the same description. A similar exception applies in respect of services under Sch 3, para 7, which provides that the RTPA does not apply to an agreement to which there are no parties other than a person who agrees to supply services and another person for whom they are to be supplied, and where no restrictions are accepted other than in respect of the supply of services of the same description to other persons or the obtaining of services of the same description from other persons.

9.10 EXCEPTIONS RELATING TO LICENSING OF INTELLECTUAL PROPERTY RIGHTS

There are specific exceptions under the RTPA for agreements concerning intellectual property rights to which there are only two parties. For example, an agreement between two parties will not come within the terms of the RTPA where it:

---

1   Section 27A of the RTPA and the Restrictive Trade Practices (Non-notifiable Agreements) (Turnover Threshold) Amendment Order 1997, SI 1997/2944.
2   Section 9(3) of the RTPA.
3   Section 9(4) of the RTPA.
4   Section 18(2) and (3) of the RTPA.

–   concerns patents (but is not a patent pooling agreement) and no restrictions are accepted other than in relation to the invention which is the subject of the patent application[1];

–   concerns know-how relating to the operation of processes of manufacture and no restrictions are accepted other than in respect of the descriptions of goods to be produced by those processes[2]; or

–   concerns know-how relating to techniques or processes to be applied in the provision of services and no restrictions are accepted other than restrictions which relate exclusively to the form or manner in which services incorporating those techniques or processes are to be made available or supplied[3].

These provisions may, however, be very narrowly interpreted, and any restriction which does not relate specifically to the permitted areas will cause the benefit of the exception to be lost. In addition, they are not cumulative, so that where an agreement relates to both patents and know-how (or any other combination of intellectual property rights) none of these provisions will apply[4].

There is also a specific exception relating to copyright, which covers licences granted by the owner of copyright, the assignment of copyright and agreements for such licences or assignments[5]. The RTPA will not apply to such agreements where no restrictions relating to goods or services are accepted other than in respect of the work or other subject matter in which the copyright subsists or will subsist. As in the case of the other intellectual property right exceptions described above, the exception will be narrowly interpreted, and the inclusion of any restriction which does not specifically relate to the work or other subject matter in which the copyright subsists may mean that the RTPA will apply. However, in contrast to the other exceptions considered above, agreements which include more than two parties may benefit from this exception.

Even where none of the specific exceptions relating to intellectual property licences apply, a licensing agreement may escape the application of the RTPA under the Ravenseft doctrine. This doctrine was developed by the Office of Fair Trading following the judgment in *Re Ravenseft Properties Ltd's Application*, where it was held that the RTPA did not apply to restrictions contained in a lease of land[6]. The court gave two grounds for its decision. First, the granting of a lease was not the supply of a good or service under the RTPA, provided that there was no commercial nexus between the parties, and that the landlord did not also supply services in relation to the leased property. Secondly, a person buying or leasing land had no previous right to be there and so lost no right or freedom (and was therefore subject to no restriction for the purposes of the RTPA) in taking possession of the land subject to limitations on its use.

The Office of Fair Trading has indicated that in its view:

---

1   Schedule 3, para 5 of the RTPA.
2   Schedule 3, para 3 of the RTPA.
3   Schedule 3, para 8 of the RTPA.
4   *Registrar of Restrictive Trade Agreements v Schweppes Ltd (No 2)* (1971) LR 7 RP 336.
5   Schedule 3, para 5A of the RTPA.
6   *Re Ravenseft Properties Ltd's Application* [1978] QB 52.

(i) the *Ravenseft* case means that a licence of intellectual property rights is not the supply of goods or services for the purposes of the RTPA[1];

(ii) a party does not accept a restriction for the purposes of the RTPA where, in the words of the Office of Fair Trading[2], either:

   (a) it accepts a 'restriction' on its power to grant a licence or a franchise (although any accompanying restriction on the supply of goods or services could fall within the terms of the RTPA); or

   (b) it accepts a 'restriction' which simply limits rights it would not have without the arrangement (this is called the open door principle).

The *Ravenseft* doctrine may mean that many intellectual property licences escape the application of the RTPA. However, it is important to note its limitations. Exclusive licences may still be relevant restrictions, because they include a limitation on the licensor using the intellectual property rights himself (which would not come within the terms of the doctrine). Any restriction on the licensee's ability to supply or obtain goods or services which are not dependent on the intellectual property rights licensed will not fall within the doctrine. Further, it is by no means certain that the *Ravenseft* doctrine would apply to the licensing of know-how. Lastly, the Office of Fair Trading's interpretation of the *Ravenseft* case has never been confirmed by the courts, which could potentially reject it. For these reasons, where it is proposed to rely on the Ravenseft doctrine, parties are often advised to make a fail-safe notification to the Office of Fair Trading, even though it is more than likely that the relevant agreement will not be found to be registrable.

9.11 THE RESALE PRICES ACT 1976

The Resale Prices Act 1976 ('RPA') prohibits both (i) minimum resale price maintenance by individual suppliers; and (ii) all forms of horizontal collective price maintenance. It should be noted that the RPA applies only to the supply of goods and not to the supply of services. It may also be argued that provisions in intellectual property licences would fall outside the RPA.

(a) Individual minimum resale price maintenance
The RPA prohibits suppliers from imposing minimum resale prices, by contract or otherwise, in relation to goods intended to be resold in the UK and any contractual terms seeking to do so are unenforceable[3]. This prohibition applies only to minimum resale price maintenance. Suppliers remain free to indicate recommended resale prices[4]. Individual maximum resale price maintenance is not prohibited under the RPA, but may be caught by the Competition Act 1980 (discussed below) or EC competition law.

---

1 The Office has taken the view that the principles laid down in the judgment in this case are of general application to proprietary rights and the grant of an industrial property licence, eg a copyright licence does not constitute the supply of a service within the meaning of the legislation (Office of Fair Trading Annual Report 1976, p 36).

2 *Restrictive Trade Practices*, a guide to the RTPA issued by the Office of Fair Trading, p 16.

3 Sections 9 and 11 of the RPA.

4 Section 9(2) of the RPA.

(b) Collective price maintenance

The RPA also prohibits agreements that impose resale prices (maximum or minimum) between two or more suppliers carrying on a business in the UK or between two or more dealers carrying on a business in the UK [1]. This prohibition applies regardless of whether the agreement is legally enforceable and covers recommendations as to resale price between suppliers or between dealers [2].

9.12   THE COMPETITION ACT 1980

Sections 2 to 10 of the Competition Act 1980 allow the Director General of Fair Trading to investigate and subsequently refer to the Monopolies and Mergers Commission 'anti-competitive practices'. According to s 2(1) of the Competition Act:

> 'a person engages in an anti-competitive practice if, in the course of business, that person pursues a course of conduct which, of itself or when taken together with a course of conduct pursued by persons associated with him, has or is intended to have or is likely to have the effect of restricting, distorting or preventing competition in connection with the production, supply or acquisition of goods in the United Kingdom or any part of it or the supply or securing of services in the United Kingdom or any part of it.'

No fines are imposable for breach of the Competition Act 1980, nor does it give third parties any right to damages. However, if the Monopolies and Mergers Commission determines that an anti-competitive practice operates, or might be expected to operate against the public interest, then the Secretary of State for Trade and Industry may make an order against the relevant company to prohibit the continuance of an anti-competitive practice or any other course of conduct which is similar in form or effect to it, and to remedy any adverse effect on the public interest identified by the Monopolies and Mergers Commission [3]. In practice, however, cases which proceed this far are generally resolved by the relevant company giving an undertaking to the Director-General of Fair Trading. The main exclusions from the Competition Act are:

– agreements which are registrable under the RTPA, or courses of conduct which are required by restrictions which make the RTPA applicable;

– courses of conduct engaged in by companies which either have an annual turnover of less than £10 million or which have a market share of less than 25 per cent, and whose corporate group does not have a turnover or market share exceeding those limits;

– conditions in contracts exclusively for the supply of goods outside of the UK.

The activities or contractual terms which have been found to constitute anti-competitive practices roughly mirror those which have been condemned under Art 86 of the EC Treaty.

---

1   Sections 1 and 2 of the RPA.
2   Section 3 of the RPA.
3   Section 10 of the Competition Act 1980.

9.13 THE COMPETITION BILL

A Competition Bill (the 'Bill') is currently before Parliament and will, if enacted, bring UK competition rules closer into line with Arts 85 and 86 of the EC Treaty and will repeal the RTPA and the provisions of the Competition Act 1980 dealing with anti-competitive practices.

In particular, the Bill provides for prohibitions on:

(i)   agreements between undertakings, decisions of associations of undertakings and concerted practices intended to be implemented in the UK that may affect trade within the UK and have as their object of effect the prevention or restriction of distortion of competition within the UK[1];

(ii) abuse of a dominant position in the UK that may affect trade within the UK[2].

Breach of these prohibitions would have consequences very similar to those under EC law, including legal unenforceability[3] and fines of up to 10 per cent of the turnover of the parties involved[4]. It is also possible that third parties would have an action for damages. Small agreements and abuses of minor significance would be provisionally immune from fines (although the Director-General would be able to lift this immunity) but would remain subject to unenforceability[5]. The criteria defining small agreements and abuses of minor significance have yet to be defined.

As under the EC Competition rules, both block exemptions and individual exemptions will be possible in respect of restrictive agreements, and exemptions will be based on criteria mirroring those applicable under Art 85(3) of the EC Treaty[6]. Agreements benefiting from an individual or block exemption under Art 85(3) and agreements that would benefit from a block exemption except that they do not affect trade between Member States are excluded from the Bill's prohibition on restrictive agreements[7].

Two forms of notification will be possible: notification for guidance and notification for a decision[8]. Both will ensure immunity from fines[9].

The Bill provides that the Director-General (and ultimately the UK courts) would be obliged to ensure, as far as possible, that issues arising under its provisions are dealt with in a manner consistent with the treatment of comparable questions under EC competition law, and in particular that the principles they apply are not inconsistent with those laid down by the EC Treaty and the European Court of Justice[10]. As a result, the principles described above in relation to Arts 85 and 86 of the EC Treaty should also apply in relation to the Bill once it enters into force, albeit with some differences

---

1   Section 2 of the Bill.
2   Section 18 of the Bill.
3   Section 1(4) of the Bill.
4   Section 37 of the Bill.
5   Sections 40 and 41 of the Bill.
6   Sections 4, 6 and 9 of the Bill.
7   Section 10 of the Bill.
8   Sections 13 and 14 of the Bill.
9   Sections 13(4) and 14(4) of the Bill.
10   Sections 13(4) and 14(4) of the Bill.

as the prohibitions set out in the Bill would apply to agreements and practices even absent an effect on trade between Member States, provided competition in the UK was affected. It is also possible that export bans would not be regarded as problematic under the prohibitions set out in the Bill as the achievement of a single market within the EC, one of the objectives of EC competition law and the justification of its hostile attitude to export bans, may not be regarded as one of the objectives of UK competition law.

The Bill provides for a wide range of enforcement powers for the Director-General, including rights to: order the production of documents; enter premises to inspect and copy documents (including the premises of persons not party to an infringing agreement or abuse); apply to the High Court for search warrants; implement interim measures; impose penalty payments; and make directions as he considers appropriate to bring infringements to an end[1].

Agreements made, decisions taken and practices adopted before the entry into force of the Bill's prohibition on anti-competitive agreements are exempt from that prohibition during a transitional period, which in most cases will be one year, although this transitional period may be lifted by the Director-General following an investigation[2]. There is no transitional period, however, for agreements that become void for failure to register under the RTPA[3]. Agreements made after the enactment of the Bill but before its entry into force may be notified to the Director-General who may grant a prospective exemption under the Bill that would also operate as an exemption under the RTPA[4].

---

1   Chapter III of the Bill.
2   Schedule 13 to and ss 6, 7, 8 and 9 of the Bill.
3   Schedule 13 to and s 8(1)(a) of the Bill.
4   Schedule 13 to and s 11 of the Bill.

Chapter 10

INTERNATIONAL TREATIES

10.1 Introduction – 10.2 The Berne Convention – 10.3 The Universal Copyright Convention ('UCC') – 10.4 TRIPs ('Trade Related Aspects of Intellectual Property') and the World Trade Organisation ('WTO') – 10.5 WIPO Copyright Treaty – 10.6 Members of the Berne Convention as at 26 March 1998 – 10.7 The Berne Convention for the Protection of Literary and Artistic Works, with its revisions

10.1   INTRODUCTION

No examination of the English and EU law of copyright and databases would be complete without a consideration of the framework of international treaties within which individual domestic laws subsist. This chapter therefore seeks to give an outline sketch of the most important international treaties which relate to the protection of databases.

The protection of copyright on an international basis was a natural extension of the protection of those rights by individual jurisdictions. The value of any intellectual property right is greatly reduced if it is not recognised on an international basis. By their very nature copyright works are easily copied and transferred; physical and national borders are no bar to this transfer. Improvements in communication created the need for nation States to agree to respect the copyrights of foreign nationals and to enforce those copyrights in their own jurisdictions. Prior to the Berne Convention, such agreements were by international treaty negotiated separately by individual nations. The Berne Convention paved the way for an increasingly successful international approach to such problems.

10.2   THE BERNE CONVENTION

10.2.1   Introduction

The Berne Convention was the result of diplomatic conferences between 1884 and 1886. It set up a union for the harmonisation of copyrights. The Berne Union has grown steadily since its inception when there were ten founding members[1] to 130 members as at 26 March 1998[2].

There have been two additions and five revisions[3] to the Berne Convention, in each case gradually increasing the level of protection enjoyed by authors.

---

1   Belgium, France, Germany, UK, Haiti, Italy, Liberia, Spain, Switzerland and Tunisia.
2   See **10.6**.
3   See **10.7**

10.2.2   The protection

Countries to which the Berne Convention applies constitute a union for the protection of the rights of authors in their literary and artistic works[1].

Article 2 of the Berne Convention defines the expression 'literary and artistic works' very broadly so as to encompass, as far as possible, every form of artistic and literary effort. The Berne Convention, which has as its origin the European system of copyright protection, seeks to protect the intellectual efforts of the creator of the work as opposed to the publisher. It is the expression of that product that the Berne Convention seeks to protect, whether in the form of words, drawings, symbols, music, three-dimensional objects or other recorded forms. The Berne Convention does not, however, require that expression to have been recorded for it to qualify for protection. The Database Directive, by contrast, does not use the term 'literary' or 'artistic work'. It merely states that the database 'shall be protected by copyright'[2]. However, in the UK this provision has been implemented by treating all databases as defined by the Database Directive as types of literary works.

Although the Berne Convention does not specify how the 'expression' is to be evidenced, provision is made permitting countries in the Berne Union to have the right to prescribe that the work is not protected until it is 'fixed in some material form'[3].

The Berne Convention makes no mention of databases even though, by the end of the nineteenth century, the production of commercial directories was well established. Perhaps in keeping with the Berne Convention's elevated desire of protecting an author's literary effort, reference was only made to 'encyclopaedias and anthologies'.

Article 2(5) of the Berne Convention provides that:

> 'Collections of *literary or artistic* [our emphasis] works such as encyclopaedias and anthologies which, by reason of the selection and arrangement of their contents, constitute intellectual creations shall be protected as such, without prejudice to the copyright in each of the works forming part of such collections.'

Accordingly, if the contents of a database are *in themselves* 'literary or artistic works' then, under the Berne Convention, the database structure can also be classified for protection. The requirement that the contents should in themselves be 'literary or artistic works' would seem to deny directories and similar works protection even though there may have been considerable and original effort in their construction. This requirement is not reflected in the Database Directive: creativity in selection is separate from, and not dependent on, the quality of the contents.

The concept in Art 2(5) of the Berne Convention that such collections constitute the 'intellectual creations' of their authors has been followed through into the Database Directive, which provides in Art 3(1):

> 'in accordance with this Directive, databases which by reason of the selection or arrangement of their contents constitute the author's own intellectual creation shall be protected as such by copyright.'

---

1   Article 1 of the Berne Convention.
2   Article 3(1) of the Database Directive.
3   Article 2(2) of the Berne Convention.

This requirement that the author's 'own intellectual creation' is represented in the database introduces a different standard for copyright in databases to that applicable to non-database 'tables or compilations', which only require originality. By way of contrast, prior to the Database Directive a database would have been protected under UK law as a 'table or compilation'[1] but not under US law which requires that the database demonstrates by its 'selection, coordination or arrangement'[2] that it is entitled to copyright protection.

Article 3(2) of the Database Directive provides that the copyright protection of databases under the Database Directive shall not extend to their contents and shall be without prejudice to any right subsisting in those contents themselves. This is consistent with Art 2(5) of the Berne Convention which provides that collections of literary works shall be protected as such, 'without prejudice to the copyright in each of the works forming part of such collections'.

The relevant rights granted to authors by the Berne Convention are as follows:

The **droit moral**:

> 'Independently of the author's economic rights, and even after the transfer of the said rights, the author shall have the right to claim authorship of the work and to object to any distortion, mutilation or other modification of, or other derogatory action in relation to, the said work, which would be prejudicial to his honour or reputation.'[3]

The moral rights granted to an author by the Berne Convention are the inalienable rights to be identified as an author of the work and to preserve his reputation as such by preventing or objecting to derogatory treatment of the work. These rights relate to the author's reputation and are thus personal to him. It is for this reason that they are inalienable, for if a publisher acquired the moral rights he would not have the same, or any, interest in enforcing it. Protection of moral rights are outside the scope of the Database Directive but are intended to be exercised in accordance with national legislation and the Berne Convention.[4]

The **reproduction right**:

> 'Authors of literary and artistic works protected by this Convention shall have the exclusive right of authorizing the reproduction of these works, in any manner or form.'[5]

The right of the author to control the manner of the exploitation of his work is an essential element of copyright. Recital 30 of the Database Directive provides that the author's exclusive rights should include the manner of exploitation and distribution. The rights are framed in Art 5 of the Database Directive as the 'Restricted Acts'. The exclusive right of temporary or permanent reproduction is consistent with Art 9 of the Berne Convention. Article 5(c) of the Database Directive deals with distribution of copies to the public, a right which is not dealt with by the Berne Convention (being concerned with the protection of authors as opposed to publishers).

---

1   CDPA, s 3(1)(a).
2   *Feist Publications Inc v Rural Telephone Service Co* 499 US 340 (1991).
3   Article 6bis of the Berne Convention.
4   Database Directive, Recital 28.
5   Article 9 of the Berne Convention.

The **translation right**:

> 'Authors of literary and artistic works protected by this Convention shall enjoy the exclusive right of making and of authorizing the translation of their works throughout the term of protection of their rights in the original works.'[1]

The corresponding provision in the Database Directive is to be found in Art 5(b).

The **broadcasting right**:

> '(I)   Authors of literary and artistic works shall enjoy the exclusive right of authorizing:
>   (i)   the broadcasting of their works or the communication thereof to the public by any other means of wireless diffusion of signs, sounds or images;
>   (ii)   any communication to the public by wire or by rebroadcasting of the broadcast of the work, when this communication is made by an organization other than the original one;
>   (iii) the public communication by loudspeaker or any other analogous instrument transmitting, by signs, sounds or images, the broadcast of the work.'[2]

The Database Directive does not refer to 'broadcasting' as one of the restricted acts in Art 5. It does, however, refer in Art 5(d) to communication and display, which should encompass broadcasting. This interpretation is consistent with the Berne Convention and indeed with the objective of the restrictions under the Database Directive, which are to preserve the methods of exploitation in the expression of the database.

The increasing use of technology to transfer large amounts of information means that databases are now widely used in broadcast services. For example, Teletext and Ceefax constantly send by broadcast pages of information which can be read by viewers who have televisions capable of capturing the information; cable and satellite operators now provide similar services.

The **right of adaptation**:

> 'Authors of literary or artistic works shall enjoy the exclusive right of authorizing adaptations, arrangements and other alterations of their works.'[3]

Article 5(b) of the Database Directive gives the rightholder the exclusive right of 'adaptation, arrangement or other alteration' which, together with Art 5(e), gives the rightholder the exclusive right in the result if displayed or performed to the public.

10.2.3   The public performance right

Article 5(d) of the Database Directive makes one of the restricted acts 'performance to the public'. Art 11 of the Berne Convention deals with the rights of public performance for authors of dramatic or dramatico-musical or musical works. Since the Database Directive specifies that it is the expression of the database (and not its contents) which is to be protected by copyright, it is difficult to imagine how any database would fall within the definition of dramatic or dramatico-musical or musical work.

---

1   Article 8 of the Berne Convention.
2   Article 11bis of the Berne Convention.
3   Article 12 of the Berne Convention.

10.2.4   Exceptions

The exceptions which the Berne Convention provides to the above rights relate to items of daily news[1] and quotations from published works[2], with provision for national legislators to make provision exempting political speeches and speeches delivered in the course of legal proceedings[3], official texts[4], public lectures[5], newspaper articles and broadcasts[6], reports of current events[7] and for educational purposes[8]. The Database Directive only provides for one mandatory exemption, which is for the use of the database by a lawful user[9]. The remaining exceptions under Art 6(2) of the Database Directive permit Member States to make provisions limiting the restricted acts permitted by Art 5 of the Database Directive in accordance with national legislation. The balance between the interests of the rightholder and the user is set out in Art 6(3) of the Database Directive which provides:

'In accordance with the Berne Convention[10] for the protection of Literary and Artistic Works, this Article may not be interpreted in such a way as to allow its application to be used in a manner which unreasonably prejudices the rightholder legitimate interests or conflicts with the normal exploitation of the database.'

Since any exemption will prejudice the interest of the rightholder, it will presumably be a matter for the determination of national courts and of the competition authorities to determine whether or not this is unreasonably prejudicial. The aims and tests of the Berne Convention will thereby be used as a measure of reasonableness.

10.3   THE UNIVERSAL COPYRIGHT CONVENTION ('UCC')

10.3.1   Introduction

The Berne Convention, which was principally promoted by European countries, was based upon a system of protection for the rights of the author, whilst the American system based on the common law emphasised the rights of the publisher. Accordingly, the desire of UNESCO was to create a bridge between the Berne Union and the United States (and other countries who had adopted the American system). These efforts culminated in the adoption of the UCC.

The UCC is sufficiently liberal on the one hand to cope with these very different copyright principles, but on the other hand to provide security for Berne Union members who were concerned that some countries would opt for the UCC in place of the Berne Union and thereby take advantage of its more liberal approach. To resolve this problem it was provided in Art 17 of the UCC that countries which were members of the Berne Union on 1 January 1951 were required to remain members of the Berne

---

1   Article 2(8) of the Berne Convention.
2   Article 10(1) of the Berne Convention.
3   Article 2bis(1) of the Berne Convention.
4   Article 2(4) of the Berne Convention.
5   Article 2bis(2) of the Berne Convention.
6   Article 10bis(1) of the Berne Convention.
7   Article 10bis(2) of the Berne Convention.
8   Article 10(2) of the Berne Convention.
9   Article 6(1) of the Database Directive.
10   See Article 9(2) of the Berne Convention.

Convention despite later membership of the UCC, so that to leave one would be to leave both.

To overcome requirements, for example in the United States, of formality in copyright registration, the UCC adopted the © mark which, together with a requirement for stating the date of the first publication and the name of the copyright proprietor, was accepted as satisfying the requirements of formality.

The other major problem faced by the UCC was the basis for copyright term protection. Berne Union countries provided for protection based upon the author's life, the minimum term for which was life of the author plus 25 years. The United States, on the other hand, provided that protection stemmed from the date of publication. Initially, this was a period of 28 years renewable for a further period of 28 years. The problem was overcome by requiring that a UCC country would grant foreign nationals a minimum period of copyright based upon the life of the author plus 25 years even though its own nationals may only be protected for a period stemming from the date of publication. A diplomatic conference was held in Paris in 1971 which resulted in the 1971 revisions to the UCC, liberalising a number of the provisions in so far as they applied to the less developed countries.

10.3.2   The protection

The UCC requires contracting States to provide 'adequate and effective protection' for the rights of authors and other copyright proprietors. The question of whether or not the protection is adequate is determined by the national jurisdiction in which protection is sought. A low level of protection can be sufficient providing it is considered to be 'adequate'. Article 2 of the UCC provides some level of measure, in that contracting States are obliged to provide protection for works published by nationals in other contracting States at the same level as works first published in their own State. Unpublished works acquire the same level of protection as a contracting State would afford to its own nationals.

To qualify for protection the work must fulfil four criteria, ie it must:

(1)   be a copyright work;
(2)   be within the copyright term;
(3)   comply with formalities; and
(4)   be a work of a national of a contracting State or have first been published in a
       contracting State.

(a) A copyright work
Works are specified in Art 1 of the UCC as 'literary, scientific and artistic works, including writings, musical, dramatic and cinematographic works, and paintings, engravings and sculptures'. No reference is made anywhere in the UCC to databases or to tables or compilations or even, as in the Berne Convention, to anthologies. Arguably, therefore, a database may not be protected if it does not fulfil the requirements of copyright of a contracting State.

(b) Within copyright
Article 4 of the UCC provides that copyright protection shall be the minimum of the life of the author plus 25 years or, where protection is computed from the date of publication, 25 years from that date.

(c) Formalities

The UCC introduced the marking requirements as a formality for seeking copyright protection. There are three requirements, namely:

(1)   the name of the copyright proprietor;
(2)   the year of first publication; and
(3)   the © mark.

These formalities are intended to satisfy equivalent or even more stringent formalities of any other contracting State. Thus, if these formalities are complied with, the fact that the copyright has not been registered at the Library of Congress would not prevent a British national claiming copyright in the United States.

(d) Nationality

Works are afforded protection if the author is a national of a contracting State. The question of who is the author will be dependent upon national laws of the countries in which the work is created or first published. For example, the UK provides that works created by an employee in the course of his employment shall belong to the employer.

The place of first publication is also of importance since there is provision in the UCC for additional rights or obligations dependent upon the area of first publication. For example, a work first published by a British national (which does not require any formalities) in the United States could be required to be registered under American law since it was the country of first publication.

Generally, however, where a work is first published in a country which is not a contracting State then all national considerations will be determined by the author's nationality.

10.3.3   Exceptions

There are two notable exceptions provided by the UCC, namely: (a) the system of compulsory licences; and (b) the translation right.

(a) Compulsory licences

The UCC provides for the granting of compulsory licences. The system depends upon the proposed licensee making application to the copyright owner and being refused a licence or, alternatively, being unable after proper investigation to find the proper copyright owner. The system of compulsory licence is more favourable to developing countries than to the developed countries.

(b) The translation right

This is the right to permit the translation of copyright works from one language to another after a specified period. Translation right shares with the system of compulsory licences, the rules which are more favourable to the less developed countries than the developed ones.

10.4   TRIPs ('TRADE RELATED ASPECTS OF INTELLECTUAL PROPERTY') AND THE WORLD TRADE ORGANISATION ('WTO')

10.4.1   History

The root of TRIPs is firmly established in trade as opposed to intellectual property. During the 1978 round of GATT (the General Agreement on Tariff and Trade), developed countries expressed their growing concern at the damage done to world trade by counterfeiting.

It was proposed at the 1978 GATT Conference that a customs code of practice be established to limit the trade in counterfeit products by having them seized at national borders. The proposal failed through lack of time. However, the impetus was such that, by the time the Uruguay round of GATT opened in 1985, there was sufficient support from developed countries to propose a comprehensive agreement relating to intellectual property generally. The rationale was that international trade was being adversely affected not only by the constant problem of counterfeiting, but also by the disparity of the rights in intellectual properties between one country and another.

It was felt that GATT, with its ability to impose trade sanctions, was a suitable forum for harmonising intellectual property rules. GATT had the advantage over WIPO in that GATT could use its financial muscle to encourage less developed countries to harmonise those rules where otherwise they might be reluctant to do so. TRIPs was negotiated over a period spanning seven years.

The TRIPs Agreement which became part of the final act of the Uruguay round was adopted at Marrakesh in 1994 with a host of other agreements bringing to an end the Uruguay round of GATT which had started in 1985. The final act also established the WTO. It is a condition of membership of the WTO that the provisions of TRIPs are adopted by all Member States.

Of all international treaties relating to intellectual property rights, TRIPs is probably the most far reaching. By supplementing, with additional obligations, the Paris, Berne, Rome and Washington Conventions it has sought to bring in additional rules, obligations and remedies, rather than change existing ones. The TRIPs Agreement has general obligations and also deals in particular with:

–   copyright and related rights;
–   trademarks;
–   geographical indications;
–   industrial designs;
–   patents;
–   layout designs for integrated circuit; and
–   trade secrets.

A new feature of TRIPs was to introduce a so-called most-favoured nations Article. This provision requires contracting parties immediately to grant the same level of benefits to the nationals of all the contracting parties as it does to the nationals of the most-favoured of any foreign States whose intellectual property rights are being respected. This will apply even if those rights are in excess of rights granted to nationals of the home State.

When TRIPs was being negotiated there was an attempt by a number of the negotiating parties to introduce provisions relating to the exhaustion of rights. In the end the matter was left open subject to Arts 3 and 4 of TRIPs (national treatment and most-favoured nation treatment). The European Commission has adopted provisions relating to the exhaustion of rights in Art 5(c) of the Database Directive which states:

'The first sale in the community of a copy of the database by the rightholder or with his consent shall exhaust the right to control resale of that copy within the community.'

Copyright and related rights are dealt with in TRIPs Part II, section 1. Articles 10 and 11 of TRIPs seek to clarify the position of computer programs, databases and rental rights.

Article 10.2 provides:

'Compilations of data or other material, whether in machine readable or other form, which by reason of the selection or arrangement of their contents constitute intellectual creations shall be protected as such. Such protection, which shall not extend to the data or material itself, shall be without prejudice to any copyright subsisting in the data or material itself.'

The Article contains most of the elements of Art 3 of the Database Directive.

A further new development for TRIPs was the inclusion at Art 40 of provisions to control anti-competitive practices in contractual licences. Article 40.2 provides that:

'Nothing in this Agreement shall prevent members from specifying in their legislation licensing practices or conditions that may in particular cases constitute an abuse of intellectual property rights, having an adverse effect on competition in the relevant market.'

This Article gives a number of examples of behaviour which might be considered to be anti-competitive, for example exclusive grant back clauses, no challenge clauses and coercive licensing packages.

There are provisions in this Article for consultation to take place between Member States who have cause to complain of anti-competitive practices by nationals of another Member State.

On 22 December 1995, WTO entered into an agreement with WIPO for co-operation between them concerning transfer of information and technical assistance.

10.5   WIPO COPYRIGHT TREATY

10.5.1   Introduction

As of 1 January 1996 there were 157 Member States who were a party to the Convention establishing WIPO. The Member States are composed of members of the Paris or Berne Unions, members of the United Nations, any special agency of the United Nations, the International Atomic Energy Agency, or any State which has been invited by the General Assembly of WIPO to become a party to the Convention.

At a diplomatic conference on copyright and neighbouring rights held in Geneva in December 1996 the members of WIPO adopted a treaty called the 'WIPO Copyright Treaty'.

The WIPO Copyright Treaty introduced new international rules to clarify the interpretation of existing intellectual property rights. Many of these rights had already been dealt with by the Commission, for example the restrictions on the right of rental and clarification of the law of copyright in computer programs.

In particular, Art 5 of the WIPO Copyright Treaty provides that:

'Compilations of data or other material, in any form, which by reason of the selection or arrangement of their contents constitute intellectual creations, are protected as such. This protection does not extend to the data or the material itself and is without prejudice to any copyright subsisting in the data or material contained in the compilation.'

It was decided at the conference that Art 5 of the WIPO Copyright Treaty was consistent with the scope of protection provided for under Art 2 of the Berne Convention and on a 'par with the relevant provisions of the TRIPs agreement'.

Article 5 of the WIPO Copyright Treaty is of course consistent with Art 3(1) of the Database Directive. It was perhaps natural to consider that WIPO should then consider the *sui generis* right created by chapter 3 of the Database Directive. At a meeting on database protection held at WIPO headquarters in Geneva, Switzerland between 17–19 September 1997 the question of creating a new database right similar to that created by the Database Directive was hotly and at times acrimoniously debated. The meeting took matters no further and action at an international level was indefinitely postponed.

The United States delegation in particular urged delay in the proposal to form a new intellectual property right to protect databases even on the most fundamental policy issues. They were supported by nearly all developing nations and by developed nations outside Europe such as Japan, Canada, Australia and Singapore. Many of the delegates felt that databases were sufficiently protected by existing copyright, unfair competition and contract laws.

The strength of feeling against a new form of intellectual property right to protect databases was so strong at the WIPO meeting that it is conceivable that no new treaty will be formulated in the foreseeable future. Indeed, the WIPO delegates considered that the EU had moved too fast in enacting legislation creating the new database right before other members of WIPO were ready to create reciprocal rules.

10.5.2 Enforcement

It is a principal tenet of international treaties that there be reciprocity in enforcement. The ability of nationals of one country to enforce their intellectual property rights in another country is a fundamental feature of international trade. Since the *sui generis* right in databases is not recognised outside the EU, the Database Directive provides that the *sui generis* right only applies to EU nationals.

Article 11 of the Database Directive provides protection in the EU for 'nationals of a Member State or persons who have their habitual residence in the territory of the Community'. No further clarification is given as to the meaning of 'habitual residence': the same expression is used in the recitals[1] without clarification. The important item in both paras 1 and 2 of Art 11 of the Database Directive would appear

---

1   Recital 56.

to be the notion that the rightholder is established in the Community in place of some other country and, in the case of a firm or company, that that establishment is financial. Clearly, the Commission envisaged (in Art 11(3) of the Database Directive) concluding reciprocal arrangements with third countries to extend the *sui generis* right on an international basis. In view of the meeting held at WIPO in September 1997[1] those arrangements may not take place for some time.

The Berne Convention provides only that copies of infringing works are liable to seizure[2]. There is no specific requirement as to the nature of any other remedy required to be adopted by members of the Berne Union.

It was not until TRIPs that enforcement was dealt with in detail. Part III of TRIPs relates specifically to the enforcement of intellectual property rights, Art 41 providing that:

'1. Members shall ensure that enforcement procedures as specified in this Part are available under their national laws so as to permit effective action against any act of infringement of intellectual property rights covered by this Agreement, including expeditious remedies to prevent infringements and remedies which constitute a deterrent to further infringements. These procedures shall be applied in such a manner as to avoid the creation of barriers to legitimate trade and to provide for safeguards against their abuse.'

The remedies open to a rightholder will depend to a great extent on the provisions which are available to him in the country in which he intends to enforce his rights. Generally, it will be necessary (or at least wise) for the rightholder before commencing an action to be able to establish that:

– he is entitled to the rights in the country where he is a national or where the work was first published;
– the work is a database or a compilation of data which fulfils the criteria necessary for a copyright work in the country in which it is sought to enforce the rights; and
– the rights in the copyright in the database (regardless of the data it contains) are being infringed in that country.

Whether or not additional requirements are necessary will depend on the country in which the action is brought. It is worth considering carefully therefore before any licence agreement is entered into where it would be most convenient to bring an action and which law is to govern the agreement. These matters should then be recorded in the agreement. The nature of any proceedings will depend on national laws. Chapter 8 sets out an overview of how such matters would be dealt with within Europe.

How matters will be resolved with regard to the international framework for the legal protection of databases remains a moot point. The one prediction that can be made with some certainty is that the Database Directive and the Database Regulations will not be the last word on the subject.

---

1   Recital 56.
2   Article 16.

10.6   MEMBERS OF THE BERNE CONVENTION AS AT 26 MARCH 1998

State	Date on which State became party to the Convention	Latest Act[1] of the Convention to which State is party and date on which State became a party to that Act
Albania	6 March 1994	Paris: 6 March 1994
Algeria	19 April 1998	Paris: 19 April 1998[2]
Argentina	10 June 1967	Brussels: 10 June 1967
		Paris, Articles 22 to 38: 8 October 1980
Australia	14 April 1928	Paris: 1 March 1978
Austria	1 October 1920	Paris: 21 August 1982
Bahamas	10 July 1973	Brussels: 10 July 1973
		Paris, Articles 22 to 38: 8 January 1977
Bahrain	2 March 1997	Paris: 2 March 1997
Barbados	30 July 1983	Paris: 30 July 1983
Belarus	12 December 1997	Paris: 12 December 1997
Belgium	5 December 1887	Brussels: 1 August 1951
		Stockholm, Articles 22 to 38: 12 February 1975
Benin	3 January 1961[3]	Paris: 12 March 1975
Bolivia	4 November 1993	Paris: 4 November 1993
Bosnia and Herzegovina	1 March 1992	Paris: 1 March 1992[4]
Botswana	15 April 1998	Paris: 15 April 1998
Brazil	9 February 1922	Paris: 20 April 1975
Bulgaria	5 December 1921	Paris: 4 December 1974
Burkina Faso	19 August 1963[5]	Paris: 24 January 1976
Cameroon	21 September 1964[3]	Paris, Articles 1 to 21: 10 October 1974
		Paris, Articles 22 to 38: 10 November 1973
Canada	10 April 1928	Paris: 26 June 1998
Cap Verde	7 July 1997	Paris: 7 July 1997
		Stockholm, Articles 22 to 38: 7 July 1970
Central African Republic	3 September 1977	Paris: 3 September 1977
Chad	25 November 1971	Brussels: 25 November 1971[6,7]
		Stockholm, Articles 22 to 38: 25 November 1971
Chile	5 June 1970	Paris: 10 July 1975
China[8]	15 October 1992	Paris: 15 October 1992
Colombia	7 March 1988	Paris: 7 March 1988
Congo	8 May 1962[3]	Paris: 5 December 1975
Costa Rica	10 June 1978	Paris: 10 June 1978
Côte d'Ivoire	1 January 1962	Paris, Articles 1 to 21: 10 October 1974
		Paris, Articles 22 to 38: 4 May 1974
Croatia	8 October 1991	Paris: 8 October 1991[4]
Cuba	20 February 1997	Paris: 20 February 1997[2]
Cyprus	24 February 1964[3]	Paris: 27 July 1983[4]
Czech Republic	1 January 1993	Paris: 1 January 1993
Democratic Republic of the Congo	8 October 1963[3]	Paris: 31 January 1975
Denmark	1 July 1903	Paris: 30 June 1979
Dominican Republic	24 December 1997	Paris: 24 December 1997
Ecuador	9 October 1991	Paris: 9 October 1991
Egypt	7 June 1977	Paris: 7 June 1977[2]
El Salvador	19 February 1994	Paris: 19 February 1994
Equatorial Guinea	26 June 1997	Paris: 26 June 1997
Estonia[9]	26 October 1994	Paris: 26 October 1994
Fiji[3]	1 December 1971	Brussels: 1 December 1971
		Stockholm, Articles 22 to 38: 15 March 1972
Finland	1 April 1928	Paris: 1 November 1986

State	*Date on which State became party to the Convention*	*Latest Act[1] of the Convention to which State is party and date on which State became a party to that Act*
France	5 December 1887	Paris, Articles 1 to 21: 10 October 1974
		Paris, Articles 22 to 38: 15 December 1972
Gabon	26 March 1962	Paris: 10 June 1975
Gambia	7 March 1993	Paris: 7 March 1993
Georgia	16 May 1995	Paris: 16 May 1995
Germany	5 December 1887	Paris, Articles 1 to 21: 10 October 1974[10]
		Paris, Articles 22 to 38: 22 January 1974
Ghana	11 October 1991	Paris: 11 October 1991
Greece	9 November 1920	Paris: 8 March 1976
Guatemala	28 July 1997	Paris: 28 July 1997
Guinea	20 November 1980	Paris: 20 November 1980
Guinea-Bissau	22 July 1991	Paris: 22 July 1991
Guyana	25 October 1994	Paris: 25 October 1994
Haiti	11 January 1996	Paris: 11 January 1996
Holy See	12 September 1935	Paris: 24 April 1975
Honduras	25 January 1990	Paris: 25 January 1990
Hungary	14 February 1922	Paris, Articles 1 to 21: 10 October 1974
		Paris, Articles 22 to 38: 15 December 1972
Iceland	7 September 1947	Rome: 7 September 1947
		Paris, Articles 22 to 38: 28 December 1984
India	1 April 1928	Paris, Articles 1 to 21: 6 May 1984[11,12]
Indonesia	5 September 1997	Paris: 5 September 1997[2]
Ireland	5 October 1927	Brussels: 5 July 1959
		Stockholm, Articles 22 to 38: 21 December 1970
Israel	24 March 1950	Brussels: 1 August 1951
		Stockholm, Articles 22 to 38: 29 January 29 or 26 February 1970[13]
Italy	5 December 1887	Paris: 14 November 1979
Jamaica	1 January 1994	Paris: 1 January 1994
Japan	15 July 1899	Paris: 24 April 1975
Kenya	11 June 1993	Paris: 11 June 1993
Latvia	11 August 1995[14]	Paris: 11 August 1995
Lebanon	30 September 1947	Rome: 30 September 1947
Lesotho	28 September 1989	Paris: 28 September 1989[2]
Liberia	8 March 1989	Paris: 8 March 1989[2]
Libya	28 September 1976	Paris: 28 September 1976[2]
Liechtenstein	30 July 1931	Brussels: 1 August 1951
		Stockholm, Articles 22 to 38: 25 May 1972
Lithuania	14 December 1994	Paris: 14 December 1994[2]
Luxembourg	20 June 1888	Paris: 20 April 1975
Madagascar	1 January 1966	Brussels: 1 January 1966
Malawi	12 October 1991	Paris: 12 October 1991
Malaysia	1 October 1990	Paris: 1 October 1990
Mali	19 March 1962[3]	Paris: 5 December 1977
Malta	21 September 1964	Rome: 21 September 1964
		Paris, Articles 22 to 38: 12 December 1977[2]
Mauritania	6 February 1973	Paris: 21 September 1976
Mauritius	10 May 1989	Paris: 10 May 1989[2]
Mexico	11 June 1967	Paris: 17 December 1974
Monaco	30 May 1889	Paris: 23 November 1974
Mongolia	12 March 1998	Paris: 12 March 1998[2,15]
Morocco	16 June 1917	Paris: 17 May 1987
Namibia	21 March 1990	Paris: 24 December 1993
Netherlands	1 November 1912	Paris, Articles 1 to 21: 30 January 1986[16]
		Paris, Articles 22 to 38: 10 January 1975[17]

State	*Date on which State became party to the Convention*	*Latest Act[1] of the Convention to which State is party and date on which State became a party to that Act*
New Zealand	24 April 1928	Rome: 4 December 1947
Niger	2 May 1962[18]	Paris: 21 May 1975
Nigeria	14 September 1993	Paris: 14 September 1993
Norway	13 April 1896	Paris, Articles 1 to 21: 11 October 1995[10]
		Paris, Articles 22 to 38: 13 June 1974
Pakistan	5 July 1948	Rome: 5 July 1948[6]
		Stockholm, Articles 22 to 38: 29 January or 26 February 1970[13]
Panama	8 June 1996	Paris: 8 June 1996
Paraguay	2 January 1992	Paris: 2 January 1992
Peru	20 August 1988	Paris: 20 August 1988
Philippines	1 August 1951	Paris: Articles 1 to 21: 18 June 1997
		Paris, Articles 22 to 38: 16 July 1980
Poland	28 January 1920	Paris, Articles 1 to 21: 22 October 1994
		Paris, Articles 22 to 38: 4 August 1990
Portugal	29 March 1911	Paris: 12 January 1979[18]
Republic of Korea	21 August 1996	Paris: 21 August 1996
Republic of Moldova	2 November 1995	Paris: 2 November 1995
Romania	1 January 1927	Rome: 6 August 1936[6]
		Stockholm, Articles 22 to 38: 29 January or 26 February 1970[2,13]
Russian Federation	13 March 1995	Paris: 13 March 1995
Rwanda	1 March 1984	Paris: 1 March 1984
Saint Kitts and Nevis	9 April 1995	Paris: 9 April 1995
Saint Lucia	24 August 1993	Paris: 24 August 1993[2]
Saint Vincent and the Grenadines	29 August 1995	Paris: 29 August 1995
Senegal	25 August 1962	Paris: 12 August 1975
Slovakia	1 January 1993	Paris: 1 January 1993
Slovenia	25 June 1991	Paris: 25 June 1991[4]
South Africa	3 October 1928	Brussels: 1 August 1951
		Paris, Articles 22 to 38: 24 March 1975[2]
Spain	5 December 1887	Paris, Articles 1 to 21: 10 October 1974
		Paris, Articles 22 to 38: 19 February 1974
Sri Lanka	20 July 1959[3]	Rome: 20 July 1959
		Paris, Articles 22 to 38: 23 September 1978
Suriname	23 February 1977	Paris: 23 February 1977
Sweden	1 August 1904	Paris, Articles 1 to 21: 10 October 1974
		Paris, Articles 22 to 38: 20 September 1973
Switzerland	5 December 1887	Paris: 25 September 1993
Thailand	17 July 1931	Paris, Articles 1 to 21: 2 September 1995[19]
		Paris, Articles 22 to 38: 29 December 1980[2]
The former Yugoslav Republic of Macedonia	8 September 1991	Paris: 8 September 1991
Togo	30 April 1975	Paris: 30 April 1975
Trinidad and Tobago	16 August 1988	Paris: 16 August 1988
Tunisia	5 December 1887	Paris: 16 August 1975[2]
Turkey	1 January 1952	Paris: 1 January 1996
Ukraine	25 October 1995	Paris: 25 October 1995
United Kingdom	5 December 1887	Paris: 2 January 1990[20]
United Republic of Tanzania	25 July 1994	Paris: 25 July 1994[2]
United States of America	1 March 1989	Paris: 1 March 1989
Uruguay	10 July 1967	Paris: 28 December 1979
Venezuela	30 December 1982	Paris: 30 December 1982[2]

State	Date on which State became party to the Convention	Latest Act[1] of the Convention to which State is party and date on which State became a party to that Act
Yugoslavia	17 June 1930	Paris: 2 September 1975[4]
Zambia	2 January 1992	Paris: 2 January 1992
Zimbabwe	18 April 1980	Rome: 18 April 1980
		Paris, Articles 22 to 38: 30 December 1981

Notes

1. 'Paris' means the Berne Convention for the Protection of Literary and Artistic Works as revised at Paris on 24 July 1971 (Paris Act); 'Stockholm' means the said Convention as revised at Stockholm on 14 July 1967 (Stockholm Act); 'Brussels' means the said Convention as revised at Brussels on 26 June 1948 (Brussels Act); 'Rome' means the said Convention as revised at Rome on 2 June 1928 (Rome Act); 'Berlin' means the said Convention as revised at Berlin on 13 November 1908 (Berlin Act).

2. With the declaration provided for in Art 33(2) relating to the International Court of Justice.

3. Date on which the declaration of continued adherence was sent, after the accession of the State to independence.

4. Subject to the reservation concerning the right of translation.

5. Burkina Faso, which had acceded to the Berne Convention (Brussels Act) as from 19 August 1963, denounced the said Convention as from 20 September 1970. Later on, Burkina Faso acceded again to the Berne Convention (Paris Act); this accession took effect on 24 January 1976.

6. This State deposited its instrument of ratification of (or of accession to) the Stockholm Act in its entirety; however, Arts 1 to 21 (substantive clauses) of the said Act have not entered into force.

7. In accordance with the provision of Art 29 of the Stockholm Act applicable to the States outside the Union which accede to the said Act, this State is bound by Arts 1 to 20 of the Brussels Act.

8. The Paris Act applies also to the Hong Kong Special Administrative Region with effect from 1 July 1997.

9. Estonia acceded to the Berne Convention (Berlin Act 1908) with effect from 9 June 1927. It lost its independence on 6 August 1940, and regained it on 20 August 1991.

10. This State has declared that it admits the application of the Appendix of the Paris Act to works of which it is the State of origin by States which have made a declaration under Art VI(1)(i) of the Appendix or a notification under Art I of the Appendix. The declarations took effect on 18 October 1973, for Germany, on 8 March 1974, for Norway and on 27 September 1971, for the UK.

11. This State declared that its ratification shall not apply to the provisions of Art 14bis(2)(b) of the Paris Act (presumption of legitimation for some authors who have brought contributions to the making of the cinematographic work).

12. This State notified the designation of the competent authority provided by Art 15(4) of the Paris Act.

13. These are the alternative dates of entry into force which the Director General of WIPO communicated to the States concerned.

14. Latvia acceded to the Berne Convention (Rome Act 1928) with effect from 15 May 1937. It lost its independence on 21 July 1940, and regained it on 21 August 1991.

15. Pursuant to Arts 1 of the Appendix of the Paris Act, this State availed itself of the faculties provided for in Arts II and III of the said Appendix. The relevant declaration is effective until 10 October 2004.

16. Ratification for the Kingdom in Europe.

17. Ratification for the Kingdom in Europe. Articles 22 to 38 of the Paris Act apply also to the Netherlands Antilles and Aruba.

18. Pursuant to the provisions of Art 14bis(2)(c) of the Paris Act, this State has made a declaration to the effect that the undertaking by authors to bring contributions to the making of a cinematographic work must be in a written agreement. This declaration was received on 5 November 1986.

19 Pursuant to Art I of the Appendix of the Paris Act, this State availed itself of the faculty provided for in Art II of the said Appendix. The relevant declaration is effective until 10 October 2004.
20 The UK extended the application of the Paris Act to the Isle of Man with effect from 18 March 1996.

10.7   THE BERNE CONVENTION FOR THE PROTECTION OF LITERARY AND ARTISTIC WORKS, WITH ITS REVISIONS

Berne Convention	9 September 1886
Additional Act of Paris	4 May 1896
Berlin Revision	13 November 1908
Additional Protocol of Berne	20 March 1914
Rome Revision	2 June 1928
Brussels Revision	26 June 1948
Stockholm Revision	14 July 1967
Paris Revision	24 July 1971

Chapter 11

TRANSITIONAL PROVISIONS

11.1 Under the Database Directive – 11.2 Under the Database Regulations – 11.3 The effect on pre-1998 databases and the effect on non-database compilations

11.1   UNDER THE DATABASE DIRECTIVE[1]

The transitional provisions in the Database Directive are found in Art 14 – Application over time.

Article 14(2) provides that where a pre-1998 database was protected by a copyright system in a Member State on the date the Database Directive was published (ie 27 March 1996) the database shall continue to enjoy this protection for the remaining copyright term applicable under that Member State's arrangements. This provision probably has most effect in the UK where copyright has a low threshold of originality. In many Member States, including for example Germany, copyright protection has always required an element of intellectual creation and so many databases, which would have been protected in the UK, would not have benefited from copyright protection under German copyright law.

Article 14(3) provides that the *sui generis* database right shall apply to all databases completed not more than 15 years before 1 January 1998 and has been directly imported into the Database Regulations as reg 30. Accordingly, databases completed before 1 January 1983 are capable of qualifying for protection by the new database right as from 1 January 1998.

Article 14(4) provides that the Database Directive shall be without prejudice to any acts concluded and rights acquired before 1 January 1998. This is a narrower provision than that implemented into the UK by the Database Regulations, reg 28 (see comments under **11.2.2** below).

Article 14(5) provides that qualifying databases completed not more than 15 years prior to 1 January 1998 shall enjoy the *sui generis* right for a 15-year term. Taken literally, Art 14(5) requires that this term shall run from 1 January 1999, which would have left such databases unprotected during 1998. This construction has apparently been accepted to have resulted from a drafting error in the Database Directive, and has been implemented in the UK as 15 years from 1 January 1998 by reg 30 of the Database Regulations.

---

1   Directive 96/9/EC, see Appendix 3.

11.2   UNDER THE DATABASE REGULATIONS

The transitional provisions can be found in Part IV of the Database Regulations, consisting of regs 26–30.

The provisions at first sight appear to be straightforward but on closer reading they create a complicated structure of rights for owners of databases created on or before 1 January 1998.

11.2.1   Database Regulations, reg 27 – general rule

The Database Regulations are to apply to all databases (as defined in reg 6) irrespective of their dates of creation subject to the exceptions set out in regs 28 and 29. They do not apply to non-database tables or compilations[1].

11.2.2   Database Regulations, reg 28 – general savings

The Database Regulations shall not:

(a)   affect any agreement made before 1 January 1998;
(b)   cause any act to be done before 1 January 1998 to be an infringement of database right; or
(c)   cause any act done after 1 January 1998 to be an infringement of database right where the act was done pursuant to an agreement made before 1 January 1998.

These are all practical savings from the Database Regulations that will prevent agreements and acts performed under such agreements from becoming unlawful retrospectively. Regulation 28 goes beyond the saving provisions provided for in the Database Directive. Article 14(4) of the Database Directive states that the Database Directive will not affect 'any acts concluded and rights acquired before [1 January 1998]'. Acts done after 1 January 1998 will only be saved from the provisions of the Database Directive if they relate to rights acquired pre-1998. The Database Regulations do not specify that post-1998 acts which are subject to these savings must be pursuant to rights acquired pre-1998: only that they be pursuant to a pre-1998 agreement. For example, we might assume that before 1 January 1998 two parties had entered into an agreement pursuant to which one party had agreed to access and transfer the contents of a third party's database onto a different medium. Such access and transfer whenever undertaken would not, by virtue of reg 28, be a breach of database right (assuming that the access and transfer would not have infringed any rights if undertaken before 1 January 1998). This is because the access and transfer was carried out pursuant to a pre-1998 agreement. The access and transfer would, however, appear to be outside the savings provided for under the Database Directive, as the acts of access and transfer do not relate to rights acquired before 1 January 1998 but are merely acts done under an agreement made before 1 January 1998.

---

1   As to this distinction, see Chapter 7.

11.2.3 Database Regulations, reg 29 – saving for copyright in certain existing databases

This regulation provides that where a database (as defined in reg 6) was created on or before 27 March 1996 (ie the date the Database Directive was published) *and* was a copyright work immediately before 1 January 1998 copyright in it shall continue to subsist for the remainder of its copyright term.

Under the provisions of the CDPA, before 1 January 1998 a table or compilation could qualify for copyright protection as a 'literary work'[1] if it satisfied the implied requirement of originality.

Originality in this context means that the collection, as a work, must be the product of a degree of skill, judgement or labour in collating information into a database but need not be the expression of original or inventive thought[2]. For example, the courts have found that literary copyright subsists in many simple works, including for example: pools coupons[3], books of telegraphic code[4], a directory of lawyers[5] and in a grid pattern and a letter sequence competition[6]. The standard of originality required of databases pre-1 January 1998 was lower than the test now required[7].

Databases (as defined by reg 6) which were made and qualified for copyright before 27 March 1996 will continue to enjoy this protection for the duration specified under s 12 of the CDPA. This means that such databases will have copyright protection for the period of 70 years from the end of the calendar year in which the author (if known) dies[8]. If the author is unknown, copyright will expire at the end of 70 years from the end of the calendar year in which the database was made[9]. If the database was computer-generated, meaning that it was generated by computer in circumstances such that there is no human author of the work[10], copyright in the database will expire at the end of 50 years from the end of the calendar year in which the database was made.

If a database (as defined by reg 6) did not qualify for copyright before 27 March 1996 it will not qualify under the more onerous test imposed by the Database Regulations. The owner will, instead, have to prove that the database qualifies for database right[11].

The provisions of reg 29 may create an interesting patchwork of rights in pre-27 March 1996 databases that qualify for copyright but are subsequently added to or altered after that date. Any alterations made after 27 March 1996 will be subject to the new provisions and will therefore need to satisfy the more onerous copyright

---

1   Section 3(1) of the CDPA.
2   *Ladbroke (Football) Ltd v William Hill (Football) Ltd* [1963] WLR 273.
3   *Ladbroke (Football) Ltd v William Hill (Football) Ltd* [1963] WLR 273.
4   *DP Anderson & Co Ltd v The Lieber Code Co* [1917] 2 KB 469.
5   *Waterlow Publishers Ltd v Rose* 12 December 1989.
6   *Express Newspapers plc v Liverpool Daily Post & Echo plc* [1985] WLR 1089.
7   Discussed in detail at Chapter 5.
8   Section 12(2) of the CDPA.
9   Section 12(3) of the CDPA.
10   Section 178 of the CDPA.
11   Discussed in detail at Chapter 5.

originality test imposed by the Database Regulations[1]. If this test is not satisfied, the post-27 March 1996 work will not qualify for copyright protection but may qualify for database right.

Saving copyright in pre-27 March 1996 databases may seem a generous concession, but in practice many commercial databases quickly become out of date and the original elements of such databases that attract continuing copyright may soon become of little value to their owners unless they are frequently revised and kept up to date. Such revisions may result in adaptations of the original database, as adaptation is now re-defined by reg 7, so that subsequent infringements will be of the post-1996 adaptation.

11.2.4   Database right: term applicable to certain existing databases

Regulation 30 reinforces the intention of the general rule expressed in reg 27 and then goes further. It provides that any database created on or after 1 January 1983 that qualifies for database right from 1 January 1998 shall benefit from this right for 15 years from 1 January 1998. This will avoid the need to prove the precise date of completion of pre-1 January 1998 databases (other than disputes as to whether the database was completed before or after 1 January 1983).

The database will only have database right protection if the maker of the database (who may not be the author) proves that the database was completed on or after 1 January 1983 and that 'substantial investment' has been put into its making and any subsequent alterations. If no substantial investment has been put into its making, the maker will have no enforceable right to prevent unauthorised extraction or re-utilisation of the database, or of alterations to it, by a third party.

11.2.5   Database right: rights conferred on maker

In bringing an action for infringement an owner of a database (who may be the author, the maker or both) will need to be aware what protection he has in each part of the database and be careful to plead his case correctly. Essentially, the owner of a pre-27 March 1996 database is likely to enjoy less protection for his latest alterations made post-27 March 1996 than he can claim for his pre-27 March 1996 database, unless he can satisfy the new database right and copyright in database tests. These tests will require that, for database right, there must be substantial investment in the amendments made, and, for copyright, that they are intellectually creative.

Where a database qualifies for both copyright protection and database right, in addition to the rights conferred on the database's author by copyright, the maker of the database will have the right to prevent the extraction (ie transfer of the database's contents onto a different medium) or re-utilisation (making accessible to the public) of all or a substantial part of the database, pursuant to reg 16. It is important to note that the author of a database (under copyright) and the maker of a database (under the database right) need not be the same person. An author is the person who creates the copyright work[2]. The maker of a database is the person who has not only taken the

---

1   Regulation 6.
2   Section 9(1) of the CDPA.

initiative in obtaining, verifying or presenting the contents of the database but has also assumed the risk of investing in that obtaining, verification or presentation[1].

11.3 THE EFFECT ON PRE-1998 DATABASES AND THE EFFECT ON NON-DATABASE COMPILATIONS

11.3.1 Databases created between 28 March 1996 and 31 December 1997

UK databases which are literary works and were created after 27 March 1996 but before 1 January 1998 get the rawest copyright deal under the Database Regulations. Databases made after 27 March 1996, and so not saved by the provisions of reg 29, but created before 1 January 1998, will no longer have copyright protection unless they can satisfy the intellectual creation criterion set out in reg 6. If they cannot satisfy this test they may still qualify for protection under the database right. However, if substantial investment cannot be proved and no other legal protection is available, for example for breach of confidence or breach of contract, such databases will not have any protection against unauthorised third party users.

11.3.2 Non-database compilations

Non-database collections, whenever created, may continue to enjoy copyright protection without further reference to the Database Regulations for the full 70-year copyright term as tables or compilations under s 3(1)(a) of the CDPA. They will not be required to meet the Database Regulations' intellectual creativity criterion of originality, but they will be excluded from the possibility of protection by database right.

11.3.3 Computer-generated compliations

For collections compiled as computer-generated works, whose authors are to be taken to be the persons by whom the arrangements necessary for the creation of such works were undertaken[2], the position on protection by copyright is unclear but the date of creation of the collection may prove to be important.

If the collection was created on or before 27 March 1996, the Database Regulations' requirement of intellectual creativity will not apply to protection by copyright, whether or not the collection is a database as defined by the Database Regulations. For all such collections, there remains the possibility that a court may find insufficient skill and labour to have been applied in the production of the work, notwithstanding that intellectual creativity may not be required.

The same rule and possibility will apply to computer-generated collections made after 27 March 1996, except for those which are databases as defined by the Database Regulations. For such databases, skill and labour in their production will be insufficient and it will be necessary to show that, by reason of the selection or

---

1   Database Regulations, reg 4.
2   Sections 9(3) and 178 of the CDPA.

arrangement of the contents of the database, the database constitutes its author's own intellectual creation. If there is no intellectual creativity in the selection or arrangement of the contents of a computer-generated database created after 27 March 1996, the database cannot be protected by copyright.

For computer-generated databases made after 1 January 1983, whether or not they qualify for copyright protection under either the skill and labour criterion or the intellectual creativity criterion, there remains the possibility of protection by database right. Instead of the author's skill or labour, or alternatively intellectual creativity, database right requires substantial investment by the maker. This requirement is discussed fully in Chapter 5.

Appendix 1

COUNCIL DIRECTIVE 91/250/EEC

of 14 May 1991

on the Legal Protection of Computer Programs[1]

THE COUNCIL OF THE EUROPEAN COMMUNITIES,

Having regard to the Treaty establishing the European Economic Community and in particular Article 100a thereof, having regard to the proposal from the Commission, in cooperation with the European Parliament, having regard to the opinion of the Economic and Social Committee,

(1)   Whereas computer programs are at present not clearly protected in all Member States by existing legislation and such protection, where it exists, has different attributes;

(2)   Whereas the development of computer programs requires the investment of considerable human, technical and financial resources while computer programs can be copied at a fraction of the cost needed to develop them independently;

(3)   Whereas computer programs are playing an increasingly important role in a broad range of industries and computer program technology can accordingly be considered as being of fundamental importance for the Community's industrial development;

(4)   Whereas certain differences in the legal protection of computer programs offered by the laws of the Member States have direct and negative effects on the functioning of the common market as regards computer programs and such differences could well become greater as Member States introduce new legislation on this subject;

(5)   Whereas existing differences having such effects need to be removed and new ones prevented from arising, while differences not adversely affecting the functioning of the common market to a substantial degree need not be removed or prevented from arising;

(6)   Whereas the Community's legal framework on the protection of computer programs can accordingly in the first instance be limited to establishing that Member States should accord protection to computer programs under copyright law as literary works and, further, to establishing who and what should be protected, the exclusive rights on which protected persons should be able to rely in order to authorise or prohibit certain acts and for how long the protection should apply;

(7)   Whereas, for the purpose of this Directive, the term 'computer program' shall include programs in any form, including those which are incorporated into hardware; whereas this term also includes preparatory design work leading to the development of a computer program provided that the nature of the preparatory work is such that a computer program can result from it at a later stage;

(8)   Whereas, in respect of the criteria to be applied in determining whether or not a computer program is an original work, no tests as to the qualitative or aesthetic merits of the program should be applied;

(9)   Whereas the Community is fully committed to the promotion of international standardisation;

---

[1]   Implemented by the Copyright (Computer Programs) Regulations 1992 (see Appendix 2).

(10) Whereas the function of a computer program is to communicate and work together with other components of a computer system and with users and, for this purpose, a logical and, where appropriate, physical interconnection and interaction is required to permit all elements of software and hardware to work with other software and hardware and with users in all the ways in which they are intended to function;

(11) Whereas the parts of the program which provide for such interconnection and interaction between elements of software and hardware are generally known as 'interfaces';

(12) Whereas the functional interconnection and interaction is generally known as 'interoperability'; whereas such interoperability can be defined as the ability to exchange information and mutually to use the information which has been exchanged;

(13) Whereas, for the avoidance of doubt, it has to be made clear that only the expression of a computer program is protected and that ideas and principles which underlie any element of a program, including those which underlie its interfaces, are not protected by copyright under this Directive;

(14) Whereas, in accordance with this principle of copyright, to the extent that logic, algorithms and programming languages comprise ideas and principles, those ideas and principles are not protected under this Directive;

(15) Whereas, in accordance with the legislation and jurisprudence of the Member States and the international copyright conventions, the expression of those ideas and principles is to be protected by copyright;

(16) Whereas, for the purposes of this Directive, the term 'rental'[1] means the making available for use, for a limited period of time and for profit-making purposes, of a computer program or a copy thereof; whereas this term does not include public lending, which, accordingly, remains outside the scope of this Directive;

(17) Whereas the exclusive rights of the author to prevent the unauthorised reproduction of his work have to be subject to a limited exception in the case of a computer program to allow the reproduction technically necessary for the use of that program by the lawful acquirer;

(18) Whereas this means that the acts of loading and running necessary for the use of a copy of a program which has been lawfully acquired, and the act of correction of its errors, may not be prohibited by contract, whereas, in the absence of specific contractual provisions, including when a copy of the program has been sold, any other act necessary for the use of the copy of a program may be performed in accordance with its intended purpose by a lawful acquirer of that copy;

(19) Whereas a person having a right to use a computer program should not be prevented from performing acts necessary to observe, study or test the functioning of the program, provided that these acts do not infringe the copyright in the program;

(20) Whereas the unauthorised reproduction, translation, adaptation or transformation of the form of the code in which a copy of a computer program has been made available constitutes an infringement of the exclusive rights of the author;

(21) Whereas, nevertheless, circumstances may exist when such a reproduction of the code and translation of its form within the meaning of Article 4(a) and (b) are indispensable to obtain the necessary information to achieve the interoperability of an independently created program with other programs;

(22) Whereas, it has therefore to be considered that in these limited circumstances only, performance of the acts of reproduction and translation by or on behalf of a person having a right to use a copy of the program is legitimate and compatible with fair practice and must therefore be deemed not to require the authorisation of the right-holder;

(23) Whereas an objective of this exception is to make it possible to connect all components of a computer system, including those of different manufacturers, so that they can work together;

---

1   See footnote 1 at p 155.

(24) Whereas such an exception to the author's exclusive rights may not be used in a way which prejudices the legitimate interests of the rightholder or which conflicts with a normal exploitation of the program;

(25) Whereas, in order to remain in accordance with the provisions of the Berne Convention for the Protection of Literary and Artistic Works, the term of protection should be the life of the author and fifty years from the first of January of the year following the year of his death or, in the case of an anonymous or pseudonymous work, 50 years from the first of January of the year following the year in which the work is first published[1];

(26) Whereas protection of computer programs under copyright laws should be without prejudice to the application, in appropriate cases, of other forms of protection; whereas, however, any contractual provisions contrary to Article 6 of the exceptions provided for in Article 5(2) and (3) should be null and void;

(27) Whereas the provisions of this Directive are without prejudice to the application of the competition rules under Articles 85 and 86 of the Treaty if a dominant supplier refuses to make information available which is necessary for interoperability as defined in this Directive;

(28) Whereas the provisions of this Directive should be without prejudice to specific requirements of Community law already enacted in respect of the publication of interfaces in the telecommunications sector or Council Decisions relating to standardisation in the field of information technology and telecommunication;

(29) Whereas this Directive does not affect derogations provided for under national legislation in accordance with the Berne Convention on points not covered by this Directive,

HAS ADOPTED THIS DIRECTIVE:

Article 1

Object of protection

1. In accordance with the provisions of this Directive, Member States shall protect computer programs, by copyright, as literary works within the meaning of the Berne Convention for the Protection of Literary and Artistic Works[2]. For the purposes of this Directive, the term 'computer programs' shall include their preparatory design material[3].

2. Protection in accordance with this Directive shall apply to the expression in any form of a computer program. Ideas and principles which underlie any element of a computer program, including those which underlie its interfaces, are not protected by copyright under this Directive[4].

3. A computer program shall be protected if it is original in the sense that it is the author's own intellectual creation. No other criteria shall be applied to determine its eligibility for protection[5].

---

1   See footnote 1 at p 157.

2   Computer programs were already protected as literary works prior to this Directive under the CDPA, s 3(1)(b). Accordingly, the Software Regulations do not make reference to this.

3   The Software Regulations, reg 3, do, however, extend protection to preparatory material by amending the CDPA, s 3(1).

4   No specific amendment to English law has been introduced to reflect this. This provision is already the case as a result of the CDPA, s 3(2) ('copyright does not subsist in a ... literary work unless and until it is recorded...') and case-law – *Donoghue v Allied Newspapers* [1938] Ch 106.

5   This relates to Recital 8, stating that no qualitative tests or aesthetic merit tests should be applied to determine eligibility. Again, under English law (unlike some civil law States) no amendment was necessary to reflect this. The Software Regulations do not give effect to the earlier statement in this Article, which requires protection only to be extended if the computer programs are the result of the author's intellectual creation. As the usual English law test for copyright is lower than this, there is a question as to whether the Software Directive has been correctly implemented into English law.

Article 2

Authorship of computer programs

1. The author of a computer program shall be the natural person or group of natural persons who has created the program[1] or, where the legislation of the Member State permits, the legal person designated as the rightholder by that legislation. Where collective works are recognized by the legislation of a Member State, the person considered by the legislation of the Member State to have created the work shall be deemed to be its author[2].

2. In respect of a computer program created by a group of natural persons jointly, the exclusive rights shall be owned jointly[3].

3. Where a computer program is created by an employee in the execution of his duties or following the instructions given by his employer, the employer exclusively shall be entitled to exercise all economic rights in the program so created, unless otherwise provided by contract[4].

Article 3

Beneficiaries of protection

Protection shall be granted to all natural or legal persons eligible under national copyright legislation as applied to literary works[5].

Article 4

Restricted Acts[6]

Subject to the provisions of Articles 5 and 6, the exclusive rights of the rightholder within the meaning of Article 2, shall include the right to do or to authorise:

(a) the permanent or temporary reproduction of a computer program by any means and in any form, in part or in whole. Insofar as loading, displaying, running, transmission or storage of the computer program necessitate such reproduction, such acts shall be subject to authorisation by the rightholder[7];

(b) the translation, adaptation, arrangement and any other alteration of a computer program and the reproduction of the results thereof, without prejudice to the rights of the person who alters the program[8];

---

1   See CDPA, s 9(1) and (3).
2   Under CDPA, s 10, a collaboration would lead to joint authorship.
3   See footnote 2 above. The CDPA, s 10 does not distinguish between work created jointly by natural persons and others.
4   See CDPA, s 11(2).
5   See CDPA, ss 1(3) and 153.
6   See CDPA, s 16 for acts restricted by copyright.
7   There is no direct equivalent to this provision in CDPA, or the Software Regulations. However, the CDPA, s 17(2) clarifies that 'copying' includes storing of work in any medium by electronic means and s 17(6) provides that copying includes copying which is transient or incidental to some other use of the work. These approximate to Art 4(a).
8   The Software Regulations, reg 5, amend the CDPA, s 21(3) to provide for this. Under s 21, 'adaptation' is defined as meaning an arrangement, altered version or translation. The CDPA, s 21(4) already defined 'translation' in this context as including 'a version of the program in which it is converted into or out of a computer language or code or into a different computer language or code'. Section 21(4) did exempt translations incidental to running a program. This was inconsistent with Art 4(a) of the Software Directive and repealed by the Software Regulations.

(c)   any form of distribution to the public, including the rental[1], of the original computer program or of copies thereof. The first sale in the Community of a copy of a program by the rightholder or with his consent shall exhaust the distribution right within the Community of that copy, with the exception of the right to control further rental of the program or a copy thereof[2].

Article 5

Exceptions to the restricted acts[3]

1.   In the absence of specific contractual provisions, the acts referred to in Article 4(a) and (b) shall not require authorisation by the rightholder where they are necessary for the use of the computer program by the lawful acquirer in accordance with its intended purpose, including for error correction[4].

2.   The making of a back-up copy by a person having a right to use the computer program may not be prevented by contract insofar as it is necessary for that use[5].

3.   The person having a right to use a copy of a computer program shall be entitled, without the authorisation of the rightholder, to observe, study or test the functioning of the program in order to determine the ideas and principles which underlie any element of the program if he does so while performing any of the acts of loading, displaying, running, transmitting or storing the program which he is entitled to do[6].

Article 6

Decompilation[7,8]

1.   The authorisation of the rightholder shall not be required where reproduction of the code and translation of its form within the meaning of Article 4(a) and (b) are indispensable to obtain the information necessary to achieve the interoperability of an independently created computer program with other programs, provided that the following conditions are met:

(a)   these acts are performed by the licensee or by another person having a right to use a copy of a program, or on their behalf by a person authorised to do so;

---

1   The CDPA, s 178 defines 'rental' as '... any arrangement under which a copy of a work is made available:
     (a) for payment (in money or money's worth), or
     (b) in the course of a business, as part of services or amenities for which payment is made on terms that it will or may be required.'

2   The exhaustion of the right to control distribution to the public is provided for by the Software Regulations, reg 1, amending the CDPA, s 18. Section 18 is clearer than the Software Directive, referring to 'the act of putting into circulation' and not 'subsequent distribution, sale, hiring ... loan or ... importation ... of those copies into the United Kingdom ...'. The CDPA, s 27(3A) (as introduced by the Software Regulations, reg 6) further provides that a copy of a computer program which has previously been sold in a Member State with the copyright owner's consent, is not an 'infringing copy'.

3   The exceptions in Art 5 apply to a person having a 'right to use'. This is provided for by the CDPA, s 50A(2) (introduced by the Software Regulations, reg 8), which uses the term 'lawful user'. In particular, a lawful user need not be a licensee.

4   See CDPA, s 50C, introduced by the Software Regulations, reg 8 for the equivalent provision.

5   See CDPA, s 50A, introduced by the Software Regulations, reg 8 for the equivalent provision.

6   There is no direct equivalent to this provision in the CDPA.

7   Decompilation is defined by CDPA, s 50B(1) (introduced by the Software Regulations, reg 8) as '[taking a] ... copy of a computer program expressed in a low level language:
     (a) to convert it into a version expressed in a higher level language; or
     (b) incidentally in the course of so converting the program, to copy it.'

8   The decompilation right is provided for more succinctly in the CDPA, s 50B, again introduced by the Software Regulations, reg 8.

(b)   the information necessary to achieve interoperability has not previously been readily available to the persons referred to in subparagraph (a); and

(c)   these acts are confined to the parts of the original program which are necessary to achieve interoperability.

2.   The provisions of paragraph 1 shall not permit the information obtained through its application:

(a)   to be used for goals other than to achieve the interoperability of the independently created computer program;

(b)   to be given to others, except when necessary for the interoperability of the independently created computer program; or

(c)   to be used for the development, production or marketing of a computer program substantially similar in its expression, or for any other act which infringes copyright.

3.   In accordance with the provisions of the Berne Convention for the protection of Literary and Artistic Works, the provisions of this Article may not be interpreted in such a way as to allow its application to be used in a manner which unreasonably prejudices the right holder's legitimate interests or conflicts with a normal exploitation of the computer program.

Article 7

Special measures of protection

1.   Without prejudice to the provisions of Articles 4, 5 and 6, Member States shall provide, in accordance with their national legislation, appropriate remedies against a person committing any of the acts listed in subparagraphs (a), (b) and (c) below[1]:

(a)   any act of putting into circulation a copy of a computer program knowing, or having reason to believe, that it is an infringing copy[2];

(b)   the possession, for commercial purposes, of a copy of a computer program knowing, or having reason to believe, that it is an infringing copy[2];

(c)   any act of putting into circulation, or the possession for commercial purposes of, any means the sole intended purpose of which is to facilitate the unauthorised removal or circumvention of any technical device which may have been applied to protect a computer program[3].

2.   Any infringing copy of a computer program shall be liable to seizure in accordance with the legislation of the Member State concerned[4].

3.   Member States may provide for the seizure of any means referred to in paragraph 1(c).

---

1   See Chapter IV of the CDPA, for remedies in general.

2   See footnote 2 at p 155 for the CDPA definition of 'infringing copy'.

3   The CDPA, s 296 provides that remedies for infringement of copyright also extend to the circulation of devices designed to circumvent copy protection. The Software Regulations, reg 10, amend this to provide that possession of such a device for commercial purposes (as distinct from actually circulating such a device) would lead to infringement remedies.

4   See CDPA, s 100.

Article 8

Term of protection

1. Protection shall be granted for the life of the author and for fifty[1] years after his death or after the death of the last surviving author; where the computer program is an anonymous or pseudonymous work, or where a legal person is designated as the author by national legislation in accordance with Article 2(1), the term of protection shall be fifty years from the time that the computer program is first lawfully made available to the public. The term of protection shall be deemed to begin on the first of January of the year following the above-mentioned events[2].

2. Member States which already have a term of protection longer than provided for in paragraph 1 are allowed to maintain their present term until such time as the term of protection for copyright works is harmonised by Community law in a more general way.

Article 9

Continued application of other legal provisions

1. The provisions of this Directive shall be without prejudice to any other legal provisions such as those concerning patent rights, trade-marks, unfair competition, trade secrets, protection of semi-conductor products or the law of contract. Any contractual provisions contrary to Article 6 or to the exceptions provided for in Article 5(2) and (3) shall be null and void[3].

2. The provisions of this Directive shall apply also to programs created before January 1, 1993 without prejudice to any acts concluded and rights acquired before that date[4].

Article 10

Final provisions

1. Member States shall bring into force the laws, regulations and administrative provisions necessary to comply with this Directive before January 1, 1993.
    When Member States adopt these measures, the latter shall contain a reference to this Directive or shall be accompanied by such reference on the occasion of their official publication. The methods of making such a reference shall be laid down by the Member States.

2. Member States shall communicate to the Commission the provisions of national law which they adopt in the field governed by the Directive.

Article 11

This Directive is addressed to the Member States.

---

1   Article 1 of Directive 93/98/EEC (the Copyright Term Directive) as implemented by reg 5 of SI 1995/3297 amends the duration of copyright to the author's life plus 70 years, except for:
    – works of unknown authorship (where the period is 70 years from creation or 70 years from making available to the public, provided that this happened within 70 years of creation); and
    – computer-generated works (where the period is 50 years from creation provided the author is an EEA national and the work's 'country of origin' is an EEA State).
    (See s 12 of the CDPA).
2   See CDPA, s 12 for equivalent provisions.
3   Introduced by the Software Regulations, reg 11 (see CDPA, s 296A).
4   See the Transitional and Saving provisions introduced by the Software Regulations, reg 12.

Appendix 2

COPYRIGHT (COMPUTER PROGRAMS) REGULATIONS 1992[1]

(SI 1992/3233)

1. Citation, commencement and extent

(1) These Regulations may be cited as the Copyright (Computer Programs) Regulations 1992 and shall come into force on January 1, 1993.

(2) These Regulations extend to Northern Ireland.

2. The Copyright, Designs and Patents Act 1988 shall be amended as follows.

Amendments of Part I (copyright) of the Copyright, Designs and Patents Act 1988

3. 'Literary work' extended to include preparatory design material for a computer program[2]

In section 3(1) (meaning of literary, dramatic and musical works) in the definition of 'literary work', omit the 'and' immediately preceding paragraph (b) and at the end of that paragraph insert ', and

(c) preparatory design material for a computer program'.

4. Restriction of infringement by issue of copies of computer programs within the Community[3]

(1) In section 18 (infringement by issue of copies to the public), in subsection (2)—

    (a) after the words 'work are' insert 'except where the work is a computer program'; and

    (b) for the words ', films and computer programs' substitute the words 'and films'.

(2) After subsection (2) of that section insert:

'(3) References in this Part to the issue to the public of copies of a work where the work is a computer program are to the act of putting into circulation copies of that program not previously put into circulation in the United Kingdom or any other member State, by or with the consent of the copyright owner, and not to—

    (a) any subsequent distribution, sale, hiring or loan of those copies, or

    (b) any subsequent importation of those copies into the United Kingdom,

except that the restricted act of issuing copies to the public includes any rental of copies to the public.'

---

1   The Software Regulations implement the provisions of the Software Directive (see Appendix 1).

2   Amendment reflects Software Directive, Art 1(1).

3   Amendment reflects Software Directive, Art 4(c).

5. Meaning of 'adaptation' in relation to a computer program[1]

(1) In section 21 (infringement by making adaptation), in subsection (3) (meaning of 'adaptation') in paragraph (a) after 'literary' insert 'work, other than a computer program,'.

(2) After that paragraph of that subsection insert—

'(ab) in relation to a computer program, means an arrangement or altered version of the program or a translation of it;'

(3) In subsection (4) of that section (meaning of 'translation' in relation to computer programs), omit the words ', otherwise than incidentally in the course of running the program'.

6. Meaning of 'infringing copy'[2]

In section 27 (meaning of 'infringing copy'), in subsection (3) (imported articles) at the beginning insert 'Subject to subsection (A)' and after that subsection insert:

'(3A) A copy of a computer program which has previously been sold in any other member State, by or with the consent of the copyright owner, is not an infringing copy for the purposes of subsection (3).'.

7. Exclusion of decompilation of computer programs from fair dealing

In section 29 (research and private study), after subsection (3) insert—

'(4) It is not fair dealing—

    (a)   to convert a computer program expressed in a low level language into a version expressed in a higher level language,[3] or

    (b)   incidentally in the course of so converting the program, to copy it, (these acts being permitted if done in accordance with section 50B (decompilation)).'.

8. New permitted acts in relation to computer programs[4]

After section 50 insert—

'Computer programs: lawful users

50A. Back up copies

(1) It is not an infringement of copyright for a lawful user of a copy of a computer program to make any back up copy of it which it is necessary for him to have for the purposes of his lawful use.

(2) For the purposes of this section and sections 50B and 50C a person is a lawful user of a computer program if (whether under a licence to do any acts restricted by the copyright in the program or otherwise), he has a right to use the program.

(3) Where an act is permitted under this section, it is irrelevant whether or not there exists any term or condition in an agreement which purports to prohibit or restrict the act (such terms being, by virtue of section 296A, void).

---

1   Amendment reflects Software Directive, Art 4(b). See also CDPA, s 21(4) for an explanation of 'translation'.

2   See footnote 3 at p 158.

3   See footnote 1 above.

4   Amended to reflect the Software Directive, Art 6.

50B. Decompilation

(1) It is not an infringement of copyright for a lawful user of a copy of a computer program expressed in a low level language—

    (a)   to convert it into a version expressed in a higher level language, or

    (b)   incidentally in the course of so converting the program, to copy it,

(that is, to 'decompile' it), provided that the conditions in subsection (2) are met.

(2) The conditions are that—

    (a)   it is necessary to decompile the program to obtain the information necessary to create an independent program which can be operated with the program decompiled or with another program ('the permitted objective'); and

    (b)   the information so obtained is not used for any purpose other than the permitted objective.

(3) In particular, the conditions in subsection (2) are not met if the lawful user—

    (a)   has readily available to him the information necessary to achieve the permitted objective;

    (b)   does not confine the decompiling to such acts as are necessary to achieve the permitted objective;

    (c)   supplies the information obtained by the decompiling to any person to whom it is not necessary to supply it in order to achieve the permitted objective; or

    (d)   uses the information to create a program which is substantially similar in its expression to the program decompiled or to do any act restricted by copyright.

(4) Where an act is permitted under this section, it is irrelevant whether or not there exists any term or condition in an agreement which purports to prohibit or restrict the act (such terms being, by virtue of section 296A, void).

50C. Other acts permitted to lawful users

(1) It is not an infringement of copyright for a lawful user of a copy of a computer program to copy or adapt it, provided that the copying or adapting—

    (a)   is necessary for his lawful use; and

    (b)   is not prohibited under any term or condition of an agreement regulating the circumstances in which his use is lawful.

(2) It may, in particular, be necessary for the lawful use of a computer program to copy it or adapt it for the purpose of correcting errors in it.

(3) This section does not apply to any copying or adapting permitted under section 50A or 50B.'.

9. In section 179 (index of defined expressions) in the appropriate place in the alphabetical order insert—

'lawful user (in sections 50A to 50C)   section 50A(2)'.

Amendments of Part VII (miscellaneous and general) of the Copyright, Designs and Patents Act 1988

10. Devices designed to circumvent copy-protection applied to computer programs[1]

In section 296 (devices designed to circumvent copy-protection), after subsection (2) insert—

'(2A) Where the copies being issued to the public as mentioned in subsection (1) are copies of a computer program, subsection (2) applies as if for the words "or advertises for sale or hire" there were substituted "advertises for sale or hire or possesses in the course of a business".'

11. Avoidance of certain terms relating to computer programs

After section 296 insert—

'Computer programs

296A. Avoidance of certain terms[2]

(1) Where a person has the use of a computer program under an agreement, any term or condition in the agreement shall be void in so far as it purports to prohibit or restrict—

    (a) the making of any back up copy of the program which it is necessary for him to have for the purposes of the agreed use;

    (b) where the conditions in section 50B(2) are met, the decompiling of the program; or

    (c) the use of any device or means to observe, study or test the functioning of the program in order to understand the ideas and principles which underlie any element of the program.

(2) In this section, decompile, in relation to a computer program, has the same meaning as in section 50B.'.

Transitional provisions and savings

12. Computer programs created before 1st January 1993[3]

(1) Subject to paragraph (2), the amendments of the Copyright, Designs and Patents Act 1988 made by these Regulations apply in relation to computer programs created before 1st January 1993 as they apply to computer programs created on or after that date.

(2) Nothing in these Regulations affects any agreement or any term or condition of an agreement where the agreement, term or condition is entered into before 1st January 1993.

---

1   Amended to reflect the Software Directive, Art 7(c) which extended the original provisions of the CDPA, by providing that commercial possession (as opposed to circulation) of such a device would require a remedy.

2   See the Software Directive, Recital 22.

3   Amendment reflects the Software Directive, Art 10.

Appendix 3

DIRECTIVE 96/9 OF THE EUROPEAN PARLIAMENT AND OF THE COUNCIL

of 11 March 1996

on the Legal Protection of Databases[1]

THE EUROPEAN PARLIAMENT AND THE COUNCIL OF THE EUROPEAN UNION,

Having regard to the Treaty establishing the European Community, and in particular Articles 57(2), 66 and 100a thereof,

Having regard to the proposal from the Commission[2],

Having regard to the opinion of the Economic and Social Committee[3],

Acting in accordance with the procedure laid down in Article 189b of the Treaty[4],

(1) Whereas databases are at present not sufficiently protected in all Member States by existing legislation; such protection, where it exists, has different attributes;

(2) Whereas such differences in the legal protection of databases offered by the legislation of the Member States have direct negative effects on the functioning of the internal market as regards databases and in particular on the freedom of natural and legal persons to provide on-line database goods and services on the basis of harmonised legal arrangements throughout the Community; whereas such differences could well become more pronounced as Member States introduce new legislation in this field, which is now taking on an increasingly international dimension;

(3) Whereas existing differences distorting the functioning of the internal market need to be removed and new ones prevented from arising, while differences not adversely affecting the functioning of the internal market or the development of an information market within the Community need not be removed or prevented from arising;

(4) Whereas copyright protection for databases exists in varying forms in the Member States accordingly to legislation or case-law, and, whereas, if differences in legislation in the scope and conditions of protection remain between the Member States, such unharmonised intellectual property rights can have the effect of preventing the free movement of goods or services within the Community;

(5) Whereas copyright remains an appropriate form of exclusive right for authors who have created databases;

---

1   Implemented by the Database Regulations, SI 1997/3032, see Appendix 4.
2   [1992] OJ C156/4, [1993] OJ C308/1.
3   [1993] OJ C19/3.
4   Opinion of the European Parliament, 23 June 1993 ([1993] OJ C194/144), Common Position of the Council of 10 July 1995 ([1995] OJ C288/14), Decision of the European Parliament of 14 December 1995 ([1996] OJ C17/1) and Council Decision of 26 February 1996.

(6)   Whereas nevertheless, in the absence of a harmonised system of unfair-competition legislation or of case-law, other measures are required in addition to prevent the unauthorised extraction and/or re-utilisation of the contents of the database;

(7)   Whereas the making of databases requires the investment of considerable human, technical and financial resources, while such databases can be copied or accessed at a fraction of the cost needed to design them independently;

(8)   Whereas the unauthorised extraction and/or re-utilisation of the contents of a database constitute acts which can have serious economic and technical consequences;

(9)   Whereas databases are a vital tool in the development of an information market within the Community; whereas this tool will also be of use in many other fields;

(10) Whereas the exponential growth, in the Community and worldwide, in the amount of information generated and processed annually in all sectors of commerce and industry calls for investment in all the Member States in advanced information processing systems;

(11) Whereas there is at present a very great imbalance in the level of investment in the database sector both as between the Member States and between the Community and the world's largest database producing third countries;

(12) Whereas such an investment in modern information storage and processing systems will not take place within the Community unless a stable and uniform legal protection regime is introduced for the protection of the rights of makers of databases;

(13) Whereas this Directive protects collections, sometimes called 'compilations'[1], of works, data or other materials which are arranged, stored and accessed by means which include electronic, electromagnetic or electro-optical processes or analogous processes;

(14) Whereas protection under this Directive should be extended to cover non-electronic databases;

(15) Whereas the criteria used to determine whether a database should be protected by copyright should be defined to the fact that the selection or the arrangements of the contents of the database is the author's own intellectual creation; whereas no such protection should cover the structure of the database;

(16) Whereas no criterion other than originality in the sense of the author's intellectual creation should be applied to determine the eligibility of the database for copyright protection, and in particular no aesthetic or qualitative criteria should be applied;

(17) Whereas the term 'database' should be understood to include literary, artistic, musical or other collections of works or collections of other material such as texts, sound, images, numbers, facts and data; whereas it should cover collections of independent works, data or other materials which are systematically or methodically arranged and can be individually accessed; whereas this means that a recording or an audiovisual, cinematographic, literary or musical work as such does not fall within the scope of this Directive;

(18) Whereas this Directive is without prejudice to the freedom of authors to decide whether, or in what manner, they will allow their works to be included in a database, in particular whether or not the authorisation given is exclusive; whereas the protection of databases by the *sui generis* right is without prejudice to existing rights over their contents, and whereas in particular where an author or the holder of a related right permits some of his works or subject matter to be included in a database pursuant to a non-exclusive agreement, a third party may make use of those works or subject matter subject to the required consent of the author or of the holder of the related right without the *sui generis* right of the maker of the database being invoked to prevent him doing so, on condition that

---

1   This is refined by Recital 17: the compilation must be systematically or methodically arranged and capable of individual access. The Database Regulations, reg 5 clarify that compilations and databases are mutually exclusive.

those works or subject matter are neither extracted from the database nor re-utilised on the basis thereof;

(19) Whereas as a rule, the compilation of several recordings of musical performances on a CD does not come within the scope of this Directive, both because, as a compilation, it does not meet the conditions for copyright protection and because it does not represent a substantial enough investment to be eligible under the *sui generis* right;

(20) Whereas protection under this Directive may also apply to the materials necessary for the operation or consultation of certain databases such as thesaurus and indexation systems;

(21) Whereas the protection provided for in this Directive relates to databases in which works, data or other materials have been arranged systematically or methodically; whereas it is not necessary for those materials to have been physically stored in an organised manner;

(22) Whereas electronic databases within the meaning of this Directive may also include devices such as CD-ROM and CD-i;

(23) Whereas the term 'database' should not be taken to extend to computer programs used in the making or operation of a database, which are protected by Council Directive 91/250 of May 14, 1991 on the legal protection of computer programs[1];

(24) Whereas the rental and lending of databases in the field of copyright and related rights are governed exclusively by Council Directive 92/100 of November 19, 1992 on rental right and lending right and on certain rights related to copyright in the field of intellectual property[2];

(25) Whereas the term of copyright is already governed by Council Directive 93/98 of October 29, 1993 harmonising the term of protection of copyright and certain related rights[3];

(26) Whereas works protected by copyright and subject matter protected by related rights, which are incorporated into a database, remain nevertheless protected by the respective exclusive rights and may not be incorporated into, or extracted from, the database without the permission of the rightholder or his successors in title;

(27) Whereas copyright in such works and related rights in subject matter thus incorporated into a database are in no way affected by the existence of a separate right in the selection or arrangement of these works and subject matter in a database;

(28) Whereas the moral rights of the natural person who created the database belong to the author and should be exercised according to the legislation of the Member States and the provisions of the Berne Convention for the Protection of Literary and Artistic Works; whereas such moral rights remain outside the scope of this Directive;

(29) Whereas the arrangements applicable to databases created by employees are left to the discretion of the Member States; whereas therefore nothing in this Directive prevents Member States from stipulating in their legislation that where a database is created by an employee in the execution of his duties or following the instructions given by his employer, the employer exclusively shall be entitled to exercise all economic rights in the database so created, unless otherwise provided by contract;

(30) Whereas the author's exclusive rights should include the right to determine the way in which his work is exploited and by whom, and in particular to control the distribution of his work to unauthorised persons;

(31) Whereas the copyright protection of databases includes making databases available by means other than the distribution of copies;

(32) Whereas Member States are required to ensure that their national provisions are at least materially equivalent in the case of such acts subject to restrictions as are provided for by this Directive;

---

1   [1991] OJ L122/42 Directive.
2   [1992] OJ L346/61.
3   [1993] OJ L290/9.

(33) Whereas the question of exhaustion of the right of distribution does not arise in the case of on-line databases, which come within the field of provision of services; whereas this also applies with regard to a material copy of such a database made by the user of such a service with the consent of the rightholder, whereas, unlike CD-ROM or CD-i, where the intellectual property is incorporated in a material medium, namely an item of goods, every on-line service is in fact an act which will have to be subject to authorisation where the copyright so provides;

(34) Whereas nevertheless, once the rightholder has chosen to make available a copy of the database to a user, whether by an on-line service or by other means of distribution, that lawful user must be able to access and use the database for the purposes and in the way set out in the agreement with the rightholder, even if such access and use necessitate performance of otherwise restricted acts;

(35) Whereas a list should be drawn up of exceptions to restricted acts, taking into account the fact that copyright as covered by this Directive applies only to the selection or arrangements of the contents of a database; whereas Member States should be given the option of providing for such exceptions in certain cases; whereas, however, this option should be exercised in accordance with the Berne Convention and to the extent that the exceptions relate to the structure of the database; whereas a distinction should be drawn between exceptions, for private use and exceptions for reproduction for private purposes, which concerns provisions under national legislation of some Member States on levies on blank media or recording equipment;

(36) Whereas the term 'scientific research' within the meaning of this Directive covers both the natural sciences and the human sciences;

(37) Whereas Article 10(1) of the Berne Convention is not affected by this Directive;

(38) Whereas the increasing use of digital recording technology exposes the database maker to the risk that the contents of this database may be copied and rearranged electronically, without his authorisation, to produce a database of identical content which, however, does not infringe any copyright in the arrangement of his database;

(39) Whereas in addition to aiming to protect the copyright in the original selection or arrangement of the contents of a database, this Directive seeks to safeguard the position of makers of databases against misappropriation of the results of the financial and professional investment made in obtaining and collecting the contents by protecting the whole or substantial parts of a database against certain acts by a user or competitor;

(40) Whereas the object of this *sui generis* right is to ensure protection of any investment in obtaining, verifying or presenting the contents of a database for the limited duration of the right; whereas such investment may consist in the deployment of financial resources and/or the expending of time, effort and energy;

(41) Whereas the objective of the *sui generis* right is to give the maker of a database the option of preventing the unauthorised extraction and/or re-utilisation of all or a substantial part of the contents of that database; the maker of a database is the person who takes the initiative and the risk of investing; whereas this excludes subcontractors in particular from the definition of maker;

(42) Whereas the special right to prevent unauthorised extraction and/or re-utilisation relates to acts by the user which go beyond his legitimate rights and thereby harm the investment; whereas the right to prohibit extraction and/or re-utilisation of all or a substantial part of the contents relates not only to the manufacture of a parasitical competing product but also to any user who, through his acts, causes significant detriment, evaluated qualitatively or quantitatively, to the investment;

(43) Whereas in the case of on-line transmission, the right to prohibit re-utilisation is not exhausted either as regards the database or as regards a material copy of the database or of part thereof made by the addressee of the transmission with the consent of the rightholder;

(44) Whereas when on-screen display of the contents of a database necessitates the permanent or temporary transfer of all or a substantial part of such contents to another medium, that act should be subject to authorisation by the rightholder;

(45) Whereas the right to prevent unauthorised extraction and/or re-utilisation does not in any way constitute an extension of copyright protection to mere facts or data;

(46) Whereas the existence of a right to prevent the unauthorised extraction and/or re-utilisation of the whole or a substantial part of works, data or materials from a database should not give rise to the creation of a new right in the works, data or materials themselves;

(47) Whereas in the interests of competition between suppliers of information products and services, protection by the *sui generis* right must not be afforded in such a way as to facilitate abuses of a dominant position, in particular as regards the creation and distribution of new products and services which have an intellectual, documentary, technical, economic, or commercial added value; whereas, therefore, the provisions of this Directive are without prejudice to the application of Community or national competition rules;

(48) Whereas the objective of this Directive, which is to afford an appropriate and uniform level of protection of databases as a means to secure the remuneration of the maker of the database, is different from the aim of Directive 95/46 of the European Parliament and of the Council of October 24, 1995 on the protection of individuals with regard to the processing of personal data and on the free movement of such data[1], which is to guarantee free circulation of personal data on the basis of harmonised rules designed to protect fundamental rights, notably the right to privacy which is recognised in Article 8 of the European Convention for the Protection of Human Rights and Fundamental Freedoms; whereas the provisions of this Directive are without prejudice to data protection legislation;

(49) Whereas notwithstanding the right to prevent extraction and/or re-utilisation of all or a substantial part of a database, it should be laid down that the maker of a database or rightholder may not prevent a lawful user of the database from extracting and re-utilising insubstantial parts; whereas, however, that user may not unreasonably prejudice either the legitimate interests of the holder of the *sui generis* right or the holder of copyright or a related right in respect of the works or subject matter contained in the database;

(50) Whereas the Member States should be given the option of providing for exceptions to the right to prevent the unauthorised extraction and/or re-utilisation of a substantial part of the contents of a database in the case of extraction for private purposes, for the purposes of illustration for teaching or scientific research, or where extraction and/or re-utilisation are/is carried out in the interests of public security or for the purposes of an administrative or judicial procedure; whereas such operations must not prejudice the exclusive rights of the maker to exploit the database and their purpose must not be commercial;

(51) Whereas the Member States, where they avail themselves of the option to permit a lawful user of a database to extract a substantial part of the contents for the purposes of illustration for teaching or scientific research, may limit that permission to certain categories of teaching or scientific research institution;

(52) Whereas those Member States which have specific rules providing for a right comparable to the *sui generis* right provided for in this Directive should be permitted to retain, as far as the new right is concerned, the exceptions traditionally specified by such rules;

(53) Whereas the burden of proof regarding the date of completion of the making of a database lies with the maker of the database;

---

1   [1995] OJ L281/31.

(54) Whereas the burden of proof that the criteria exist for concluding that a substantial modification of the contents of a database is to be regarded as a substantial new investment lies with the maker of the database resulting from such investment;

(55) Whereas a substantial new investment involving a new term of protection may include a substantial verification of the contents of the database;

(56) Whereas the right to prevent unauthorised extraction and/or re-utilisation in respect of a database should apply to databases whose makers are nationals or habitual residents of third countries or to those produced by legal persons not established in a Member State, within the meaning of the Treaty, only if such third countries offer comparable protection to databases by nationals of a Member State or persons who have their habitual residence in the territory of the Community;

(57) Whereas in addition to remedies provided under the legislation of the Member States for infringements of copyright or other rights, Member States should provide for appropriate remedies against unauthorised extraction and/or re-utilisation of the contents of a database;

(58) Whereas in addition to the protection given under this Directive to the structure of the database by copyright, and to its contents against unauthorised extraction and/or re-utilisation under the *sui generis* right, other legal provisions in the Member States relevant to the supply of database goods and services continue to apply;

(59) Whereas this Directive is without prejudice to the application to databases composed of audiovisual works of any rules recognised by a Member State's legislation concerning the broadcasting of audiovisual programmes;

(60) Whereas some Member States currently protect under copyright arrangements databases which do not meet the criteria for eligibility for copyright protection laid down in this Directive; whereas, even if the databases concerned are eligible for protection under the right laid down in this Directive to prevent unauthorised extraction and/or re-utilisation of their contents, the term of protection under that right is considerably shorter than that which they enjoy under the national arrangements currently in force; whereas harmonisation of the criteria for determining whether a database is to be protected by copyright may not have the effect of reducing the term of protection currently enjoyed by the rightholders concerned; whereas a derogation should be laid down to that effect; whereas the effects of such derogation must be confined to the territories of the Member States concerned,

HAVE ADOPTED THIS DIRECTIVE:

Chapter I

SCOPE

Article 1

Scope

1. This Directive concerns the legal protection of databases in any form.

2. For the purposes of this Directive, 'database' shall mean a collection of independent works, data or other materials arranged in a systematic or methodical way and individually accessible by electronic or other means[1].

3. Protection under this Directive shall not apply to computer programs used in the making or operation of databases accessible by electronic means[2].

---

1   Reflected verbatim by the Database Regulations, reg 6, amending the CDPA, s 6.
2   This is not directly reflected in the Database Regulations.

Article 2

Limitations on the scope

This Directive shall apply without prejudice to Community provisions relating to:

(a)   the legal protection of computer programs;
(b)   rental right, lending right and certain rights related to copyright in the field of intellectual property;
(c)   the term of protection of copyright and certain related rights.

Chapter II

COPYRIGHT

Article 3

Object of protection

1.   In accordance with this Directive, databases which, by reason of the selection or arrangement of their contents, constitute the author's own intellectual creation shall be protected as such by copyright. No other criteria shall be applied to determine their eligibility for that protection[1].
2.   The copyright protection of databases provided for by this Directive shall not extend to their contents and shall be without prejudice to any rights subsisting in those contents themselves.

Article 4

Database authorship

1.   The author of a database shall be the natural person or group of natural persons who created the database[2] or, where the legislation of the Member States so permits, the legal person designated as the rightholder by that legislation.
2.   Where collective works are recognised by the legislation of a Member State, the economic rights shall be owned by the person holding the copyright[3].
3.   In respect of a database created by a group of natural persons jointly, the exclusive rights shall be owned jointly[4].

Article 5

Restricted acts[5]

In respect of the expression of the database which is protectable by copyright, the author of a database shall have the exclusive right to carry out or to authorise:

(a)   temporary or permanent reproduction by any means and in any form, in whole or in part;
(b)   translation, adaptation, arrangement and any other alteration[6];

---

1   See the Database Regulations, reg 6, amending the CDPA, s 3.
2   See CDPA, s 9(1)
3   See CDPA, s 10 – this would lead to joint ownership.
4   See footnote 3 above: the CDPA does not distinguish between work created jointly by natural persons and others.
5   See CDPA, s 16 for acts restricted by copyright.
6   See the Database Regulations, reg 7 amending the CDPA, s 21 which defines 'adaptation' in relation to a database as '... an arrangement ... altered version ... or translation'.

(c) any form of distribution to the public of the database or of copies thereof. The first sale in the Community of a copy of the database by the rightholder or with his consent shall exhaust the right to control resale of that copy within the Community[1];

(d) any communication, display or performance to the public;

(e) any reproduction, distribution, communication, display or performance to the public of the results of the acts referred to in (b).

Article 6

Exceptions to restricted acts

1. The performance by the lawful user of a database or of a copy thereof of any of the acts listed in Article 5 which is necessary for the purposes of access to the contents of the databases and normal use of the contents by the lawful user shall not require the authorisation of the author of the database. Where the lawful user is authorised to use only part of the database, this provision shall apply only to that part[2].

2. Member States shall have the option of providing for limitations on the rights set out in Article 5 in the following cases[3]:

   (a) in the case of reproduction for private purposes of a non-electronic database;

   (b) where there is use for the sole purpose of illustration for teaching or scientific research, as long as the source is indicated and to the extent justified by the non-commercial purpose to be achieved;

   (c) where there is use for the purposes of public security or for the purposes of an administrative or judicial procedure;

   (d) where other exceptions to copyright which are traditionally authorised under national law are involved, without prejudice to points (a), (b) and (c).

3. In accordance with the Berne Convention for the protection of Literary and Artistic Works, this Article may not be interpreted in such a way as to allow its application to be used in a manner which unreasonably prejudices the rightholder's legitimate interests or conflicts with normal exploitation of the database.

Chapter III

SUI GENERIS RIGHT[4]

Article 7

Object of protection

1. Member States shall provide for a right for the maker of a database which shows that there has been qualitatively and/or quantitatively a substantial investment in either the obtaining, verification or presentation of the contents to prevent extraction and/or re-utilisation of the whole or of a substantial part, evaluated qualitatively and/or quantitatively, of the contents of that database[5].

2. For the purposes of this Chapter[6]:

---

1 See CDPA, s 18 for restrictions on the distribution right.

2 See the Database Regulations, reg 9, amending the CDPA by inserting a new s 50D.

3 The CDPA, s 29, as amended by the Database Regulations, reg 8 states that 'fair dealing ... for research or private study' does not infringe copyright. The more detailed provisions restricting private study to non-electronic databases are not included, nor is the 'sole purposes' test of Art 2(b).

4 See the Database Regulations, Part III – 'database right'.

5 See the Database Regulations, regs 13(1) and 16(1) which reproduce this almost verbatim and the definition of 'substantial', which reproduces the qualitative/quantitative concept.

6 See the equivalent definition in the Database Regulations, reg 12(1).

(a) 'extraction' shall mean the permanent or temporary transfer of all or a substantial part of the contents of a database to another medium by any means or in any form;

(b) 're-utilisation' shall mean any form of making available to the public all or a substantial part of the contents of a database by the distribution of copies, by renting, by on-line or other forms of transmission. The first sale of a copy of a database within the Community by the rightholder or with his consent shall exhaust the right to control resale of that copy within the Community[1];

Public lending is not an act of extraction or re-utilisation[2].

3.   The right referred to in paragraph 1 may be transferred, assigned or granted under contractual licence[3].

4.   The right provided for in paragraph 1 shall apply irrespective of the eligibility of that database for protection by copyright or by other rights[4]. Moreover, it shall apply irrespective of eligibility of the contents of that database for protection by copyright or by other rights. Protection of databases under the right provided for in paragraph 1 shall be without prejudice to rights existing in respect of their contents.

5.   The repeated and systematic extraction and/or re-utilisation of insubstantial parts of the contents of the database implying acts which conflict with a normal exploitation of that database or which unreasonably prejudice the legitimate interests of the maker of the database shall not be permitted[5].

Article 8

Rights and obligations of lawful users[6]

1.   The maker of a database which is made available to the public in whatever manner may not prevent a lawful user of the database from extracting and/or re-utilising insubstantial parts of its contents, evaluated qualitatively and/or quantitatively, for any purposes whatsoever. Where the lawful user is authorised to extract and/or re-utilise only part of the database, this paragraph shall apply only to that part.

2.   A lawful user of a database which is made available to the public in whatever manner may not perform acts which conflict with normal exploitation of the database or unreasonably prejudice the legitimate interests of the maker of the database.

3.   A lawful user of a database which is made available to the public in any manner may not cause prejudice to the holder of a copyright or related right in respect of the works or subject matter contained in the database.

---

1   The distribution right is set out in the Database Regulations, reg 12(5).

2   This is expressed, in a more convoluted manner, in the Database Regulations, reg 12(2) and (3), which attempt to establish what is meant by 'public lending' and that a charge (to cover expenses) does not debar this provision from applying. Further, 'on-the-spot reference use' is, per reg 12(4), outside the definition of public lending in the Database Regulations. This seems beyond the scope of the Database Directive.

3   Ie it is a 'property' right, as provided for by reg 13(1) of the Database Regulations and reg 23 (extending the provisions of ss 90–93 of the CDPA to transactions relating to databases).

4   See the Database Regulations, reg 13(2).

5   This is reproduced almost verbatim in reg 16(2) of the Database Regulations. However, there, the key phrase 'conflict with normal exploitation ... or unreasonably prejudice' has been omitted.

6   Provided for in reg 19(1) of the Database Regulations. The restrictions on 'normal use' and 'prejudice' are not set out there.

Article 9

Exceptions to the *sui generis* right[1]

Member States may stipulate that lawful users of a database which is made available to the public in whatever manner may, without the authorisation of its maker, extract or re-utilise a substantial part of its contents:

(a)   in the case of extraction for private purposes of the contents of a non-electronic database;

(b)   in the case of extraction for the purposes of illustration for teaching or scientific research, as long as the source is indicated and to the extent justified by the non-commercial purpose to be achieved;

(c)   in the case of extraction and/or re-utilisation for the purposes of public security or an administrative or judicial procedure.

Article 10

Term of protection[2]

1.   The right provided for in Article 7 shall run from the date of completion of the making of the database. It shall expire fifteen years from the first of January of the year following the date of completion.

2.   In the case of a database which is made available to the public in whatever manner before expiry of the period provided for in paragraph 1, the term of protection by that right shall expire fifteen years from the first of January of the year following the date when the database was first made available to the public.

3.   Any substantial change, evaluated qualitatively or quantitatively, to the contents of a database, including any substantial change resulting from the accumulation of successive additions, deletions or alterations, which would result in the database being considered to be a substantial new investment, evaluated qualitatively or quantitatively, shall qualify the database resulting from that investment for its own term of protection.

Article 11

Beneficiaries of protection under the *sui generis* right[3]

1.   The right provided for in Article 7 shall apply to databases whose makers or rightholders are nationals of a Member State or who have their habitual residence in the territory of the Community.

2.   Paragraph 1 shall also apply to companies and firms formed in accordance with the law of a Member State and having their registered office, central administration or principal place of business within the Community; however, where such a company or firm has only its registered office in the territory of the Community, its operations must be genuinely linked on an ongoing basis with the economy of a Member State.

3.   Agreements extending the right provided for in Article 7 to databases made in third countries and falling outside the provisions of paragraphs 1 and 2 shall be concluded by the Council acting on a proposal from the Commission. The term of any protection extended to databases by virtue of that procedure shall not exceed that available pursuant to Article 10.

---

1   Regulation 20 of the Database Regulations provides that use for teaching/research purposes are exemptions to the *sui generis* right. The exemption is *not* limited to scientific research. The 'private use' exemption is not reproduced. Schedule 1 to the Regulations contains exemptions falling within Art 9(c).

2   Reproduced in reg 17 of the Database Regulations.

3   This is provided for in reg 18 of the Database Regulations, which also clarifies that qualifying residence must be at the time of creation of the database.

Chapter IV

COMMON PROVISIONS

Article 12

Remedies[1]

Member States shall provide appropriate remedies in respect of infringements of the rights provided for in this Directive.

Article 13

Continued application of other legal provisions[2]

This Directive shall be without prejudice to provisions concerning in particular copyright, rights related to copyright or any other rights or obligations subsisting in the data, works or other materials incorporated into a database, patent rights, trade marks, design rights, the protection of national treasures, laws on restrictive practices and unfair competition, trade secrets, security, confidentiality, data protection and privacy, access to public documents, and the law of contract.

Article 14

Application over time

1. Protection pursuant to this Directive as regards copyright shall also be available in respect of databases created prior to the date referred to in Article 16(1) which on that date fulfil the requirements laid down in this Directive as regards copyright protection of databases[3].
2. Notwithstanding paragraph 1, where a database protected under copyright arrangements in a Member State on the date of publication of this Directive does not fulfil the eligibility criteria for copyright protection laid down in Article 3(1), this Directive shall not result in any curtailing in that Member State of the remaining term of protection afforded under those arrangements.
3. Protection pursuant to the provisions of this Directive as regards the right provided for in Article 7 shall also be available in respect of databases the making of which was completed not more than fifteen years prior to the date referred to in Article 16(1) and which on that date fulfil the requirements laid down in Article 7[4].
4. The protection provided for in paragraphs 1 and 3 shall be without prejudice to any acts concluded and rights acquired before the date referred to in those paragraphs[5].
5. In the case of a database the making of which was completed not more than fifteen years prior to the date referred to in Article 16(1), the term of protection by the right provided for in Article 7 shall expire fifteen years from the first of January following that date[6].

Article 15

Binding nature of certain provisions

Any contractual provision contrary to Articles 6(1)[7] and 8 shall be null and void.

---

1   Regulation 23 of the Database Regulations extends the remedies provisions of the CDPA to infringements of database right.
2   The Database Regulations do not expressly provide for this.
3   Regulation 29 of the Database Regulations makes equivalent provision.
4   Provided for by reg 30 of the Database Regulations.
5   The saving provision is reproduced by reg 28 of the Database Regulations.
6   See footnote 4 above.
7   See CDPA, s 50D(2), as introduced by the Database Regulations, reg 9.

Article 16

Final Provisions

1. Member States shall bring into force the laws, regulations and administrative provisions necessary to comply with this Directive before January 1, 1998.

    When Member States adopt these provisions, they shall contain a reference to this Directive or shall be accompanied by such reference on the occasion of their official publication. The methods of making such reference shall be laid down by Member States.

2. Member States shall communicate to the Commission the text of the provisions of domestic law which they adopt in the field governed by this Directive.

3. Not later than at the end of the third year after the date referred to in paragraph 1, and every three years thereafter, the Commission shall submit to the European Parliament, the Council and the Economic and Social Committee a report on the application of this Directive, in which, *inter alia*, on the basis of specific information supplied by the Member States, it shall examine in particular the application of the *sui generis* right, including Articles 8 and 9, and shall verify especially whether the application of this right has led to abuse of a dominant position or other interference with free competition which would justify appropriate measures being taken, including the establishment of non-voluntary licensing arrangements. Where necessary, it shall submit proposals for adjustment of this Directive in line with developments in the area of databases.

Article 17

This Directive is addressed to the Member States.

Done at Strasbourg, 11 March 1996.

Appendix 4

COPYRIGHT AND RIGHTS IN DATABASES REGULATIONS 1997[1]

(SI 1997/3032)

PART I

Introductory Provisions

1. Citation, commencement and extent

(1) These Regulations may be cited as the Copyright and Related Rights in Databases Regulations 1997.

(2) These Regulations come into force on 1st January 1998.

(3) These Regulations extend to the whole of the United Kingdom.

2. Implementation of Directive

(1) These Regulations make provision for the purpose of implementing—

    (a) Council Directive No. 96/9/EC of 11 March 1996[2] on the legal protection of databases, and

    (b) certain obligations of the United Kingdom created by or arising under the EEA Agreement so far as relating to the implementation of that Directive.

(2) In this Regulation 'the EEA Agreement' means the Agreement on the European Economic Area signed at Oporto on 2nd May 1992[3], as adjusted by the Protocol signed at Brussels on 17th March 1993[4].

3. Interpretation

In these Regulations 'the 1988 Act' means the Copyright, Designs and Patents Act 1988.

4. Scheme of the Regulations

(1) The 1988 Act is amended in accordance with the provisions of Part II of these Regulations, subject to the savings and transitional provisions in Part IV of these Regulations.

(2) Part III of these Regulations has effect subject to those savings and transitional provisions.

---

1   Implementing the Database Directive – see Appendix 3.
2   OJ No L77, 27 March 1996, p 20.
3   CM 2073.
4   CM 2183.

PART II[1]

Amendment of the Copyright, Designs and Patents Act 1988

5. Copyright in databases

In section 3(1), in the definition of 'literary work'—

(a) in paragraph (a) after 'compilation' insert 'other than a database'[2];
(b) at the end of paragraph (b) leave out 'and';
(c) at the end of paragraph (c) insert 'and
     (d) a database.'

6. Meaning of 'database'

After section 3 insert—

3A. 'Databases'

(1)[3] In this Part 'database' means a collection of independent works, data or other materials which—

  (a) are arranged in a systematic or methodical way, and
  (b) are individually accessible by electronic or other means.

(2) For the purposes of this Part a literary work consisting of a database is original if, and only if, by reason of the selection or arrangement of the contents of the database the database constitutes the author's own intellectual creation.'[4]

7. Meaning of 'adaptation' in relation to database[5]

In section 21 (infringement by making adaptation or act done in relation to adaptation) in subsection (3) —

(a) in paragraph (a), for 'other than a computer program or' substitute 'other than a computer program or a database, or in relation to a', and
(b) after paragraph (ab) insert—

'(ac) in relation to a database, means an arrangement or altered version of the database or a translation of it;'.

---

1   This part is exclusively concerned with amendment of the CDPA to the extent necessary to make its provisions consistent with the Database Directive as regards copyright protection of databases.
2   The Database Regulations distinguish between a 'compilation' and a 'database' as defined at s 3A. It is therefore possible for a collection of works which fall outside the definition of database (perhaps because they lack the necessary requirement of 'independence') to attract copyright protection on a 'compilation'. This latter term is not defined.
3   This implements Art 1(2) of the Database Directive verbatim. However, Art 1(3) of the Database Directive goes on to exclude from a database any computer programs which are used in 'the making or operation of databases accessible electronically'. The Regulations do not reflect this exclusion. This distinction could be of significance, in that lawful users of databases benefit from different provisions to lawful users of computer programs.
4   The criterion of intellectual creativity reflects Art 3(1) of the Database Directive.
5   Implementing the Database Directive, Art 5(6).

8. Research[1]

(1) In section 29 (research and private study), in subsection (1), after 'literary' insert 'work, other than a database, or a'.

(2) After subsection (1) of that section insert—

'(1A) Fair dealing with a database for the purposes of research or private study does not infringe any copyright in the database provided that the source is indicated.'.

(3) After subsection (4) of that section insert—

'(5) The doing of anything in relation to a database for the purposes of research for a commercial purpose is not fair dealing with the database.'.

9. Permitted acts in relation to databases[2]

After section 50C insert—

'Databases: permitted acts

50D. Acts permitted to lawful users of databases

(1) It is not an infringement of copyright in a database for a person who has a right to use the database or any part of the database, (whether under a licence to do any of the acts restricted by the copyright in the database or otherwise) to do, in the exercise of that right, anything which is necessary for the purposes of access to and use of the contents of the database or of that part of the database.

(2) Where an act which would otherwise infringe copyright in a database is permitted under this section, it is irrelevant whether or not there exists any term or condition in any agreement which purports to prohibit or restrict the act (such terms being, by virtue of section 296B, void).'.

10. Avoidance of certain terms

After section 296A insert—

'Databases

296B. Avoidance of certain terms relating to databases

Where under an agreement a person has a right to use a database or part of a database, any term or condition in the agreement shall be void in so far as it purports to prohibit or restrict the performance of any act which would but for section 50D infringe the copyright in the database'.

11. Defined expressions

In section 179 (index of defined expressions), in the appropriate place in alphabetical order insert—

---

1   This reflects certain of the optional exemptions set out in the Database Directive, Art 6(2). However, the research exemption in the Database Directive is limited to 'scientific' research (in the natural and human sciences): the exemption in the Database Regulations is wider than this. Furthermore, the Database Directive requires the 'sole purpose' to be research. Again, the Database Regulations do not reproduce this restriction. Persons who intend to rely on the research exemption under the Database Regulations, therefore, should be aware that there are questions as to the extent to which the Regulations adequately implement the Database Directive. A cautious interpretation based on the Database Directive is the safest course.

2   Implementing the Database Directive, Art 6(1).

'database   section 3A(1)'
'original (in relation to a database)   section 3A(2)'

PART III[1]

Database Right

12. Interpretation[2]

(1) In this Part—

'database' has the meaning given by section 3A(1) of the 1988 Act (as inserted by Regulation 6);

'extraction', in relation to any contents of a database means the permanent or temporary transfer of those contents to another medium by any means or in any form;

'investment' includes any investment, whether of financial, human or technical resources;

'jointly', in relation to the making of the database shall be construed in accordance with Regulation 14(6);

'lawful user', in relation to a database, means any person who (whether under a licence to do any of the acts restricted by any database right in the database or otherwise) has a right to use the database;

'maker', in relation to a database, shall be construed in accordance with Regulation 14;

're-utilisation', in relation to any contents of a database, means making those contents available to the public by any means;

'substantial', in relation to any investment, extraction or re-utilisation, means substantial in terms of quantity or quality or a combination of both.

(2) The making of a copy of a database available for use on terms that it will or may be returned otherwise than for direct or indirect economic or commercial advantage[3], through an establishment which is accessible to the public shall not be taken for the purposes of this Part to constitute extraction or re-utilisation of the contents of the database.

(3) Where the making of a copy of a database available through an establishment which is accessible to the public gives rise to a payment, the amount of which does not go beyond what is necessary to cover the costs of the establishment, there is no direct or indirect economic or commercial advantage for the purposes of paragraph (2).

(4) Paragraph (2) does not apply to the making of a copy of a database available for on-the-spot reference use.

(5) Where a copy of a database has been sold within the EEA by, or with the consent of, the owner of the database right in the database, the further sale within the EEA of that copy shall not be taken for the purposes of this Part to constitute extraction or re-utilisation of the contents of the database[4].

---

1   The Database Regulations reflect the Database Directive in dealing with copyright and the *sui generis* right in separate sections.

2   The definition of 'extraction' and 're-utilisation' follows Art 7(2) of the Database Directive closely. The definition of 'investment' reflects Recital 7 of the Database Directive and that of 'substantial' reflects Art 7(1).

3   This reflects the statement in Art 7(2) of the Database Directive that public lending is not an act of extraction or re-utilisation and hence not restricted. However, the Database Regulations go further than the Directive in trying to define 'public lending'.

4   Reflecting Art 7(2)(b) of the Database Directive.

13. Database right

(1) A property right ('database right') subsists, in accordance with this Part, in a database if there has been a substantial investment in obtaining, verifying or presenting the contents of the database[1].

(2) For the purposes of paragraph (1) it is immaterial whether or not the database or any of its contents are copyright works, within the meaning of Part I of the 1988 Act[2].

(3) This Regulation has effect subject to Regulation 18[3].

14. The maker of a database[4]

(1) Subject to paragraphs (2) to (4), the person who takes the initiative in obtaining, verifying or presenting the contents of a database and assumes the risk of investing in that obtaining, verification or presentation shall be regarded as the maker of, and as having made, the database.

(2) Where a database is made by an employee in the course of his employment, his employer shall be regarded as the maker of the database, subject to any agreement to the contrary[5].

(3) Subject to paragraph (4), where a database is made by Her Majesty or by an officer or servant of the Crown in the course of his duties, Her Majesty shall be regarded as the maker of the database.

(4) Where a database is made by or under the direction or control of the House of Commons or the House of Lords—

   (a)   the House by whom, or under whose direction or control, the database is made shall be regarded as the maker of the database, and

   (b)   if the database is made by or under the direction or control of both Houses, the two Houses shall be regarded as joint makers of the database.

(5) For the purposes of this Part a database is made jointly if two or more persons acting together in collaboration take the initiative in obtaining, verifying or presenting the contents of the database and assume the risk of investing in that obtaining, verification or presentation.

(6) Reference in this Part to the maker of a database shall, except as otherwise provided, be construed, in relation to a database which is made jointly, as references to all the makers of the database.

15. First ownership of database right

The maker of a database is the first owner of database right in it.

---

1   Reflecting almost verbatim Art 7(1) of the Database Directive.

2   Reflecting Art 7(4) of the Database Directive.

3   Which sets out the 'territorial' restrictions or the persons to whom Member States are to extend database rights.

4   This definition expands on Recital 41 of the Database Directive, which states:

      'the maker of a database is the person who takes the initiative and the risk of investing'.

      Recital 41 goes on to exclude subcontractors expressly from the definition of maker, on the grounds that a subcontractor, by the nature of his relationship with his principal, does not take the initiative and risk necessary to gain ownership of database right. This is not reflected in the Database Regulations.

5   This provision is permitted by Recital 29 of the Database Directive.

16. Acts infringing database right[1]

(1)   Subject to the provisions of this Part, a person infringes database right in a database if, without the consent of the owner of the right, he extracts or re-utilises all or a substantial part of the contents of the database.

(2)   For the purposes of this Part, the repeated and systematic extraction or re-utilisation of insubstantial parts of the contents of a database may amount to the extraction or re-utilisation of a substantial part of those contents[2].

17. Term of protection[3]

(1)   Database right in a database expires at the end of the period of fifteen years from the end of the calendar year in which the making of the database was completed.

(2)   Where a database is made available to the public before the end of the period referred to in paragraph (1), database right in the database shall expire fifteen years from the end of the calendar year in which the database was first made available to the public.

(3)   Any substantial change to the contents of a database, including a substantial change resulting from the accumulation of successive additions, deletions or alterations, which would result in the database being considered to be a substantial new investment shall qualify the database resulting from that investment for its own term of protection.

(4)   This Regulation has effect subject to Regulation 30.

18. Qualification for database right[4]

(1)   Database right does not subsist in a database unless, at the material time, its maker, or if it was made jointly, one or more of its makers, was—

(a)   an individual who was a national of an EEA state or habitually resident within the EEA,

(b)   a body which was incorporated under the law of an EEA state and which, at that time, satisfied one of the conditions in paragraph (2), or

(c)   a partnership or other unincorporated body which was formed under the law of an EEA state and which, at that time, satisfied the condition in paragraph (2)(a).

(2)   The conditions mentioned in paragraph (1)(b) and (c) are—

(a)   that the body has its central administration or principal place of business within the EEA, or

(b)   that the body has its registered office within the EEA and the body's operations are linked on an ongoing basis with the economy of an EEA state.

(3)   Paragraph (1) does not apply in any case falling within Regulation 14.

(4)   In this Regulation—

(a)   'EEA' and 'EEA state' have the meaning given by section 172A of the 1988 Act;

(b)   'the material time' means the time when the database was made, or if the making extended over a period, a substantial part of that period.

---

1   Reflecting Art 7(1) of the Database Directive.
2   This is easier to follow if read in conjunction with Art 7(5) of the Database Directive and Recital 42. These clarify that what is prohibited are acts which 'go beyond ... [the] legitimate rights [of the lawful user] and thereby harm the investment [of the maker]'.
3   Reflecting Art 10 of the Database Directive.
4   Reflecting Art 11 of the Database Directive.

19. Avoidance of certain terms affecting lawful users

(1)   A lawful user of a database which has been made available to the public in any manner shall be entitled to extract or re-utilise insubstantial parts of the contents of the database for any purpose[1].

(2)   Where under an agreement a person has a right to use a database, or part of a database, which has been made available to the public in any manner, any term or condition in the agreement shall be void in so far as it purports to prevent that person from extracting or re-utilising insubstantial parts of the contents of the database, or of that part of the database, for any purpose[2].

20. Exceptions to database right[3]

(1)   Database right in a database which has been made available to the public in any manner is not infringed by fair dealing with a substantial part of its contents if—

(a)   that part is extracted from the database by a person who is apart from this paragraph a lawful user of the database,

(b)   it is extracted for the purpose of illustration for teaching or research and not for any commercial purpose, and

(c)   the source is indicated.

(2)   The provisions of Schedule 1[4] specify other acts which may be done in relation to a database notwithstanding the existence of database right.

21. Acts permitted on assumption as to expiry of database right[5]

(1)   Database right in a database is not infringed by the extraction or re-utilisation of a substantial part of the contents of the database at a time when, or in pursuance of arrangements made at a time when—

(a)   it is not possible by reasonable inquiry to ascertain the identity of the maker, and

(b)   it is reasonable to assume that database right has expired.

(2)   In the case of a database alleged to have been made jointly, paragraph (1) applies in relation to each person alleged to be one of the makers.

22. Presumptions relevant to database right[6]

(1)   The following presumptions apply in proceedings brought by virtue of this Part of these Regulations with respect to a database.

---

1   Reflecting Art 8(1) of the Database Directive.
2   Reflecting Art 15 of the Database Directive.
3   This mirrors the exception for copyright, see footnote 1 at p 176, save that, for copyright, there is no requirement that the database be made available to the public. Nor do the exceptions to database right include the 'private study' exception which is available for copyright. The effect of this is to deprive the private study exception for copyright of its effect. As most databases which attract copyright will also satisfy the criterion for database right, a lawful user will not be able to rely on the private user exception without infringing database right. The situation will change on expiry of the database right, when the public user exception will become available. The comments at footnote 1 at p 176 about differences between the Database Directive and the Database Regulations also apply here.
4   Schedule 1 expands on the exception permitted under Art 9(c) for 'public security or an administrative or judicial procedure'.
5   The Database Directive does not make provision for this.
6   The Database Directive does not make provision for this.

(2) Where a name purporting to be that of the maker appeared on copies of the database as published, or on the database when it was made, the person whose name appeared shall be presumed, until the contrary is proved—

(a) to be the maker of the database, and
(b) to have made it in circumstances not falling within Regulation 14(2) to (4).

(3) Where copies of the database as published bear a label or a mark stating—

(a) that a named person was the maker of the database, or
(b) that the database was first published in a specified year,

the label or mark shall be admissible as evidence of the facts stated and shall be presumed to be correct until the contrary is proved.

(4) In the case of a database alleged to have been made jointly, paragraphs (2) and (3), so far as is applicable, apply in relation to each person alleged to be one of the makers.

23. Application of copyright provisions to database right

The following provisions of the 1988 Act—

sections 90 to 93 (dealing with rights in copyright works[1]);
sections 96 to 98 (rights and remedies of copyright owner[2]);
sections 101 and 102 (rights and remedies of exclusive licensee);

apply in relation to database right and databases in which that right subsists as they apply in relation to copyright and copyright works.

24. Licensing of database right

The provisions of Schedule 2 have effect with respect to the licensing of database right.

25. Database right: jurisdiction of Copyright Tribunal

(1) The Copyright Tribunal has jurisdiction under this Part to hear and determine proceedings under the following provisions of Schedule 2—

(a) paragraph 3, 4 or 5 (reference of licensing scheme);
(b) paragraph 6 or 7 (application with respect to licence under licensing scheme);
(c) paragraph 10, 11 or 12 (reference or application with respect to licence by licensing body).

(2) The provisions of Chapter VIII of Part I of the 1988 Act (general provisions relating to the Copyright Tribunal) apply in relation to the Tribunal when exercising any jurisdiction under this Part.

(3) Provision shall be made by rules under section 150 of the 1988 Act prohibiting the Tribunal from entertaining a reference under paragraph 3, 4 or 5 of Schedule 2 (reference of licensing scheme) by a representative organisation unless the Tribunal is satisfied that the organisation is reasonably representative of the class of persons which it claims to represent.

---

1   This implements Art 7(3) of the Database Directive.
2   This implements Art 12 of the Database Directive.

PART IV

Savings and Transitional Provisions

26. Introductory

(1) In this Part 'commencement' means the commencement of these Regulations.

(2) Expressions used in this Part which are defined for the purposes of Part I of the 1988 Act have the same meaning as in that Part.

27. General Rule

Subject to Regulations 28 and 29, these Regulations apply to databases made before or after commencement.

28. General Savings[1]

(1) Nothing in these Regulations affects any agreement made before commencement.

(2) No act done—

(a) before commencement, or

(b) after commencement, in pursuance of an agreement made before commencement,

shall be regarded as an infringement of database right in a database.

29. Saving for copyright in certain existing databases[2]

(1) Where a database—

(a) was created on or before 27th March 1996, and

(b) is a copyright work immediately before commencement,

copyright shall continue to subsist in the database for the remainder of its copyright term.

(2) In this Regulation 'copyright term' means the period of the duration of copyright under section 12 of the 1988 Act (duration of copyright in literary, dramatic, musical or artistic work).

30. Database right: term applicable to certain existing databases[3]

Where:

(a) the making of a database was completed on or after 1st January 1983, and

(b) on commencement, database right begins to subsist in the database,

database right shall subsist in the database for the period of fifteen years beginning with 1st January 1998.

---

1   Reflecting Art 14(4) of the Database Directive.

2   This implements Art 14(1) and (2) of the Database Directive. The intent of Art 14(2) is to protect existing databases which do not satisfy the intellectual creativity criterion of the Directive, but which would otherwise attract copyright protection in a Member State. Regulation 29 does not make this distinction clear.

3   Reflecting Art 14(3) and (5) of the Database Directive.

SCHEDULE 1

Regulation 20(2)

EXCEPTIONS TO DATABASE RIGHT FOR PUBLIC ADMINISTRATION

1. Parliamentary and judicial proceedings

Database right in a database is not infringed by anything done for the purposes of parliamentary or judicial proceedings or for the purposes of reporting such proceedings.

2. Royal Commissions and statutory inquiries

(1) Database right in a database is not infringed by anything done for—

    (a)   the purposes of the proceedings of a Royal Commission or statutory inquiry, or

    (b)   the purpose of reporting any such proceedings held in public.

(2) Database right in a database is not infringed by the issue to the public of copies of the report of a Royal Commission or statutory inquiry containing the contents of the database.

(3) In this paragraph 'Royal Commission' and 'statutory inquiry' have the same meaning as in section 46 of the 1988 Act.

3. Material open to public inspection or on official register

(1) Where the contents of a database are open to public inspection pursuant to a statutory requirement, or are on a statutory register, database right in the database is not infringed by the extraction of all or a substantial part of the contents containing factual information of any description, by or with the authority of the appropriate person, for a purpose which does not involve re-utilisation of all or a substantial part of the contents.

(2) Where the contents of a database are open to public inspection pursuant to a statutory requirement, database right in the database is not infringed by the extraction or re-utilisation of all or a substantial part of the contents, by or with the authority of the appropriate person, for the purpose of enabling the contents to be inspected at a more convenient time or place or otherwise facilitating the exercise of any right for the purpose of which the requirement is imposed.

(3) Where the contents of a database which is open to public inspection pursuant to a statutory requirement, or which is on a statutory register, contain information about matters of general scientific, commercial or economic interest, database right in the database is not infringed by the extraction or re-utilisation of all or a substantial part of the contents, by or with the authority of the appropriate person, for the purpose of disseminating that information.

(4) In this paragraph—

'appropriate person' means the person required to make the contents of the database open to public inspection or, as the case may be, the person maintaining the register;

'statutory register' means a register maintained in pursuance of a statutory requirement; and

'statutory requirement' means a requirement imposed by provision made by or under an enactment.

4. Material communicated to the Crown in the course of public business

(1)   This paragraph applies where the contents of a database have in the course of public business been communicated to the Crown for any purpose, by or with the licence of the owner of the database right and a document or other material thing recording or embodying the contents of the database is owned by or in the custody or control of the Crown.

(2)   The Crown may, for the purpose for which the contents of the database were communicated to it, or any related purpose which could reasonably have been anticipated by the owner of the database right in the database, extract or re-utilise all or a substantial part of the contents without infringing database right in the database.

(3)   The Crown may not re-utilise the contents of a database by virtue of this paragraph if the contents have previously been published otherwise than by virtue of this paragraph.

(4)   In sub-paragraph (1) 'public business' includes any activity carried on by the Crown.

(5)   This paragraph has effect subject to any agreement to the contrary between the Crown and the owner of the database right in the database.

5. Public Records

The contents of a database which are comprised in public records within the meaning of the Public Records Act 1958, the Public Records (Scotland) Act 1937 or the Public Records Act (Northern Ireland) 1923 which are open to public inspection in pursuance of that Act, may be re-utilised by or with the authority of any officer appointed under that Act, without infringement of database right in the database.

6. Acts done under statutory authority

(1)   Where the doing of a particular act is specifically authorised by an Act of Parliament, whenever passed, then, unless the Act provides otherwise, the doing of that act does not infringe database right in a database.

(2)   Sub-paragraph (1) applies in relation to an enactment contained in Northern Ireland legislation as it applies in relation to an Act of Parliament.

(3)   Nothing in this paragraph shall be construed as excluding any defence of statutory authority otherwise available under or by virtue of any enactment.

SCHEDULE 2

Regulation 24

LICENSING OF DATABASE RIGHT

1. Licensing scheme and licensing bodies

(1)   In this Schedule a 'licensing scheme' means a scheme setting out—

(a)   the classes of case in which the operator of the scheme, or the person on whose behalf he acts, is willing to grant database right licences, and

(b)   the terms on which licences would be granted in those classes of case;

and for this purpose a 'scheme' includes anything in the nature of a scheme, whether described as a scheme or as a tariff or by any other name.

(2) In this Schedule a 'licensing body' means a society or other organisation which has as its main object, or one of its main objects, the negotiating or granting, whether as owner or prospective owner of a database right or as agent for him, of database right licences, and whose objects include the granting of licences covering the databases of more than one maker.

(3) In this paragraph 'database right licences' means licences to do, or authorise the doing of, any of the things for which consent is required under Regulation 16.

2.   Paragraphs 3 to 8 apply to licensing schemes which are operated by licensing bodies and cover databases of more than one maker so far as they relate to licences for extracting or re-utilising all or a substantial part of the contents of a database; and references in those paragraphs to a licensing scheme shall be construed accordingly.

3.   Reference of proposed licensing scheme to tribunal

(1) The terms of a licensing scheme proposed to be operated by a licensing body may be referred to the Copyright Tribunal by an organisation claiming to be representative of persons claiming that they require licences in cases of a description to which the scheme would apply, either generally or in relation to any description of case.

(2) The Tribunal shall first decide whether to entertain the reference, and may decline to do so on the ground that the reference is premature.

(3) If the Tribunal decides to entertain the reference it shall consider the matter referred and make such order, either confirming or varying the proposed scheme, either generally or so far as it relates to cases of the description to which the reference relates, as the Tribunal may determine to be reasonable in the circumstances.

(4) The order may be made so as to be in force indefinitely or for such period as the Tribunal may determine.

4.   Reference of proposed licensing scheme to tribunal

(1) If while a licensing scheme is in operation a dispute arises between the operator of the scheme and—

(a) a person claiming that he requires a licence in a case of a description to which the scheme applies, or

(b) an organisation claiming to be representative of such persons,

that person or organisation may refer the scheme to the Copyright Tribunal in so far as it relates to cases of that description.

(2) A scheme which has been referred to the Tribunal under this paragraph shall remain in operation until proceedings on the reference are concluded.

(3) The Tribunal shall consider the matter in dispute and make such order, either confirming or varying the scheme so far as it relates to cases of the description to which the reference relates, as the Tribunal may determine to be reasonable in the circumstances.

(4) The order may be made so as to be in force indefinitely or for such period as the Tribunal may determine.

5.   Further reference of scheme to tribunal

(1) Where the Copyright Tribunal has on a previous reference of a licensing scheme under paragraph 3 or 4, or under this paragraph, made an order with respect to the scheme, then, while the order remains in force—

(a) the operator of the scheme,

(b)   a person claiming that he requires a licence in a case of the description to which the order applies, or

(c)   an organisation claiming to be representative of such persons,

may refer the scheme again to the Tribunal so far as it relates to cases of that description.

(2)   A licensing scheme shall not, except with the special leave of the Tribunal, be referred again to the Tribunal in respect of the same description of cases—

(a)   within twelve months from the date of the order on the previous reference, or

(b)   if the order was made so as to be in force for 15 months or less, until the last three months before the expiry of the order.

(3)   A scheme which has been referred to the Tribunal under this section shall remain in operation until proceedings on the reference are concluded.

(4)   The Tribunal shall consider the matter in dispute and make such order, either confirming, varying or further varying the scheme so far as it relates to cases of the description to which the reference relates, as the Tribunal may determine to be reasonable in the circumstances.

(5)   The order may be made so as to be in force indefinitely or for such period as the Tribunal may determine.

6.   Application for grant of licence in connection with licensing scheme

(1)   A person who claims, in a case covered by a licensing scheme, that the operator of the scheme has refused to grant him or procure the grant to him of a licence in accordance with the scheme, or has failed to do so within a reasonable time after being asked, may apply to the Copyright Tribunal.

(2)   A person who claims, in a case excluded from a licensing scheme, that the operator of the scheme either:

(a)   has refused to grant him a licence or procure the grant to him of a licence, or has failed to do so within a reasonable time of being asked, and that in the circumstances it is unreasonable that a licence should not be granted, or

(b)   proposes terms for a licence which are unreasonable,

may apply to the Copyright Tribunal.

(3)   A case shall be regarded as excluded from a licensing scheme for the purposes of sub-paragraph (2) if:

(a)   the scheme provides for the grant of licences subject to terms excepting matters from the licence and the case falls within such an exception, or

(b)   the case is so similar to those in which licences are granted under the scheme that it is unreasonable that it should not be dealt with in the same way.

(4)   If the Tribunal is satisfied that the claim is well-founded, it shall make an order declaring that, in respect of the matters specified in the order, the applicant is entitled to a licence on such terms as the Tribunal may determine to be applicable in accordance with the scheme or, as the case may be, to be reasonable in the circumstances.

(5)   The order may be made so as to be in force indefinitely or for such period as the Tribunal may determine.

7. Application for review of order as to entitlement to licence

(1) Where the Copyright Tribunal has made an order under paragraph 6 that a person is entitled to a licence under a licensing scheme, the operator of the scheme or the original applicant may apply to the Tribunal to review its order.

(2) An application shall not be made, except with the special leave of the Tribunal—

 (a) within twelve months from the date of the order, or of the decision on a previous application under this section, or

 (b) if the order was made so as to be in force for 15 months or less, or as a result of the decision on a previous application under this section is due to expire within 15 months of that decision, until the last three months before the expiry date.

(3) The Tribunal shall on an application for review confirm or vary its order as the Tribunal may determine to be reasonable having regard to the terms applicable in accordance with the licensing scheme or, as the case may be, the circumstances of the case.

8. Effect of order of tribunal as to licensing scheme

(1) A licensing scheme which has been confirmed or varied by the Copyright Tribunal—

 (a) under paragraph 3 (reference of terms of proposed scheme), or

 (b) under paragraph 4 or 5 (reference of existing scheme to Tribunal),

shall be in force or, as the case may be, remain in operation, so far as it relates to the description of case in respect of which the order was made, so long as the order remains in force.

(2) While the order is in force a person who in a case of a class to which the order applies—

 (a) pays to the operator of the scheme any charges payable under the scheme in respect of a licence covering the case in question or, if the amount cannot be ascertained, gives an undertaking to the operator to pay them when ascertained, and

 (b) complies with the other terms applicable to such a licence under the scheme,

shall be in the same position as regards infringement of database right as if he had at all material times been the holder of a licence granted by the owner of the database right in question in accordance with the scheme.

(3) The Tribunal may direct that the order, so far as it varies the amount of charges payable, has effect from a date before that on which it is made, but not earlier than the date on which the reference was made or, if later, on which the scheme came into operation.

If such a direction is made:

 (a) any necessary repayments, or further payments, shall be made in respect of charges already paid, and

 (b) the reference in sub-paragraph (2)(a) to the charges payable under the scheme shall be construed as a reference to the charges so payable by virtue of the order.

No such direction may be made where sub-paragraph (4) below applies.

(4) Where the Tribunal has made an order under paragraph 6 (order as to entitlement to licence under licensing scheme) and the order remains in force, the person in whose favour the order is made shall if he—

 (a) pays to the operator of the scheme any charges payable in accordance with the order or, if the amount cannot be ascertained, gives an undertaking to pay the charges when ascertained, and

(b)   complies with the other terms specified in the order,

be in the same position as regards infringement of database right as if he had at all material times been the holder of a licence granted by the owner of the database right in question on the terms specified in the order.

9.   References and applications with respect to licences by licensing bodies

Paragraphs 10 to 13 (references and applications with respect to licensing by licensing bodies) apply to licences relating to database right which cover databases of more than one maker granted by a licensing body otherwise than in pursuance of a licensing scheme, so far as the licences authorise extracting or re-utilising all or a substantial part of the contents of a database; and references in those paragraphs to a licence shall be construed accordingly.

10.   Reference to tribunal of proposed licence

(1)   The terms on which a licensing body proposes to grant a licence may be referred to the Copyright Tribunal by the prospective licensee.
(2)   The Tribunal shall first decide whether to entertain the reference, and may decline to do so on the ground that the reference is premature.
(3)   If the Tribunal decides to entertain the reference it shall consider the terms of the proposed licence and make such order, either confirming or varying the terms, as it may determine to be reasonable in the circumstances.
(4)   The order may be made so as to be in force indefinitely or for such period as the Tribunal may determine.

11.   Reference to tribunal of expiring licence

(1)   A licensee under a licence which is due to expire, by effluxion of time or as a result of notice given by the licensing body, may apply to the Copyright Tribunal on the ground that it is unreasonable in the circumstances that the licence should cease to be in force.
(2)   Such an application may not be made until the last three months before the licence is due to expire.
(3)   A licence in respect of which a reference has been made to the Tribunal shall remain in operation until proceedings on the reference are concluded.
(4)   If the Tribunal finds the application well-founded, it shall make an order declaring that the licensee shall continue to be entitled to the benefit of the licence on such terms as the Tribunal may determine to be reasonable in the circumstances.
(5)   An order of the Tribunal under this section may be made so as to be in force indefinitely or for such period as the Tribunal may determine.

12.   Application for review of order as to licence

(1)   Where the Copyright Tribunal has made an order under paragraph 10 or 11, the licensing body or the person entitled to the benefit of the order may apply to the Tribunal to review its order.
(2)   An application shall not be made, except with the special leave of the Tribunal—

(a)   within twelve months from the date of the order or of the decision on a previous application under this paragraph, or
(b)   if the order was made so as to be in force for 15 months or less, or as a result of the decision on a previous application under this section is due to expire within 15 months of that decision, until the last three months before the expiry date.

(3)   The Tribunal shall on an application for review confirm or vary its order as the Tribunal may determine to be reasonable in the circumstances.

13.   Effect of order or tribunal as to licence

(1)   Where the Copyright Tribunal has made an order under paragraph 10 or 11 and the order remains in force, the person entitled to the benefit of the order shall if he—

(a)   pays to the licensing body any charges payable in accordance with the order or, if the amount cannot be ascertained, gives an undertaking to pay the charges when ascertained, and

(b)   complies with the other terms specified in the order,

be in the same position as regards infringement of database right as if he had at all material times been the holder of a licence granted by the owner of the database right in question on the terms specified in the order.

(2)   The benefit of the order may be assigned—

(a)   in the case of an order under paragraph 10, if assignment is not prohibited under the terms of the Tribunal's order; and

(b)   in the case of an order under paragraph 11, if assignment was not prohibited under the terms of the original licence.

(3)   The Tribunal may direct that an order under paragraph 10 or 11, or an order under paragraph 12 varying such an order, so far as it varies the amount of charges payable, has effect from a date before that on which it is made, but not earlier than the date on which the reference or application was made or, if later, on which the licence was granted or, as the case may be, was due to expire.

If such a direction is made—

(a)   any necessary repayments, or further payments, shall be made in respect of charges already paid, and

(b)   the reference in sub-paragraph (1)(a) to the charges payable in accordance with the order shall be construed, where the order is varied by a later order, as a reference to the charges so payable by virtue of the later order.

14.   General considerations: unreasonable discrimination

In determining what is reasonable on a reference or application under this Schedule relating to a licensing scheme or licence, the Copyright Tribunal shall have regard to—

(a)   the availability of other schemes, or the granting of other licences, to other persons in similar circumstances, and

(b)   the terms of those schemes or licences,

and shall exercise its powers so as to secure that there is no unreasonable discrimination between licensees, or prospective licensees, under the scheme or licence to which the reference or application relates and licensees under other schemes operated by, or other licences granted by, the same person.

15.   Powers exercisable in consequence of competition report

(1)   Where the matters specified in a report of the Monopolies and Mergers Commission as being those which in the Commission's opinion operate, may be expected to operate or have operated against the public interest include—

(a) conditions in licences granted by the owner of database right in a database restricting the use of the database by the licensee or the right of the owner of the database right to grant other licences, or

(b) a refusal of an owner of database right to grant licences on reasonable terms,

the powers conferred by Part I of Schedule 8 to the Fair Trading Act 1973 (powers exercisable for purpose of remedying or preventing adverse effects specified in report of Commission) include power to cancel or modify those conditions and, instead or in addition, to provide that licences in respect of the database right shall be available as of right.

(2) The references in sections 56(2) and 72(2) of that Act, and sections 10(2) and 12(5) of the Competition Act 1980, to the powers specified in that Part of that Schedule shall be construed accordingly.

(3) The terms of a licence available by virtue of this paragraph shall, in default of agreement, be settled by the Copyright Tribunal on an application by the person requiring the licence; and terms so settled shall authorise the licensee to do everything in respect of which a licence is so available.

(4) Where the terms of a licence are settled by the Tribunal, the licence has effect from the date on which the application to the Tribunal was made.

Appendix 5

COPYRIGHT, DESIGNS AND PATENTS ACT 1988 AS AMENDED[1] TO REFLECT THE COMPUTER PROGRAMS AND DATABASE REGULATIONS (EXTRACTS)

3   Literary, dramatic and musical works

(1)   In this Part—

'literary work' means any work, other than a dramatic or musical work, which is written, spoken or sung, and accordingly includes—

(a)   a table or compilation *other than a database*[2] ~~and~~

(b)   a computer program ~~and~~

(c)   preparatory design material for a computer program[3] *and*

(d)   a database[2].

'dramatic work' includes a work of dance or mime; and

'musical work' means a work consisting of music, exclusive of any words or action intended to be sung, spoken or performed with the music.

(2)   Copyright does not subsist in a literary, dramatic or musical work unless and until it is recorded, in writing or otherwise; and references in this Part to the time at which such a work is made are to the time at which it is so recorded.

(3)   It is immaterial for the purposes of subsection (2) whether the work is recorded by or with the permission of the author; and where it is not recorded by the author, nothing in that subsection affects the question whether copyright subsists in the record as distinct from the work recorded.

3A   (1)   In this Part 'database' means a collection of independent works, data or materials which—

(a)   are arranged in a systematic or methodical way, and

(b)   are individually accessible by electronic or other means.

---

1   Amendments made by the Software Regulations are shown by single underlining (for inserted text) or single strike-through (for deleted text). Amendments made by the Database Regulations are shown in italics: additions are also underlined and deletions marked by a strike-through.

All amendments made by the Software Regulations are subject to reg 12(2): agreements made before 1 January 1993 are not to be affected. Similarly, all amendments made by the Database Regulations are subject to reg 27(1): agreements made before 1 January 1998 are not to be affected.

2   Text added by the Database Regulations, regs 4 and 5.

3   Text added by the Software Regulations, regs 2 and 3.

(2)   For the purposes of this Part, a literary work consisting of a database is original if, and only if, by reason of the selection or arrangement of the contents of the database the database constitutes the author's own intellectual creation[1].

18   Infringement by issue of copies to the public[2]

(1)   The issue to the public of copies of the work is an act restricted by the copyright in every description of copyright work.

(2)   References in this Part to the issue to the public of copies of a work are except where the work is a computer program to the act of putting into circulation copies not previously put into circulation, in the United Kingdom or elsewhere, and not to—

(a)   any subsequent distribution, sale, hiring or loan of those copies, or

(b)   any subsequent importation of those copies into the United Kingdom;

except that in relation to sound recordings and films the restricted act of issuing copies to the public includes any rental of copies to the public.

(3)   References in this Part to the issue to the public of copies of a work where the work is a computer program are to the act of putting into circulation copies of that program not previously put into circulation in the United Kingdom or any other Member State, by or with the consent of the copyright owner, and not to—

(a)   any subsequent distribution, sale, hiring or loan of those copies, or

(b)   any subsequent importation of those copies into the United Kingdom,

except that the restricted act of issuing copies to the public includes any rental of copies to the public.

21   Infringement by making adaptation or act done in relation to adaptation

(1)   The making of an adaptation of the work is an act restricted by the copyright in a literary, dramatic or musical work.

For this purpose an adaptation is made when it is recorded, in writing or otherwise.

(2)   The doing of any of the acts specified in sections 17 to 20, or subsection (1) above, in relation to an adaptation of the work is also an act restricted by the copyright in a literary, dramatic or musical work.

For this purpose it is immaterial whether the adaptation has been recorded, in writing or otherwise, at the time the act is done.

(3)   In this Part 'adaptation'—

(a)   in relation to a literary work, other than a computer program[3] or *a database or in relation to a*[4] dramatic work means—

(i)   a translation of the work;

(ii)   a version of a dramatic work in which it is converted into a non-dramatic work or, as the case may be, of a non-dramatic work in which it is converted into a dramatic work;

---

1   Text added by the Database Regulations, regs 4 and 6.
2   Text added/amended by the Software Regulations, regs 2 and 4.
3   Text added by the Software Regulations, regs 2, 5(1) and (2).
4   Text added by the Database Regulations, regs 4 and 7.

(iii)   a version of the work in which the story or action is conveyed wholly or mainly by means of pictures in a form suitable for reproduction in a book, or in a newspaper, magazine or similar periodical;

(ab)   <u>in relation to a computer program, means an arrangement or altered version of the program or a translation of it</u>[1]

(ac)   *in relation to a database, means an arrangement or altered version of the database or a translation of it*[2]

(b)   in relation to a musical work, means an arrangement or transcription of the work.

(4)   In relation to a computer program a 'translation' includes a version of the program in which it is converted into or out of a computer language or code or into a different computer language or code ~~otherwise than incidentally in the course of running the program~~.[3]

(5)   No inference shall be drawn from this section as to what does or does not amount to copying a work.

Infringing Copies

27   Meaning of 'infringing copy'

(1)   In this Part 'infringing copy', in relation to a copyright work, shall be construed in accordance with this section.

(2)   An article is an infringing copy if its making constituted an infringement of the copyright in the work in question.

(3)   <u>Subject to subsection (3A)</u>[4] an article is also an infringing copy if—

(a)   it has been or is proposed to be imported into the United Kingdom, and

(b)   its making in the United Kingdom would have constituted an infringement of the copyright in the work in question, or a breach of an exclusive licence agreement relating to that work.

(3A)   <u>A copy of a computer program which has previously been sold in any other Member State, by or with the consent of the copyright owner, is not an infringing copy for the purposes of subsection (3)</u>[5].

(4)   Where in any proceedings the question arises whether an article is an infringing copy and it is shown—

(a)   that the article is a copy of the work, and

(b)   that copyright subsists in the work or has subsisted at any time,

it shall be presumed until the contrary is proved that the article was made at a time when copyright subsisted in the work.

(5)   Nothing in subsection (3) shall be construed as applying to an article which may lawfully be imported into the United Kingdom by virtue of any enforceable Community right within the meaning of section 2(1) of the European Communities Act 1972.

(6)   In this Part 'infringing copy' includes a copy falling to be treated as an infringing copy by virtue of any of the following provisions—

section 32(5) (copies made for purposes of instruction or examination),

---

1   See footnote 3 at p 192.
2   See footnote 4 at p 193.
3   Text repealed by the Software Regulations, regs 2 and 5(3).
4   Text added by the Software Regulations, regs 2 and 6.
5   Text added by the Software Regulations, regs 2 and 6.

section 35(3) (recordings made by educational establishments for educational purposes),
section 36(5) (reprographic copying by educational establishments for purposes of instruction),
section 37(3)(b) (copies made by librarian or archivist in reliance on false declaration),
section 56(2) (further copies, adaptations, etc. of work in electronic form retained on transfer of principal copy),
section 63(2) (copies made for purpose of advertising artistic work for sale),
section 68(4) (copies made for purpose of broadcast or cable programme), or
any provision of an order under section 141 (statutory licence for certain reprographic copying by educational establishments).

29 Research and private study

(1) Fair dealing with a literary *work, other than a database or a*[1] dramatic, musical or artistic work for the purposes of research or private study does not infringe any copyright in the work or, in the case of a published edition, in the typographical arrangement.

(1A) Fair dealing with a database for the purposes of research or private study does not infringe any copyright in the database provided that the source is indicated.[2]

(2) Fair dealing with the typographical arrangement of a published edition for the purposes mentioned in subsection (1) does not infringe any copyright in the arrangement.

(3) Copying by a person other than the researcher or student himself is not fair dealing if—

    (a) in the case of a librarian, or a person acting on behalf of a librarian, he does anything which regulations under section 40 would not permit to be done under section 38 or 39 (articles or parts of published works: restriction on multiple copies of same material), or

    (b) in any other case, the person doing the copying knows or has reason to believe that it will result in copies of substantially the same material being provided to more than one person at substantially the same time and for substantially the same purpose.

(4) It is not fair dealing—

    (a) to convert a computer program expressed in a low level language into a version expressed in a higher level language, or

    (b) incidentally in the course of so converting the program, to copy it,

these acts being permitted if done in accordance with section 50B (decompilation).[3]

(5) The doing of anything in relation to a database for the purposes of research for a commercial purpose is not fair dealing with the database.[4]

Computer programs: lawful users

50 Back up copies[5]

(1) It is not an infringement of copyright for a lawful user of a copy of a computer program to make any back up copy of it which it is necessary for him to have for the purposes of his lawful use.

---

1   Text added by the Database Regulations, regs 4 and 8.
2   Text added by the Database Regulations, regs 4 and 8.
3   Text added by the Software Regulations, regs 2 and 7.
4   Text added by the Database Regulations, regs 4 and 8.
5   Text for ss 50A, 50B and 50C added by the Software Regulations, regs 2 and 8.

(2) For the purposes of this section and sections 50B and 50C a person is a lawful user of a computer program if (whether under a licence to do any acts restricted by the copyright in the program or otherwise), he has a right to use the program.

(3) Where an act is permitted under this section, it is irrelevant whether or not there exists any term or condition in an agreement which purports to prohibit or restrict the act (such terms being, by virtue of section 296A, void).

50B   Decompilation

(1) It is not an infringement of copyright for a lawful user of a copy of a computer program expressed in a low level language—

(a)   to convert it into a version expressed in a higher level language, or

(b)   incidentally in the course of so converting the program, to copy it,

(that is, to 'decompile' it), provided that the conditions in subsection (2) are met.

(2) The conditions are that—

(a)   it is necessary to decompile the program to obtain the information necessary to create an independent program which can be operated with the program decompiled or with another program ('the permitted objective'); and

(b)   the information so obtained is not used for any purpose other than the permitted objective.

(3) In particular, the conditions in subsection (2) are not met if the lawful user—

(a)   has readily available to him the information necessary to achieve the permitted objective;

(b)   does not confine the decompiling to such acts as are necessary to achieve the permitted objective;

(c)   supplies the information obtained by the decompiling to any person to whom it is not necessary to supply it in order to achieve the permitted objective; or

(d)   uses the information to create a program which is substantially similar in its expression to the program decompiled or to do any act restricted by copyright.

(4) Where an act is permitted under this section, it is irrelevant whether or not there exists any term or condition in an agreement which purports to prohibit or restrict the act (such terms being, by virtue of section 296A, void).

50C   Other acts permitted to lawful users

(1) It is not an infringement of copyright for a lawful user of a copy of a computer program to copy or adapt it, provided that the copying or adapting—

(a)   is necessary for his lawful use; and

(b)   is not prohibited under any term or condition of an agreement regulating the circumstances in which his use is lawful.

(2) It may, in particular, be necessary for the lawful use of a computer program to copy it or adapt it for the purpose of correcting errors in it.

(3) This section does not apply to any copying or adapting permitted under section 50A or 50B.

50D   *Databases: permitted acts*

(1)   *It is not an infringement of copyright in a database for a person who has a right to use the database or any part of the database (whether under a licence to do any of the acts restricted by the copyright in the database or otherwise) to do in the exercise of that right, anything which is necessary for the purposes of access to and use of the contents of the database or of that part of the database.*

(2)   *Where an act which would otherwise infringe copyright in a database is permitted under this section, it is irrelevant whether or not there exists any term or condition in any agreement which purports to prohibit or restrict the act (such terms being, by virtue of section 296B, void).*[1]

179   Index of defined expressions

The following Table shows provisions defining or otherwise explaining expressions used in this Part (other than provisions defining or explaining an expression used only in the same section)—

database	*section 3A(1)*[2]
lawful user (in sections 50A to 50C)	section 50A(2)[3]
original (in relation to a database)	*section 3A(2)*[4]

Devices designed to circumvent copy-protection

296   Devices designed to circumvent copy-protection

(1)   This section applies where copies of a copyright work are issued to the public, by or with the licence of the copyright owner, in an electronic form which is copy-protected.

(2)   The person issuing the copies to the public has the same rights against a person who, knowing or having reason to believe that it will be used to make infringing copies—

(a)   makes, imports, sells or lets for hire, offers or exposes for sale or hire, or advertises for sale or hire, any device or means specifically designed or adapted to circumvent the form of copy-protection employed, or

(b)   publishes information intended to enable or assist persons to circumvent that form of copy-protection,

as a copyright owner has in respect of an infringement of copyright.

(2A)   Where the copies being issued to the public as mentioned in subsection (1) are copies of a computer program, subsection (2) applies as if for the words 'or advertises for sale or hire' there were substituted 'advertises for sale or hire or possesses in the course of a business'.[5]

(3)   Further, he has the same rights under section 99 or 100 (delivery up or seizure of certain articles) in relation to any such device or means which a person has in his possession, custody or control with the intention that it should be used to make infringing copies of copyright works, as a copyright owner has in relation to an infringing copy.

(4)   References in this section to copy-protection include any device or means intended to prevent or restrict copying of a work or to impair the quality of copies made.

(5)   Expressions used in this section which are defined for the purposes of Part I of this Act (copyright) have the same meaning as in that Part.

---

1   Text added by the Database Regulations, regs 4 and 9.
2   Text added by the Database Regulations, regs 4 and 11.
3   Text added by the Software Regulations, regs 2 and 9.
4   See footnote 3 above.
5   Text added by the Software Regulations, regs 2 and 10.

(6)   The following provisions apply in relation to proceedings under this section as in relation to proceedings under Part I (copyright)—

(a)   sections 104 to 106 of this Act (presumptions as to certain matters relating to copyright), and

(b)   section 72 of the Supreme Court Act 1981, section 15 of the Law Reform (Miscellaneous Provisions) (Scotland) Act 1985 and section 94A of the Judicature (Northern Ireland) Act 1978 (withdrawal of privilege against self-incrimination in certain proceedings relating to intellectual property);

and section 114 of this Act applies, with the necessary modifications, in relation to the disposal of anything delivered up or seized by virtue of subsection (3) above.

Computer programs

296A   Avoidance of certain terms

(1)   Where a person has the use of a computer program under an agreement, any term or condition in the agreement shall be void in so far as it purports to prohibit or restrict—

(a)   the making of any back up copy of the program which it is necessary for him to have for the purposes of the agreed use;

(b)   where the conditions in section 50B(2) are met, the decompiling of the program; or

(c)   the use of any device or means to observe, study or test the functioning of the program in order to understand the ideas and principles which underlie any element of the program.

(2)   In this section, decompile, in relation to a computer program, has the same meaning as in section 50B.[1]

Databases

296B *Where under an agreement a person has a right to use a database or part of a database, any term or condition in the agreement shall be void in so far as it purports to prohibit or restrict the performance of any act which would but for section 50D infringe the copyright in the database.*[2]

---

1   Text added by the Software Regulations, regs 2 and 11.
2   Text added by the Database Regulations, regs 4 and 10.

Appendix 6

THE BERNE CONVENTION FOR THE PROTECTION OF LITERARY AND ARTISTIC WORKS OF SEPTEMBER 1886

2 October 1979[1]

Article 1

The countries to which this Convention applies constitute a Union for the protection of the rights of authors in their literary and artistic works.

Article 2

(1) The expression 'literary and artistic works' shall include every production in the literary, scientific and artistic domain, whatever may be the mode or form of its expression, such as books, pamphlets and other writings; lectures, addresses, sermons and other works of the same nature; dramatic or dramatico-musical works; choreographic works and entertainments in dumb show; musical compositions with or without words; cinematographic works to which are assimilated works expressed by a process analogous to cinematography; works of drawing, painting, architecture, sculpture, engraving and lithography; photographic works to which are assimilated works expressed by a process analogous to photography; works of applied art; illustrations, maps, plans, sketches and three-dimensional works relative to geography, topography, architecture or science.

(2) It shall, however, be a matter for legislation in the countries of the Union to prescribe that works in general or any specified categories of works shall not be protected unless they have been fixed in some material form.

(3) Translations, adaptations, arrangements of music and other alterations of a literary or artistic work shall be protected as original works without prejudice to the copyright in the original work.

(4) It shall be a matter for legislation in the countries of the Union to determine the protection to be granted to official texts of a legislative, administrative and legal nature, and to official translations of such texts.

(5) Collections of literary or artistic works such as encyclopaedias and anthologies which, by reason of the selection and arrangement of their contents, constitute intellectual creations shall be protected as such, without prejudice to the copyright in each of the works forming part of such collections.

---

1 Berne Convention for the Protection of Literary and Artistic Works, of September 1886. Completed at Paris on 4 May 1896, Revised at Berlin on 13 November 1908, Completed at Berne on 20 March 1914, Revised at Rome on 2 June 1928, at Brussels on 26 June 1948, at Stockholm on 14 July 1967, and at Paris on 24 July 1971, amended on 2 October 1979.

(6) The works mentioned in this article shall enjoy protection in all countries of the Union. This protection shall operate for the benefit of the author and his successors in title.

(7) Subject to the provisions of Article 7(4) of this Convention, it shall be a matter for legislation in the countries of the Union to determine the extent of the application of their laws to works of applied art and industrial designs and models, as well as the conditions under which such works, designs and models shall be protected. Works protected in the country of origin solely as designs and models shall be entitled in another country of the Union only to such special protection as is granted in that country to designs and models; however, if no such special protection is granted in that country, such works shall be protected as artistic works.

(8) The protection of this Convention shall not apply to news of the day or to miscellaneous facts having the character of mere items of press information.

Article 2 bis

(1) It shall be a matter for legislation in the countries of the Union to exclude, wholly or in part, from the protection provided by the preceding Article political speeches and speeches delivered in the course of legal proceedings.

(2) It shall also be a matter for legislation in the countries of the Union to determine the conditions under which lectures, addresses and other works of the same nature which are delivered in public may be reproduced by the press, broadcast, communicated to the public by wire and made the subject of public communication as envisaged in Article 11bis (1) of this Convention, when such use is justified by the informatory purpose.

(3) Nevertheless, the author shall enjoy the exclusive right of making a collection of his works mentioned in the preceding paragraphs.

Article 3

(1) The protection of this Convention shall apply to:

(a) authors who are nationals of one of the countries of the Union, for their works, whether published or not;
(b) authors who are not nationals of one of the countries of the Union, for their works first published in one of those countries, or simultaneously in a country outside the Union and in a country of the Union.

(2) Authors who are not nationals of one of the countries of the Union but who have their habitual residence in one of them shall, for the purposes of this Convention, be assimilated to nationals of that country.

(3) The expression 'published works' means works published with the consent of their authors, whatever may be the means of manufacture of the copies, provided that the availability of such copies has been such as to satisfy the reasonable requirements of the public, having regard to the nature of the work. The performance of a dramatic, dramatico-musical, cinematographic or musical work, the public recitation of a literary work, the communication by wire or the broadcasting of literary or artistic works, the exhibition of a work of art and the construction of a work of architecture shall not constitute publication

(4) A work shall be considered as having been published simultaneously in several countries if it has been published in two or more countries within thirty days of its first publication.

Article 4

The protection of this Convention shall apply, even if the conditions of Article 3 are not fulfilled, to:

(a)   authors of cinematographic works the maker of which has his headquarters or habitual residence in one of the countries of the Union;

(b)   authors of works of architecture, erected in a country of the Union or of other artistic works incorporated in a building or other structure located in a country of the Union.

Article 5

(1) Authors shall enjoy, in respect of works for which they are protected under this Convention, in countries of the Union other than the country of origin, the rights which their respective laws do now or may hereafter grant to their nationals, as well as the rights specially granted by this Convention.

(2) The enjoyment and the exercise of these rights shall not be subject to any formality; such enjoyment and such exercise shall be independent of the existence of protection in the country of origin of the work. Consequently, apart from the provisions of this Convention, the extent of protection, as well as the means of redress afforded to the author to protect his rights, shall be governed exclusively by the laws of the country where protection is claimed.

(3) Protection in the country of origin is governed by domestic law. However, when the author is not a national of the country of origin of the work for which he is protected under this Convention, he shall enjoy in that country the same rights as national authors.

(4) The country of origin shall be considered to be:

(a)   in the case of works first published in a country of the Union, that country; in the case of works published simultaneously in several countries of the Union which grant different terms of protection, the country whose legislation grants the shortest term of protection;

(b)   in the case of works published simultaneously in a country outside the Union and in a country of the Union, the latter country;

(c)   in the case of unpublished works or of works first published in a country outside the Union, without simultaneous publication in a country of the Union, the country of the Union of which the author is a national, provided that:

    (i)   when these are cinematographic works the maker of which has his headquarters or his habitual residence in a country of the Union, the country of origin shall be that country, and

    (ii)   when these are works of architecture erected in a country of the Union or other artistic works incorporated in a building or other structure located in a country of the Union, the country of origin shall be that country.

Article 6

(1) Where any country outside the Union fails to protect in an adequate manner the works of authors who are nationals of one of the countries of the Union, the latter country may restrict the protection given to the works of authors who are, at the date of the first publication thereof, nationals of the other country and are not habitually resident in one of the countries of the Union. If the country of first publication avails itself of this right, the other countries of the Union shall not be required to grant to works thus subjected to special treatment a wider protection than that granted to them in the country of first publication.

(2) No restrictions introduced by virtue of the preceding paragraph shall affect the rights which an author may have acquired in respect of a work published in a country of the Union before such restrictions were put into force.

(3) The countries of the Union which restrict the grant of copyright in accordance with this Article shall give notice thereof to the Director General of the World Intellectual Property Organization (hereinafter designated as 'the Director General') by a written declaration specifying the countries in regard to which protection is restricted, and the restrictions to which rights of authors who are nationals of those countries are subjected. The Director General shall immediately communicate this declaration to all the countries of the Union.

Article 6 bis

(1) Independently of the author's economic rights, and even after the transfer of the said rights, the author shall have the right to claim authorship of the work and to object to any distortion, mutilation or other modification of, or other derogatory action in relation to, the said work, which would be prejudicial to his honour or reputation.

(2) The rights granted to the author in accordance with the preceding paragraph shall, after his death, be maintained, at least until the expiry of the economic rights, and shall be exercisable by the persons or institutions authorized by the legislation of the country where protection is claimed. However, those countries whose legislation, at the moment of their ratification of or accession to this Act, does not provide for the protection after the death of the author of all the rights set out in the preceding paragraph may provide that some of these rights may, after his death, cease to be maintained.

(3) The means of redress for safeguarding the rights granted by this Article shall be governed by the legislation of the country where protection is claimed.

Article 7

(1) The term of protection granted by this Convention shall be the life of the author and fifty years after his death.

(2) However, in the case of cinematographic works, the countries of the Union may provide that the term of protection shall expire fifty years after the work has been made available to the public with the consent of the author, or, failing such an event within fifty years from the making of such a work, fifty years after the making.

(3) In the case of anonymous or pseudonymous works, the term of protection granted by this Convention shall expire fifty years after the work has been lawfully made available to the public. However, when the pseudonym adopted by the author leaves no doubt as to his identity, the term of protection shall be that provided in paragraph (1). If the author of an anonymous or pseudonymous work discloses his identity during the above-mentioned period, the term of protection applicable shall be that provided in paragraph (1). The countries of the Union shall not be required to protect anonymous or pseudonymous works in respect of which it is reasonable to presume that their author has been dead for fifty years.

(4) It shall be a matter for legislation in the countries of the Union to determine the term of protection of photographic works and that of works of applied art in so far as they are protected as artistic works; however, this term shall last at least until the end of a period of twenty-five years from the making of such a work.

(5) The term of protection subsequent to the death of the author and the terms provided by paragraphs (2), (3) and (4), shall run from the date of death or of the event referred to in those

paragraphs, but such terms shall always be deemed to begin on the 1st of January of the year following the death or such event.

(6) The countries of the Union may grant a term of protection in excess of those provided by the preceding paragraphs.

(7) Those countries of the Union bound by the Rome Act of this Convention, which grant, in their national legislation in force at the time of signature of the present Act, shorter terms of protection than those provided for in the preceding paragraphs, shall have the right to maintain such terms when ratifying or acceding to the present Act.

(8) In any case, the term shall be governed by the legislation of the country where protection is claimed; however, unless the legislation of that country otherwise provides, the term shall not exceed the term fixed in the country of origin of the work.

Article 7 bis

The provisions of the preceding Article shall also apply in the case of a work of joint authorship, provided that the terms measured from the death of the author shall be calculated from the death of the last surviving author.

Article 8

Authors of literary and artistic works protected by this Convention shall enjoy the exclusive right of making and of authorizing the translation of their works throughout the term of protection of their rights in the original works.

Article 9

(1) Authors of literary and artistic works protected by this Convention shall have the exclusive right of authorizing the reproduction of these works, in any manner or form.

(2) It shall be a matter for legislation in the countries of the Union to permit the reproduction of such works in certain special cases, provided that such reproduction does not conflict with a normal exploitation of the work and does not unreasonably prejudice the legitimate interests of the author.

(3) Any sound or visual recording shall be considered as a reproduction for the purposes of this Convention.

Article 10

(1) It shall be permissible to make quotations from a work which has already been lawfully made available to the public, provided that their making is compatible with fair practice, and their extent does not exceed that justified by the purpose, including quotations from newspaper articles and periodicals in the form of press summaries.

(2) It shall be a matter for legislation in the countries of the Union, and for special agreements existing or to be concluded between them, to permit the utilization, to the extent justified by the purpose, of literary or artistic works by way of illustration in publications, broadcasts or sound or visual recordings for teaching, provided such utilization is compatible with fair practice.

(3) Where use is made of works in accordance with the preceding paragraphs of this Article, mention shall be made of the source, and of the name of the author, if it appears thereon.

Article 10 bis

(1) It shall be a matter for legislation in the countries of the Union to permit the reproduction by the press, the broadcasting or the communication to the public by wire, of articles published in newspapers or periodicals on current economic, political or religious topics, and of broadcast works of the same character, in cases in which the reproduction, broadcasting or such communication thereof is not expressly reserved. Nevertheless, the source must always be clearly indicated; the legal consequences of a breach of this obligation shall be determined by the legislation of the country where protection is claimed.

(2) It shall also be a matter for legislation in the countries of the Union to determine the conditions under which, for the purpose of reporting current events by means of photography, cinematography, broadcasting or communication to the public by wire, literary or artistic works seen or heard in the course of the event may, to the extent justified by the informatory purpose, be reproduced and made available to the public.

Article 11

(1) Authors of dramatic, dramatico-musical and musical works shall enjoy the exclusive right of authorizing:

(i)   the public performance of their works, including such public performance by any means or process;
(ii)   any communication to the public of the performance of their works.

(2) Authors of dramatic or dramatico-musical works shall enjoy, during the full term of their rights in the original works, the same rights with respect to translations thereof.

Article 11 bis

(1) Authors of literary and artistic works shall enjoy the exclusive right of authorizing:

(i)   the broadcasting of their works or the communication thereof to the public by any other means of wireless diffusion of signs, sounds or images;
(ii)   any communication to the public by wire or by rebroadcasting of the broadcast of the work, when this communication is made by an organization other than the original one;
(iii) the public communication by loudspeaker or any other analogous instrument transmitting, by signs, sounds or images, the broadcast of the work.

(2) It shall be a matter for legislation in the countries of the Union to determine the conditions under which the rights mentioned in the preceding paragraph may be exercised, but these conditions shall apply only in the countries where they have been prescribed. They shall not in any circumstances be prejudicial to the moral rights of the author, nor to his right to obtain equitable remuneration which, in the absence of agreement, shall be fixed by competent authority.

(3) In the absence of any contrary stipulation, permission granted in accordance with paragraph (1) of this Article shall not imply permission to record, by means of instruments recording sounds or images, the work broadcast. It shall, however, be a matter for legislation in the countries of the Union to determine the regulations for ephemeral recordings made by a broadcasting organization by means of its own facilities and used for its own broadcasts. The preservation of these recordings in official archives may, on the ground of their exceptional documentary character, be authorized by such legislation.

Article 11 ter

(1) Authors of literary works shall enjoy the exclusive right of authorizing:

(i)   the public recitation of their works, including such public recitation by any means or process;

(ii) any communication to the public of the recitation of their works.

(2) Authors of literary works shall enjoy, during the full term of their rights in the original works, the same rights with respect to translations thereof.

Article 12

Authors of literary or artistic works shall enjoy the exclusive right of authorizing adaptations, arrangements and other alterations of their works.

Article 13

(1) Each country of the Union may impose for itself reservations and conditions on the exclusive right granted to the author of a musical work and to the author of any words, the recording of which together with the musical work has already been authorized by the latter, to authorize the sound recording of that musical work, together with such words, if any; but all such reservations and conditions shall apply only in the countries which have imposed them and shall not, in any circumstances, be prejudicial to the rights of these authors to obtain equitable remuneration which, in the absence of agreement, shall be fixed by competent authority.

(2) Recordings of musical works made in a country of the Union in accordance with Article 13(3) of the Convention signed at Rome on June 2, 1928, and at Brussels on June 26, 1948, may be reproduced in that country without the permission of the author of the musical work until a date two years after that country becomes bound by this Act.

(3) Recordings made in accordance with paragraphs (1) and (2) of this Article and imported without permission from the parties concerned into a country where they are treated as infringing recordings shall be liable to seizure.

Article 14

(1) Authors of literary or artistic works shall have the exclusive right of authorizing:

(i)   the cinematographic adaptation and reproduction of these works, and the distribution of the works thus adapted or reproduced;

(ii) the public performance and communication to the public by wire of the works thus adapted or reproduced.

(2) The adaptation into any other artistic form of a cinematographic production derived from literary or artistic works shall, without prejudice to the authorization of the author of the cinematographic production, remain subject to the authorization of the authors of the original works.

(3) The provisions of Article 13(1) shall not apply.

Article 14 bis

(1) Without prejudice to the copyright in any work which may have been adapted or reproduced, a cinematographic work shall be protected as an original work. The owner of copyright in a cinematographic work shall enjoy the same rights as the author of an original work, including the rights referred to in the preceding Article.

(2) (a) Ownership of copyright in a cinematographic work shall be a matter for legislation in the country where protection is claimed.

(b) However, in the countries of the Union which, by legislation include among the owners of copyright in a cinematographic work authors who have brought contributions to the making of the work, such authors, if they have undertaken to bring such contributions, may not, in the absence of any contrary or special stipulation, object to the reproduction, distribution, public performance, communication to the public by wire, broadcasting or any other communication to the public, or to the subtitling or dubbing of texts, of the work.

(c) The question whether or not the form of the undertaking referred to above should, for the application of the preceding subparagraph (b), be in a written agreement or a written act of the same effect shall be a matter for the legislation of the country where the maker of the cinematographic work has his headquarters or habitual residence. However, it shall be a matter for the legislation of the country of the Union where protection is claimed to provide that the said undertaking shall be in a written agreement or a written act of the same effect. The countries whose legislation so provides shall notify the Director General by means of a written declaration, which will be immediately communicated by him to all the other countries of the Union.

(d) By 'contrary or special stipulation' is meant any restrictive condition which is relevant to the aforesaid undertaking.

(3) Unless the national legislation provides to the contrary, the provisions of paragraph (2) (b) above shall not be applicable to authors of scenarios, dialogues and musical works created for the making of the cinematographic work, nor to the principal director thereof. However, those countries of the Union whose legislation does not contain rules providing for the application of the said paragraph (2)(b) to such director shall notify the Director General by means of a written declaration, which will be immediately communicated by him to all the other countries of the Union.

Article 14ter

(1) The author, or after his death the persons or institutions authorized by national legislation, shall, with respect to original works of art and original manuscripts of writers and composers, enjoy the inalienable right to an interest in any sale of the work subsequent to the first transfer by the author of the work.

(2) The protection provided by the preceding paragraph may be claimed in a country of the Union only if legislation in the country to which the author belongs so permits, and to the extent permitted by the country where this protection is claimed.

(3) The procedure for collection and the amounts shall be matters for determination by national legislation.

Article 15

(1) In order that the author of a literary or artistic work protected by this Convention shall, in the absence of proof to the contrary, be regarded as such, and consequently be entitled to institute infringement proceedings in the countries of the Union, it shall be sufficient for his name to appear on the work in the usual manner. This paragraph shall be applicable even if this name is a pseudonym, where the pseudonym adopted by the author leaves no doubt as to his identity.

(2) The person or body corporate whose name appears on a cinematographic work in the usual manner shall, in the absence of proof to the contrary, be presumed to be the maker of the said work.

(3) In the case of anonymous and pseudonymous works, other than those referred to in paragraph (1) above, the publisher whose name appears on the work shall, in the absence of proof to the contrary, be deemed to represent the author, and in this capacity be shall be entitled to protect and enforce the author's rights. The provisions of this paragraph shall cease to apply when the author reveals his identity and establishes his claim to authorship of the work.

(4)   (a)   In the case of unpublished works where the identity of the author is unknown, but where there is every ground to presume that he is a national of a country of the Union, it shall be a matter for legislation in that country to designate the competent authority who shall represent the author and shall be entitled to protect and enforce his rights in the countries of the Union.

      (b)   Countries of the Union which make such designation under the terms of this provision shall notify the Director General by means of a written declaration giving full information concerning the authority thus designated. The Director General shall at once communicate this declaration to all other countries of the Union.

Article 16

(1) Infringing copies of a work shall be liable to seizure in any country of the Union where the work enjoys legal protection.

(2) The provisions of the preceding paragraph shall also apply to reproductions coming from a country where the work is not protected, or has ceased to be protected.

(3) The seizure shall take place in accordance with the legislation of each country.

Articles 17–18 omitted

Article 19

The provisions of this Convention shall not preclude the making of a claim to the benefit of any greater protection which may be granted by legislation in a country of the Union.

Article 20

The Governments of the countries of the Union reserve the right to enter into special agreements among themselves, in so far as such agreements grant to authors more extensive rights than those granted by the Convention, or contain other provisions not contrary to this Convention. The provisions of existing agreements which satisfy these conditions shall remain applicable.

[...]

Appendix 7

UNIVERSAL COPYRIGHT CONVENTION
as revised at Paris on 24 July 1971

Article I

Each Contracting State undertakes to provide for the adequate and effective protection of the rights of authors and other copyright proprietors in literary, scientific and artistic works, including writings, musical, dramatic and cinematographic works, and paintings, engravings and sculpture.

Article II

1. Published works of nationals of any Contracting State and works first published in that State shall enjoy in each other Contracting State the same protection as that other State accords to works of its nationals first published in its own territory, as well as the protection specially granted by this Convention.

2. Unpublished works of nationals of each Contracting State shall enjoy in each other Contracting State the same protection as that other State accords to unpublished works of its own nationals, as well as the protection specially granted by this Convention.

3. For the purpose of this Convention any Contracting State may, by domestic legislation, assimilate to its own nationals any person domiciled in that State.

Article III

1. Any Contracting State which, under its domestic law, requires as a condition of copyright, compliance with formalities such as deposit, registration, notice, notarial certificates, payment of fees or manufacture or publication in that Contracting State, shall regard these requirements as satisfied with respect to all works protected in accordance with this Convention and first published outside its territory and the author of which is not one of its nationals, if from the time of the first publication all the copies of the work published with the authority of the author or other copyright proprietor bear the symbol © accompanied by the name of the copyright proprietor and the year of first publication placed in such manner and location as to give reasonable notice of claim of copyright.

2. The provisions of paragraph 1 shall not preclude any Contracting State from requiring formalities or other conditions for the acquisition and enjoyment of copyright in respect of works first published in its territory or works of its nationals wherever published.

3. The provisions of paragraph 1 shall not preclude any Contracting State from providing that a person seeking judicial relief must, in bringing the action, comply with procedural requirements, such as that the complainant must appear through domestic counsel or that the complainant must deposit with the court or an administrative office, or both, a copy of the work involved in the litigation; provided that failure to comply with such requirements shall not affect the validity of the copyright, nor shall any such requirement be imposed upon a national

of another Contracting State if such requirement is not imposed on nationals of the State in which protection is claimed.

4. In each Contracting State there shall be legal means of protecting without formalities the unpublished works of nationals of other Contracting States.

5. If a Contracting State grants protection for more than one term of copyright and the first term is for a period longer than one of the minimum periods prescribed in article IV, such State shall not be required to comply with the provisions of paragraph 1 of this article in respect of the second or any subsequent term of copyright.

Article IV

1. The duration of protection of a work shall be governed, in accordance with the provisions of article II and this article, by the law of the Contracting State in which protection is claimed.

2.   (a)   The term of protection for works protected under this Convention shall not be less than the life of the author and twenty-five years after his death. However, any Contracting State which, on the effective date of this Convention in that State, has limited this term for certain classes of works to a period computed from the first publication of the work, shall be entitled to maintain these exceptions and to extend them to other classes of works. For all these classes the term of protection shall not be less than twenty-five years from the date of first publication.

    (b)   Any Contracting State which, upon the effective date of this Convention in that State, does not compute the term of protection upon the basis of the life of the author, shall be entitled to compute the term of protection from the date of the first publication of the work or from its registration prior to publication, as the case may be, provided the term of protection shall not be less than twenty-five years from the date of first publication or from its registration prior to publication, as the case may be.

    (c)   If the legislation of a Contracting State grants two or more successive terms of protection, the duration of the first term shall not be less than one of the minimum periods specified in sub-paragraphs (a) and (b).

3. The provisions of paragraph 2 shall not apply to photographic works or to works of applied art; provided, however, that the term of protection in those Contracting States which protect photographic works, or works of applied art in so far as they are protected as artistic works, shall not be less than ten years for each of said classes of works.

4.   (a)   No Contracting State shall be obliged to grant protection to a work for a period longer than that fixed for the class of works to which the work in question belongs, in the case of unpublished works by the law of the Contracting State of which the author is a national, and in the case of published works by the law of the Contracting State in which the work has been first published.

    (b)   For the purposes of the application of sub-paragraph (a), if the law of any Contracting State grants two or more successive terms of protection, the period of protection of that State shall be considered to be the aggregate of those terms. However, if a specified work is not protected by such State during the second or any subsequent term for any reason, the other Contracting States shall not be obliged to protect it during the second or any subsequent term.

5. For the purposes of the application of paragraph 4, the work of a national of a Contracting State, first published in a non-Contracting State, shall be treated as though first published in the Contracting State of which the author is a national.

6. For the purposes of the application of paragraph 4, in case of simultaneous publication in two or more Contracting States, the work shall be treated as though first published in the State which affords the shortest term, any work published in two or more Contracting States within thirty days of its first publication shall be considered as having been published simultaneously in said Contracting States.

Article IV bis

1. The rights referred to in article I shall include the basic rights ensuring the author's economic interests, including the exclusive right to authorize reproduction by any means, public performance and broadcasting. The provisions of this article shall extend to works protected under this Convention either in their original form or in any form recognizably derived from the original.

2. However, any Contracting State may, by its domestic legislation, make exceptions that do not conflict with the spirit and provisions of this Convention, to the rights mentioned in paragraph 1 of this article. Any State whose legislation so provides, shall nevertheless accord a reasonable degree of effective protection to each of the rights to which exception has been made.

Article V

1. The rights referred to in article I shall include the exclusive right of the author to make, publish and authorize the making and publication of translations of works protected under this Convention.

2. However, any Contracting State may, by its domestic legislation, restrict the right of translation of writings, but only subject to the following provisions:

(a) If, after the expiration of a period of seven years from the date of the first publication of a writing, a translation of such writing has not been published in a language in general use of the Contracting State, by the owner of the right of translation or with his authorization, any national of such Contracting State may obtain a non-exclusive licence from the competent authority thereof to translate the work into that language and publish the work so translated.

(b) Such national shall in accordance with the procedure of the State concerned, establish either that he has requested, and been denied, authorization by the proprietor of the right to make and publish the translation, or that, after due diligence on his part, he was unable to find the owner of the right. A licence may also be granted on the same conditions if all previous editions of a translation in a language in general use in the Contracting State are out of print.

(c) If the owner of the right of translation cannot be found, then the applicant for a licence shall send copies of his application to the publisher whose name appears on the work and, if the nationality of the owner of the right of translation is known, to the diplomatic or consular representative of the State of which such owner is a national, or to the organization which may have been designated by the government of that State. The licence shall not be granted before the expiration of a period of two months from the date of the dispatch of the copies of the application.

(d) Due provision shall be made by domestic legislation to ensure to the owner of the right of translation a compensation which is just and conforms to international standards, to ensure payment and transmittal of such compensation, and to ensure a correct translation of the work.

(e) The original title and the name of the author of the work shall be printed on all copies of the published translation. The licence shall be valid only for publication of the translation in the territory of the Contracting State where it has been applied for. Copies so published may be imported and sold in another Contracting State if a language in general use in such other State is the same language as that into which the work has been so translated, and if the domestic law in such other State makes provision for such licences and does not prohibit such importation and sale. Where the foregoing conditions do not exist, the importation and sale of such copies in a Contracting State shall be governed by its domestic law and its agreements. The licence shall not be transferred by the licensee.

(f)   The licence shall not be granted when the author has withdrawn from circulation all copies of the work.

Article V bis

1. Any Contracting State regarded as a developing country in conformity with the established practice of the General Assembly of the United Nations may, by a notification deposited with the Director-General of the United Nations Educational, Scientific and Cultural Organization (hereinafter called 'the Director-General') at the time of its ratification, acceptance or accession or thereafter, avail itself of any or all of the exceptions provided for in articles V ter and V quater.

2. Any such notification shall be effective for ten years from the date of coming into force of this Convention, or for such part of that ten-year period as remains at the date of deposit of the notification, and may be renewed in whole or in part for further periods of ten years each if, not more than fifteen or less than three months before the expiration of the relevant ten-year period, the Contracting State deposits a further notification with the Director-General. Initial notifications may also be made during these further periods of ten years in accordance with the provisions of this article.

3. Notwithstanding the provisions of paragraph 2, a Contracting State that has ceased to be regarded as a developing country as referred to in paragraph 1 shall no longer be entitled to renew its notification made under the provisions of paragraph 1 or 2, and whether or not it formally withdraws the notification such State shall be precluded from availing itself of the exceptions provided for in articles V ter and V quater at the end of the current ten-year period, or at the end of three years after it has ceased to be regarded as a developing country, whichever period expires later.

4. Any copies of a work already made under the exceptions provided for in articles V ter and V quater may continue to be distributed after the expiration of the period for which notifications under this article were effective until their stock is exhausted.

5. Any Contracting State that has deposited a notification in accordance with article XIII with respect to the application of this Convention to a particular country or territory, the situation of which can be regarded as analogous to that of the States referred to in paragraph 1 of this article, may also deposit notifications and renew them in accordance with the provisions of this article with respect to any such country or territory. During the effective period of such notifications, the provisions of articles V ter and V quater may be applied with respect to such country or territory. The sending of copies from the country or territory to the Contracting State shall be considered as export within the meaning of articles V ter and V quater.

Article V ter

1.   (a)   Any Contracting State to which article V bis (1) applies may substitute for the period of seven years provided for in article V (2) a period of three years or any longer period prescribed by its legislation. However, in the case of a translation into a language not in general use in one or more developed countries that are party to this Convention or only the 1952 Convention, the period shall be one year instead of three.

(b) A Contracting State to which article V bis (1) applies may, with the unanimous agreement of the developed countries party to this Convention or only the 1952 Convention and in which the same language is in general use, substitute, in the case of translation into that language, for the period of three years provided for in sub-paragraph (a) another period as determined by such agreement but not shorter than one year. However, this sub-paragraph shall not apply where the language in question is English, French or Spanish. Notification of any such agreement shall be made to the Director-General.

(c) The licence may only be granted if the applicant, in accordance with the procedure of the State concerned, establishes either that he has requested, and been denied, authorization by the owner of the right of translation, or that, after due diligence on his part, he was unable to find the owner of the right. At the same time as he makes his request he shall inform either the International Copyright Centre established by the United Nations Educational, Scientific and Cultural Organization or any national or regional information centre which may have been designated in a notification to that effect deposited with the Director-General by the government of the State in which the publisher is believed to have his principal place of business.

(d) If the owner of the right of translation cannot be found, the applicant for a licence shall send, by registered airmail, copies of his application to the publisher whose name appears on the work and to any national or regional information centre as mentioned in sub-paragraph (c). If no such centre is notified he shall also send a copy to the international copyright information centre established by the United Nations Educational, Scientific and Cultural Organization.

2. (a) Licences obtainable after three years shall not be granted under this article until a further period of six months has elapsed and licences obtainable after one year until a further period of nine months has elapsed. The further period shall begin either from the date of the request for permission to translate mentioned in paragraph 1(c) or, if the identity or address of the owner of the right of translation is not known, from the date of dispatch of the copies of the application for a licence mentioned in paragraph 1(d).

(b) Licences shall not be granted if a translation has been published by the owner of the right of translation or with his authorization during the said period of six or nine months.

3. Any licence under this article shall be granted only for the purpose of teaching, scholarship or research.

4. (a) Any licence granted under this article shall not extend to the export of copies and shall be valid only for publication in the territory of the Contracting State where it has been applied for.

(b) Any copy published in accordance with a licence granted under this article shall bear a notice in the appropriate language stating that the copy is available for distribution only in the Contracting State granting the licence. If the writing bears the notice specified in article III (1) the copies shall bear the same notice.

(c) The prohibition of export provided for in sub-paragraph (a) shall not apply where a governmental or other public entity of a State which has granted a licence under this article to translate a work into a language other than English, French or Spanish sends copies of a translation prepared under such licence to another country if:

(i) the recipients are individuals who are nationals of the Contracting State granting the licence, or organizations grouping such individuals;

(ii) the copies are to be used only for the purpose of teaching, scholarship or research;

    (iii) the sending of the copies and their subsequent distribution to recipients is without the object of commercial purpose; and

    (iv) the country to which the copies have been sent has agreed with the Contracting State to allow the receipt, distribution or both and the Director-General has been notified of such agreement by any one of the governments which have concluded it.

5. Due provision shall be made at the national level to ensure:

(a) that the licence provides for just compensation that is consistent with standards of royalties normally operating in the case of licences freely negotiated between persons in the two countries concerned; and

(b) payment and transmittal of the compensation; however, should national currency regulations intervene, the competent authority shall make all efforts, by the use of international machinery, to ensure transmittal in internationally convertible currency or its equivalent.

6. Any licence granted by a Contracting State under this article shall terminate if a translation of the work in the same language with substantially the same content as the edition in respect of which the licence was granted is published in the said State by the owner of the right of translation or with his authorization, at a price reasonably related to that normally charged in the same State for comparable works. Any copies already made before the licence is terminated may continue to be distributed until their stock is exhausted.

7. For works which are composed mainly of illustrations a licence to translate the text and to reproduce the illustrations may be granted only if the conditions of article V quater are also fulfilled.

8.   (a) A licence to translate a work protected under this Convention, published in printed or analogous forms of reproduction, may also be granted to a broadcasting organization having its headquarters in a Contracting State to which article V bis (1) applies, upon an application made in that State by the said organization under the following conditions:

        (i)   the translation is made from a copy made and acquired in accordance with the laws of the Contracting State;

        (ii)   the translation is for use only in broadcasts intended exclusively for teaching or for the dissemination of the results of specialized technical or scientific research to experts in a particular profession;

        (iii) the translation is used exclusively for the purposes set out in condition (ii), through broadcasts lawfully made which are intended for recipients on the territory of the Contracting State, including broadcasts made through the medium of sound or visual recordings lawfully and exclusively made for the purpose of such broadcasts;

        (iv) sound or visual recordings of the translation may be exchanged only between broadcasting organizations having their headquarters in the Contracting State granting the licence; and

        (v)   all uses made of the translation are without any commercial purpose.

    (b) Provided all of the criteria and conditions set out in sub-paragraph (a) are met, a licence may also be granted to a broadcasting organization to translate any text incorporated in an audio-visual fixation which was itself prepared and published for the sole purpose of being used in connexion with systematic instructional activities.

    (c) Subject to sub-paragraphs (a) and (b), the other provisions of this article shall apply to the grant and exercise of the licence.

9. Subject to the provisions of this article, any licence granted under this Article shall be governed by the provisions of article V, and shall continue to be governed by the provisions of article V and of this article, even after the seven-year period provided for in article V (2) has expired. However, after the said period has expired, the licensee shall be free to request that the said licence be replaced by a new licence governed exclusively by the provisions of article V.

Article V quater

1. Any Contracting State to which article V bis (1) applies may adopt the following provisions:

(a) If, after the expiration of (i) the relevant period specified in sub-paragraph (c) commencing from the date of first publication of a particular edition of a literary, scientific or artistic work referred to in paragraph 3, or (ii) any longer period determined by national legislation of the State, copies of such edition have not been distributed in that State to the general public or in connexion with systematic instructional activities at a price reasonably related to that normally charged in the State for comparable works, by the owner of the right of reproduction or with his authorization, any national of such State may obtain a non-exclusive licence from the competent authority to publish such edition at that or a lower price for use in connexion with systematic instructional activities. The licence may only be granted if such national, in accordance with the procedure of the State concerned, establishes either that he has requested, and been denied, authorization by the proprietor of the right to publish such work, or that, after due diligence on his part, he was unable to find the owner of the right. At the same time as he makes his request he shall inform either the international copyright information centre established by the United Nations Educational, Scientific and Cultural Organization or any national or regional information centre referred to in subparagraph (d).

(b) A licence may also be granted on the same conditions if, for a period of six months, no authorized copies of the edition in question have been on sale in the State concerned to the general public or in connexion with systematic instructional activities at a price reasonably related to that normally charged in the State for comparable works.

(c) The period referred to in sub-paragraph (a) shall be five years except that:

(i) for works of the natural and physical sciences, including mathematics, and of technology, the period shall be three years;

(ii) for works of fiction, poetry, drama and music, and for art books, the period shall be seven years.

(d) If the owner of the right of reproduction cannot be found, the applicant for a licence shall send, by registered air mail, copies of his application to the publisher whose name appears on the work and to any national or regional information centre identified as such in a notification deposited with the Director-General by the State in which the publisher is believed to have his principal place of business. In the absence of any such notification, he shall also send a copy to the international copyright information centre established by the United Nations Educational, Scientific and Cultural Organization. The licence shall not be granted before the expiration of a period of three months from the date of dispatch of the copies of the application.

(e) Licences obtainable after three years shall not be granted under this article:

(i) until a period of six months has elapsed from the date of the request for permission referred to in sub-paragraph (a) or, if the identity or address of the owner of the right of reproduction is unknown, from the date of the dispatch of the copies of the application for a licence referred to in sub-paragraph (d);

(ii) if any such distribution of copies of the edition as is mentioned in sub-paragraph (a) has taken place during that period.

(f)   The name of the author and the title of the particular edition of the work shall be printed on all copies of the published reproduction. The licence shall not extend to the export of copies and shall be valid only for publication in the territory of the Contracting State where it has been applied for. The licence shall not be transferable by the licensee.

(g)   Due provision shall be made by domestic legislation to ensure an accurate reproduction of the particular edition in question.

(h)   A licence to reproduce and publish a translation of a work shall not be granted under this article in the following cases:

   (i)   where the translation was not published by the owner of the right of translation or with his authorization;

   (ii)   where the translation is not in a language in general use in the State with power to grant the licence.

2. The exceptions provided for in paragraph 1 are subject to the following additional provisions:

(a)   Any copy published in accordance with a licence granted under this article shall bear a notice in the appropriate language stating that the copy is available for distribution only in the Contracting State to which the said licence applies. If the edition bears the notice specified in article III (1), the copies shall bear the same notice.

(b)   Due provision shall be made at the national level to ensure:

   (i)   that the licence provides for just compensation that is consistent with standards of royalties normally operating in the case of licences freely negotiated between persons in the two countries concerned; and

   (ii)   payment and transmittal of the compensation; however, should national currency regulations intervene, the competent authority shall make all efforts, by the use of international machinery, to ensure transmittal in internationally convertible currency or its equivalent.

(c)   Whenever copies of an edition of a work are distributed in the Contracting State to the general public or in connexion with systematic instructional activities, by the owner of the right of reproduction or with his authorization, at a price reasonably related to that normally charged in the State for comparable works, any licence granted under this article shall terminate if such edition is in the same language and is substantially the same in content as the edition published under the licence. Any copies already made before the licence is terminated may continue to be distributed until their stock is exhausted.

(d)   No licence shall be granted when the author has withdrawn from circulation all copies of the edition in question.

3.   (a)   Subject to sub-paragraph (b), the literary, scientific or artistic works to which this article applies shall be limited to works published in printed or analogous forms of reproduction.

      (b)   The provisions of this article shall also apply to reproduction in audio-visual form of lawfully made audio-visual fixations including any protected works incorporated therein and to the translation of any incorporated text into a language in general use in the State with power to grant the licence; always provided that the audio-visual fixations in question were prepared and published for the sole purpose of being used in connexion with systematic instructional activities.

Article VI

'Publication', as used in this Convention, means the reproduction in tangible form and the general distribution to the public of copies of a work from which it can be read or otherwise visually perceived.

Article VII

This Convention shall not apply to works or rights in works which, at the effective date of this Convention in a Contracting State where protection is claimed, are permanently in the public domain in the said Contracting State.

Articles VIII–XVI omitted

Article XVII

1. This Convention shall not in any way affect the provisions of the Berne Convention for the Protection of Literary and Artistic Works or membership in the Union created by that Convention.

2. In application of the foregoing paragraph, a declaration has been annexed to the present article. This declaration is an integral part of this Convention for the States bound by the Berne Convention on 1 January 1951, or which have or may become bound to it at a later date. The signature of this Convention by such States shall also constitute signature of the said declaration, and ratification, acceptance or accession by such States shall include the declaration, as well as this Convention.

[…]

Appendix 8

AGREEMENT ON TRADE-RELATED ASPECTS OF INTELLECTUAL PROPERTY RIGHTS, INCLUDING TRADE IN COUNTERFEIT GOODS

PART I: GENERAL PROVISIONS AND BASIC PRINCIPLES

Article 1

Nature and Scope of Obligations

1. Members shall give effect to the provisions of this Agreement. Members may, but shall not be obliged to, implement in their domestic law more extensive protection than is required by this Agreement, provided that such protection does not contravene the provisions of this Agreement. Members shall be free to determine the appropriate method of implementing the provisions of this Agreement within their own legal system and practice.

2. For the purposes of this Agreement, the term 'intellectual property' refers to all categories of intellectual property that are the subject of Sections 1 to 7 of Part II.

3. Members shall accord the treatment provided for in this Agreement to the nationals of other Members. In respect of the relevant intellectual property right, the nationals of other Members shall be understood as those natural or legal persons that would meet the criteria for eligibility for protection provided for in the Paris Convention (1967), the Berne Convention (1971), the Rome Convention and the Treaty on Intellectual Property in Respect of Integrated Circuits, were all Members of the WTO members of those conventions. Any Member availing itself of the possibilities provided in paragraph 3 of Article 5 or paragraph 2 of Article 6 of the Rome Convention shall make a notification as foreseen in those provisions to the Council for Trade-Related Aspects of Intellectual Property Rights.

Article 2

Intellectual Property Conventions

1. In respect of Parts II, III and IV of this Agreement, Members shall comply with Articles 1–12 and 19 of the Paris Convention (1967).

2. Nothing in Parts I to IV of this Agreement shall derogate from existing obligations that Members may have to each other under the Paris Convention, the Berne Convention, the Rome Convention and the Treaty on Intellectual Property in Respect of Integrated Circuits.

Article 3

National Treatment

1. Each Member shall accord to the nationals of other Members treatment no less favourable than that it accords to its own nationals with regard to the protection of intellectual property, subject to the exceptions already provided in, respectively, the Paris Convention (1967), the

Berne Convention (1971), the Rome Convention and the Treaty on Intellectual Property in Respect of Integrated Circuits. In respect of performers, producers of phonograms and broadcasting organizations, this obligation only applies in respect of the rights provided under this Agreement. Any Member availing itself of the possibilities provided in Article 6 of the Berne Convention and paragraph 1(b) of Article 16 of the Rome Convention shall make a notification as foreseen in those provisions to the Council for Trade-Related Aspects of Intellectual Property Rights.

2. Members may avail themselves of the exceptions permitted under paragraph 1 above in relation to judicial and administrative procedures, including the designation of an address for service or the appointment of an agent within the jurisdiction of a Member, only where such exceptions are necessary to secure compliance with laws and regulations which are not inconsistent with the provisions of this Agreement and where such practices are not applied in a manner which would constitute a disguised restriction on trade.

Article 4

Most-Favoured-Nation Treatment

With regard to the protection of intellectual property, any advantage, favour, privilege or immunity granted by a Member to the nationals of any other country shall be accorded immediately and unconditionally to the nationals of all other Members. Exempted from this obligation are any advantage, favour, privilege or immunity accorded by a Member:

(a) deriving from international agreements on judicial assistance and law enforcement of a general nature and not particularly confined to the protection of intellectual property;
(b) granted in accordance with the provisions of the Berne Convention (1971) or the Rome Convention authorizing that the treatment accorded be a function not of national treatment but of the treatment accorded in another country;
(c) in respect of the rights of performers, producers of phonograms and broadcasting organizations not provided under this Agreement;
(d) deriving from international agreements related to the protection of intellectual property which entered into force prior to the entry into force of the Agreement Establishing the WTO, provided that such agreements are notified to the Council for Trade-Related Aspects of Intellectual Property Rights and do not constitute an arbitrary or unjustifiable discrimination against nationals of other Members.

Article 5

Multilateral Agreements on Acquisition or Maintenance of Protection

The obligations under Articles 3 and 4 above do not apply to procedures provided in multilateral agreements concluded under the auspices of the World Intellectual Property Organization relating to the acquisition or maintenance of intellectual property rights.

Article 6

Exhaustion

For the purposes of dispute settlement under this Agreement, subject to the provisions of Articles 3 and 4 above nothing in this Agreement shall be used to address the issue of the exhaustion of intellectual property rights.

Article 7

Objectives

The protection and enforcement of intellectual property rights should contribute to the promotion of technological innovation and to the transfer and dissemination of technology, to the mutual advantage of producers and users of technological knowledge and in a manner conducive to social and economic welfare, and to a balance of rights and obligations.

Article 8

Principles

1. Members may, in formulating or amending their national laws and regulations, adopt measures necessary to protect public health and nutrition, and to promote the public interest in sectors of vital importance to their socio-economic and technological development, provided that such measures are consistent with the provisions of this Agreement.

2. Appropriate measures, provided that they are consistent with the provisions of this Agreement, may be needed to prevent the abuse of intellectual property rights by right holders or the resort to practices which unreasonably restrain trade or adversely affect the international transfer of technology.

PART II: STANDARDS CONCERNING THE AVAILABILITY, SCOPE AND USE OF INTELLECTUAL PROPERTY RIGHTS

SECTION 1: COPYRIGHT AND RELATED RIGHTS

Article 9

Relation to Berne Convention

1. Members shall comply with Articles 1–21 and the Appendix of the Berne Convention (1971). However, Members shall not have rights or obligations under this Agreement in respect of the rights conferred under Article 6bis of that Convention or of the rights derived therefrom.

2. Copyright protection shall extend to expressions and not to ideas, procedures, methods of operation or mathematical concepts as such.

Article 10

Computer Programs and Compilations of Data

1. Computer programs, whether in source or object code, shall be protected as literary works under the Berne Convention (1971).

2. Compilations of data or other material, whether in machine readable or other form, which by reason of the selection or arrangement of their contents constitute intellectual creations shall be protected as such. Such protection, which shall not extend to the data or material itself, shall be without prejudice to any copyright subsisting in the data or material itself.

Article 11

Rental Rights

In respect of at least computer programs and cinematographic works, a Member shall provide authors and their successors in title the right to authorize or to prohibit the commercial rental to the public of originals or copies of their copyright works. A Member shall be excepted from this obligation in respect of cinematographic works unless such rental has led to widespread copying of such works which is materially impairing the exclusive right of reproduction conferred in that Member on authors and their successors in title. In respect of computer programs, this obligation does not apply to rentals where the program itself is not the essential object of the rental.

Article 12

Term of Protection

Whenever the term of protection of a work, other than a photographic work or a work of applied art, is calculated on a basis other than the life of a natural person, such term shall be no less than fifty years from the end of the calendar year of authorized publication, or, failing such authorised publication within fifty years from the making of the work, fifty years from the end of the calendar year of making.

Article 13

Limitations and Exceptions

Members shall confine limitations or exceptions to exclusive rights to certain special cases which do not conflict with a normal exploitation of the work and do not unreasonably prejudice the legitimate interests of the right holder.

Article 14

Protection of Performers, Producers of Phonograms (Sound Recordings) and Broadcasting Organizations

1. In respect of a fixation of their performance on a phonogram, performers shall have the possibility of preventing the following acts when undertaken without their authorization: the fixation of their unfixed performance and the reproduction of such fixation. Performers shall also have the possibility of preventing the following acts when undertaken without their authorization: the broadcasting by wireless means and the communication to the public of their live performance.

2. Producers of phonograms shall enjoy the right to authorize or prohibit the direct or indirect reproduction of their phonograms.

3. Broadcasting organizations shall have the right to prohibit the following acts when undertaken without their authorization: the fixation, the reproduction of fixations, and the rebroadcasting by wireless means of broadcasts, as well as the communication to the public of television broadcasts of the same. Where Members do not grant such rights to broadcasting organizations, they shall provide owners of copyright in the subject matter of broadcasts with the possibility of preventing the above acts, subject to the provisions of the Berne Convention (1971).

4. The provisions of Article 11 in respect of computer programs shall apply mutatis mutandis to producers of phonograms and any other right holders in phonograms as determined in domestic law. If, on the date of the Ministerial Meeting concluding the Uruguay Round of Multilateral Trade Negotiations, a Member has in force a system of equitable remuneration of right holders in respect of the rental of phonograms, it may maintain such system provided that the commercial rental of phonograms is not giving rise to the material impairment of the exclusive rights of reproduction of right holders.

5. The term of the protection available under this Agreement to performers and producers of phonograms shall last at least until the end of a period of fifty years computed from the end of the calendar year in which the fixation was made or the performance took place. The term of

protection granted pursuant to paragraph 3 above shall last for at least twenty years from the end of the calendar year in which the broadcast took place.

6. Any Member may, in relation to the rights conferred under paragraphs 1–3 above, provide for conditions, limitations, exceptions and reservations to the extent permitted by the Rome Convention. However, the provisions of Article 18 of the Berne Convention (1971) shall also apply, mutatis mutandis, to the rights of performers and producers of phonograms in phonograms.

Sections 2–7 omitted

SECTION 8: CONTROL OF ANTI-COMPETITIVE PRACTICES IN CONTRACTUAL LICENCES

Article 40

1. Members agree that some licensing practices or conditions pertaining to intellectual property rights which restrain competition may have adverse effects on trade and may impede the transfer and dissemination of technology.

2. Nothing in this Agreement shall prevent Members from specifying in their national legislation licensing practices or conditions that may in particular cases constitute an abuse of intellectual property rights having an adverse effect on competition in the relevant market. As provided above, a Member may adopt, consistently with the other provisions of this Agreement, appropriate measures to prevent or control such practices, which may include for example exclusive grant back conditions, conditions preventing challenges to validity and coercive package licensing, in the light of the relevant laws and regulations of that Member.

3. Each Member shall enter, upon request, into consultations with any other Member which has cause to believe that an intellectual property right owner that is a national or domiciliary of the Member to which the request for consultations has been addressed is undertaking practices in violation of the requesting Member's laws and regulations on the subject matter of this Section, and which wishes to secure compliance with such legislation, without prejudice to any action under the law and to the full freedom of an ultimate decision of either Member. The Member addressed shall accord full and sympathetic consideration to, and shall afford adequate opportunity for, consultations with the requesting Member, and shall co-operate through supply of publicly available non-confidential information of relevance to the matter in question and of other information available to the Member, subject to domestic law and to the conclusion of mutually satisfactory agreements concerning the safeguarding of its confidentiality by the requesting Member.

4. A Member whose nationals or domiciliaries are subject to proceedings in another Member concerning alleged violation of that other Member's laws and regulations on the subject matter of this Section shall, upon request, be granted an opportunity for consultations by the other Member under the same conditions as those foreseen in paragraph 3 above.

PART III: ENFORCEMENT OF INTELLECTUAL PROPERTY RIGHTS

SECTION 1: GENERAL OBLIGATIONS

Article 41

1. Members shall ensure that enforcement procedures as specified in this Part are available under their national laws so as to permit effective action against any act of infringement of intellectual property rights covered by this Agreement, including expeditious remedies to prevent infringements and remedies which constitute a deterrent to further infringements.

These procedures shall be applied in such a manner as to avoid the creation of barriers to legitimate trade and to provide for safeguards against their abuse.

2. Procedures concerning the enforcement of intellectual property rights shall be fair and equitable. They shall not be unnecessarily complicated or costly, or entail unreasonable time-limits or unwarranted delays.

3. Decisions on the merits of a case shall preferably be in writing and reasoned. They shall be made available at least to the parties to the proceeding without undue delay. Decisions on the merits of a case shall be based only on evidence in respect of which parties were offered the opportunity to be heard.

4. Parties to a proceeding shall have an opportunity for review by a judicial authority of final administrative decisions and, subject to jurisdictional provisions in national laws concerning the importance of a case, of at least the legal aspects of initial judicial decisions on the merits of a case. However, there shall be no obligation to provide an opportunity for review of acquittals in criminal cases.

5. It is understood that this Part does not create any obligation to put in place a judicial system for the enforcement of intellectual property rights distinct from that for the enforcement of laws in general, nor does it affect the capacity of Members to enforce their laws in general. Nothing in this Part creates any obligation with respect to the distribution of resources as between enforcement of intellectual property rights and the enforcement of laws in general.

SECTION 2: CIVIL AND ADMINISTRATIVE PROCEDURES AND REMEDIES

Article 42

Fair and Equitable Procedures

Members shall make available to right holders civil judicial procedures concerning the enforcement of any intellectual property right covered by this Agreement. Defendants shall have the right to written notice which is timely and contains sufficient detail, including the basis of the claims. Parties shall be allowed to be represented by independent legal counsel, and procedures shall not impose overly burdensome requirements concerning mandatory personal appearances. All parties to such procedures shall be duly entitled to substantiate their claims and to present all relevant evidence. The procedure shall provide a means to identify and protect confidential information, unless this would be contrary to existing constitutional requirements.

Article 43

Evidence of Proof

1. The judicial authorities shall have the authority, where a party has presented reasonably available evidence sufficient to support its claims and has specified evidence relevant to substantiation of its claims which lies in the control of the opposing party, to order that this evidence be produced by the opposing party, subject in appropriate cases to conditions which ensure the protection of confidential information.

2. In cases in which a party to a proceeding voluntarily and without good reason refuses access to, or otherwise does not provide necessary information within a reasonable period, or significantly impedes a procedure relating to an enforcement action, a Member may accord judicial authorities the authority to make preliminary and final determinations, affirmative or negative, on the basis of the information presented to them, including the complaint or the allegation presented by the party adversely affected by the denial of access to information, subject to providing the parties an opportunity to be heard on the allegations or evidence.

Article 44

Injunctions

1. The judicial authorities shall have the authority to order a party to desist from an infringement, inter alia to prevent the entry into the channels of commerce in their jurisdiction of imported goods that involve the infringement of an intellectual property right, immediately after customs clearance of such goods. Members are not obliged to accord such authority in respect of protected subject matter acquired or ordered by a person prior to knowing or having reasonable grounds to know that dealing in such subject matter would entail the infringement of an intellectual property right.

2. Notwithstanding the other provisions of this Part and provided that the provisions of Part II specifically addressing use by governments, or by third parties authorized by a government, without the authorization of the right holder are complied with, Members may limit the remedies available against such use to payment of remuneration in accordance with sub-paragraph (h) of Article 31 above. In other cases, the remedies under this Part shall apply or, where these remedies are inconsistent with national law, declaratory judgments and adequate compensation shall be available.

Article 45

Damages

1. The judicial authorities shall have the authority to order the infringer to pay the right holder damages adequate to compensate for the injury the right holder has suffered because of an infringement of his intellectual property right by an infringer who knew or had reasonable grounds to know that he was engaged in infringing activity.

2. The judicial authorities shall also have the authority to order the infringer to pay the right holder expenses, which may include appropriate attorney's fees. In appropriate cases, Members may authorize the judicial authorities to order recovery of profits and/or payment of pre-established damages even where the infringer did not know or had no reasonable grounds to know that he was engaged in infringing activity.

Article 46

Other Remedies

In order to create an effective deterrent to infringement, the judicial authorities shall have the authority to order that goods that they have found to be infringing be, without compensation of any sort, disposed of outside the channels of commerce in such a manner as to avoid any harm caused to the right holder, or, unless this would be contrary to existing constitutional requirements, destroyed. The judicial authorities shall also have the authority to order that materials and implements the predominant use of which has been in the creation of the infringing goods be, without compensation of any sort, disposed of outside the channels of commerce in such a manner as to minimize the risks of further infringements. In considering such requests, the need for proportionality between the seriousness of the infringement and the remedies ordered as well as the interests of third parties shall be taken into account. In regard to counterfeit trademark goods, the simple removal of the trademark unlawfully affixed shall not be sufficient, other than in exceptional cases, to permit release of the goods into the channels of commerce.

Article 47

Right of Information

Members may provide that the judicial authorities shall have the authority, unless this would be out of proportion to the seriousness of the infringement, to order the infringer to inform the right holder of the identity of third persons involved in the production and distribution of the infringing goods or services and of their channels of distribution.

Article 48

Indemnification of the Defendant

1. The judicial authorities shall have the authority to order a party at whose request measures were taken and who has abused enforcement procedures to provide to a party wrongfully enjoined or restrained adequate compensation for the injury suffered because of such abuse. The judicial authorities shall also have the authority to order the applicant to pay the defendant expenses, which may include appropriate attorney's fees.

2. In respect of the administration of any law pertaining to the protection or enforcement of intellectual property rights, Members shall only exempt both public authorities and officials from liability to appropriate remedial measures where actions are taken or intended in good faith in the course of the administration of such laws.

Article 49

Administrative Procedures

To the extent that any civil remedy can be ordered as a result of administrative procedures on the merits of a case, such procedures shall conform to principles equivalent in substance to those set forth in this Section.

SECTION 3: PROVISIONAL MEASURES

Article 50

1. The judicial authorities shall have the authority to order prompt and effective provisional measures:

(a)   to prevent an infringement of any intellectual property right from occurring, and in particular to prevent the entry into the channels of commerce in their jurisdiction of goods, including imported goods immediately after customs clearance;

(b)   to preserve relevant evidence in regard to the alleged infringement.

2. The judicial authorities shall have the authority to adopt provisional measures in audita altera parte where appropriate, in particular where any delay is likely to cause irreparable harm to the right holder, or where there is a demonstrable risk of evidence being destroyed.

3. The judicial authorities shall have the authority to require the applicant to provide any reasonably available evidence in order to satisfy themselves with a sufficient degree of certainty that the applicant is the right holder and that his right is being infringed or that such infringement is imminent, and to order the applicant to provide a security or equivalent assurance sufficient to protect the defendant and to prevent abuse.

4. Where provisional measures have been adopted inaudita altera parte, the parties affected shall be given notice, without delay after the execution of the measures at the latest. A review, including a right to be heard, shall take place upon request of the defendant with a view to

deciding, within a reasonable period after the notification of the measures, whether these measures shall be modified, revoked or confirmed.

5. The applicant may be required to supply other information necessary for the identification of the goods concerned by the authority that will execute the provisional measures.

6. Without prejudice to paragraph 4 above, provisional measures taken on the basis of paragraphs 1 and 2 above shall, upon request by the defendant, be revoked or otherwise cease to have effect, if proceedings leading to a decision on the merits of the case are not initiated within a reasonable period, to be determined by the judicial authority ordering the measures where national law so permits or, in the absence of such a determination, not to exceed twenty working days or thirty-one calendar days, whichever is the longer.

7. Where the provisional measures are revoked or where they lapse due to any act or omission by the applicant, or where it is subsequently found that there has been no infringement or threat of infringement of an intellectual property right, the judicial authorities shall have the authority to order the applicant, upon request of the defendant, to provide the defendant appropriate compensation for any injury caused by these measures.

8. To the extent that any provisional measure can be ordered as a result of administrative procedures, such procedures shall conform to principles equivalent in substance to those set forth in this Section.

SECTION 4: SPECIAL REQUIREMENTS RELATED TO BORDER MEASURES

Article 51

Suspension of Release by Customs Authorities

Members shall, in conformity with the provisions set out below, adopt procedures to enable a right holder, who has valid grounds for suspecting that the importation of counterfeit trademark or pirated copyright goods may take place, to lodge an application in writing with competent authorities, administrative or judicial, for the suspension by the customs authorities of the release into free circulation of such goods. Members may enable such an application to be made in respect of goods which involve other infringements of intellectual property rights, provided that the requirements of this Section are met. Members may also provide for corresponding procedures concerning the suspension by the customs authorities of the release of infringing goods destined for exportation from their territories.

Article 52

Application

Any right holder initiating the procedures under Article 51 above shall be required to provide adequate evidence to satisfy the competent authorities that, under the laws of the country of importation, there is prima facie an infringement of his intellectual property right and to supply a sufficiently detailed description of the goods to make them readily recognizable by the customs authorities. The competent authorities shall inform the applicant within a reasonable period whether they have accepted the application and, where determined by the competent authorities, the period for which the customs authorities will take action.

Article 53

Security or Equivalent Assurance

1. The competent authorities shall have the authority to require an applicant to provide a security or equivalent assurance sufficient to protect the defendant and the competent

authorities and to prevent abuse. Such security or equivalent assurance shall not unreasonably deter recourse to these procedures.

2. Where pursuant to an application under this Section the release of goods involving industrial designs, patents, layout-designs or undisclosed information into free circulation has been suspended by customs authorities on the basis of a decision other than by a judicial or other independent authority, and the period provided for in Article 55 has expired without the granting of provisional relief by the duly empowered authority, and provided that all other conditions for importation have been complied with, the owner, importer, or consignee of such goods shall be entitled to their release on the posting of a security in an amount sufficient to protect the right holder for any infringement. Payment of such security shall not prejudice any other remedy available to the right holder, it being understood that the security shall be released if the right holder fails to pursue his right of action within a reasonable period of time.

Article 54

Notice of Suspension

The importer and the applicant shall be promptly notified of the suspension of the release of goods according to Article 51 above.

Article 55

Duration of Suspension

If, within a period not exceeding ten working days after the applicant has been served notice of the suspension, the customs authorities have not been informed that proceedings leading to a decision on the merits of the case have been initiated by a party other than the defendant, or that the duly empowered authority has taken provisional measures prolonging the suspension of the release of the goods, the goods shall be released, provided that all other conditions for importation or exportation have been complied with; in appropriate cases, this time-limit may be extended by another ten working days. If proceedings leading to a decision on the merits of the case have been initiated, a review, including a right to be heard, shall take place upon request of the defendant with a view to deciding, within a reasonable period, whether these measures shall be modified, revoked or confirmed. Notwithstanding the above, where the suspension of the release of goods is carried out or continued in accordance with a provisional judicial measure, the provisions of Article 50, paragraph 6 above shall apply.

Article 56

Indemnification of the Importer and of the Owner of the Goods

Relevant authorities shall have the authority to order the applicant to pay the importer, the consignee and the owner of the goods appropriate compensation for any injury caused to them through the wrongful detention of goods or through the detention of goods released pursuant to Article 55 above.

Article 57

Right of Inspection and Information

Without prejudice to the protection of confidential information, Members shall provide the competent authorities the authority to give the right holder sufficient opportunity to have any product detained by the customs authorities inspected in order to substantiate his claims. The competent authorities shall also have authority to give the importer an equivalent opportunity to have any such product inspected. Where a positive determination has been made on the merits of a case, Members may provide the competent authorities the authority to inform the right holder of the names and addresses of the consignor, the importer and the consignee and of the quantity of the goods in question.

Article 58

Ex Officio Action

Where Members require competent authorities to act upon their own initiative and to suspend the release of goods in respect of which they have acquired prima facie evidence that an intellectual property right is being infringed:

(a)   the competent authorities may at any time seek from the right holder any information that may assist them to exercise these powers;

(b)   the importer and the right holder shall be promptly notified of the suspension. Where the importer has lodged an appeal against the suspension with the competent authorities, the suspension shall be subject to the conditions, mutatis mutandis, set out at Article 55 above;

(c)   Members shall only exempt both public authorities and officials from liability to appropriate remedial measures where actions are taken or intended in good faith.

Article 59

Remedies

Without prejudice to other rights of action open to the right holder and subject to the right of the defendant to seek review by a judicial authority, competent authorities shall have the authority to order the destruction or disposal of infringing goods in accordance with the principles set out in Article 46 above. In regard to counterfeit trademark goods, the authorities shall not allow the re-exportation of the infringing goods in an unaltered state or subject them to a different customs procedure, other than in exceptional circumstances.

Article 60

De Minimis Imports

Members may exclude from the application of the above provisions small quantities of goods of a non-commercial nature contained in travellers' personal luggage or sent in small consignments.

SECTION 5: CRIMINAL PROCEDURES

Article 61

Members shall provide for criminal procedures and penalties to be applied at least in cases of wilful trademark counterfeiting or copyright piracy on a commercial scale. Remedies available shall include imprisonment and/or monetary fines sufficient to provide a deterrent, consistently with the level of penalties applied for crimes of a corresponding gravity. In appropriate cases, remedies available shall also include the seizure, forfeiture and destruction of the infringing goods and of any materials and implements the predominant use of which has been in the commission of the offence. Members may provide for criminal procedures and penalties to be applied in other cases of infringement of intellectual property rights, in particular where they are committed wilfully and on a commercial scale.

Appendix 9

WIPO COPYRIGHT TREATY[1]

Article 1 – Relation to the Berne Convention

(1) This Treaty is a special agreement within the meaning of Article 20 of the Berne Convention for the Protection of Literary and Artistic Works, as regards Contracting Parties that are countries of the Union established by that Convention. This Treaty shall not have any connection with treaties other than the Berne Convention, nor shall it prejudice any rights and obligations under any other treaties.

(2) Nothing in this Treaty shall derogate from existing obligations that Contracting Parties have to each other under the Berne Convention for the Protection of Literary and Artistic Works.

(3) Hereinafter, 'Berne Convention' shall refer to the Paris Act of July 24, 1971 of the Berne Convention for the Protection of Literary and Artistic Works.

(4) Contracting Parties shall comply with Articles 1 to 21 and the Appendix of the Berne Convention.

Article 2 – Scope of Copyright Protection

Copyright protection extends to expressions and not to ideas, procedures, methods of operation or mathematical concepts as such.

Article 3 – Application of Articles 2 to 6 of the Berne Convention

Contracting Parties shall apply mutatis mutandis the provisions of Articles 2 to 6 of the Berne Convention in respect of the protection provided for in this Treaty.

Article 4 – Computer Programs

Computer programs are protected as literary works within the meaning of Article 2 of the Berne Convention. Such protection applies to computer programs, whatever may be the mode or form of their expression.

Article 5 – Compilations of Data (Databases)

Compilations of data or other material, in any form, which by reason of the selection or arrangement of their contents constitute intellectual creations, are protected as such. This protection does not extend to the data or the material itself and is without prejudice to any copyright subsisting in the data or material contained in the compilation.

---

1   Adopted by the Diplomatic Conference on 20 December 1996.

Article 6 – Right of Distribution

(1) Authors of literary and artistic works shall enjoy the exclusive right of authorizing the making available to the public of the original and copies of their works through sale or other transfer of ownership.

(2) Nothing in this Treaty shall affect the freedom of Contracting Parties to determine the conditions, if any, under which the exhaustion of the right in paragraph (1) applies after the first sale or other transfer of ownership of the original or a copy of the work with the authorization of the author.

Article 7 – Right of Rental

(1) Authors of:

(i)   computer programs;
(ii)   cinematographic works; and
(iii) works embodied in phonograms as determined in the national law of Contracting Parties,
       shall enjoy the exclusive right of authorizing commercial rental to the public of the
       originals or copies of their works.

(2) Paragraph (1) shall not apply:

(i)   in the case of computer programs where the program itself is not the essential object of the
       rental; and
(ii)   in the case of cinematographic works, unless such commercial rental has led to
       widespread copying of such works materially impairing the exclusive right of
       reproduction.

(3) Notwithstanding the provisions of paragraph (1), a Contracting Party that, on April 15, 1994, had and continues to have in force a system of equitable remuneration of authors for the rental of copies of their works embodied in phonograms may maintain that system provided that the commercial rental of works embodied in phonograms is not giving rise to the material impairment of the exclusive rights of reproduction of authors.

Article 8 – Right of Communication to the Public

Without prejudice to the provisions of Articles 11(1)(ii), 11bis(1)(i) and (ii), 11ter(1)(ii), 14(1)(ii) and 14bis(1) of the Berne Convention, authors of literary and artistic works shall enjoy the exclusive right of authorizing any communication to the public of their works, by wire or wireless means, including the making available to the public of their works in such a way that members of the public may access these works from a place and at a time individually chosen by them.

Article 9 – Duration of the Protection of Photographic Works

In respect of photographic works, the Contracting Parties shall not apply the provisions of Article 7(4) of the Berne Convention.

Article 10 – Limitations and Exceptions

(1) Contracting Parties may, in their national legislation, provide for limitations of or exceptions to the rights granted to authors of literary and artistic works under this Treaty in certain special cases that do not conflict with a normal exploitation of the work and do not unreasonably prejudice the legitimate interests of the author.

(2) Contracting Parties shall, when applying the Berne Convention, confine any limitations of or exceptions to rights provided for therein to certain special cases that do not conflict with a normal exploitation of the work and do not unreasonably prejudice the legitimate interests of the author.

Article 11 – Obligations concerning Technological Measures

Contracting Parties shall provide adequate legal protection and effective legal remedies against the circumvention of effective technological measures that are used by authors in connection with the exercise of their rights under this Treaty or the Berne Convention and that restrict acts, in respect of their works, which are not authorized by the authors concerned or permitted by law.

Article 12 – Obligations concerning Rights Management Information

(1) Contracting Parties shall provide adequate and effective legal remedies against any person knowingly performing any of the following acts knowing or, with respect to civil remedies having reasonable grounds to know, that it will induce, enable, facilitate or conceal an infringement of any right covered by this Treaty or the Berne Convention:

(i)   to remove or alter any electronic rights management information without authority;

(ii)   to distribute, import for distribution, broadcast or communicate to the public, without authority, works or copies of works knowing that electronic rights management information has been removed or altered without authority.

(2) As used in this Article, 'rights management information' means information which identifies the work, the author of the work, the owner of any right in the work, or information about the terms and conditions of use of the work, and any numbers or codes that represent such information, when any of these items of information is attached to a copy of a work or appears in connection with the communication of a work to the public.

Article 13 – Application in Time

Contracting Parties shall apply the provisions of Article 18 of the Berne Convention to all protection provided for in this Treaty.

Article 14 – Provisions on Enforcement of Rights

(1) Contracting Parties undertake to adopt, in accordance with their legal systems, the measures necessary to ensure the application of this Treaty.

(2) Contracting Parties shall ensure that enforcement procedures are available under their law so as to permit effective action against any act of infringement of rights covered by this Treaty, including expeditious remedies to prevent infringements and remedies which constitute a deterrent to further infringements.

[…]

Appendix 10

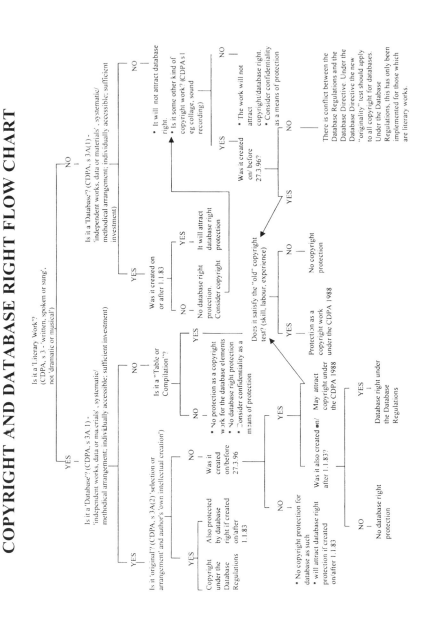

COPYRIGHT AND DATABASE RIGHT FLOW CHART

Is it a 'Literary Work'?
(CDPA, s 3 - 'written, spoken or sung',
not 'dramatic or musical')

YES — Is it a 'Database'? (CDPA, s 3A 1) -
'independent works, data or materials' - systematic/
methodical arrangement; individually accessible; sufficient investment)

NO — Is it a 'Database'? (CDPA, s 3A(1)) -
'independent works, data or materials' - systematic/
methodical arrangement; individually accessible; sufficient investment)

YES — Is it 'original'? (CDPA, s 3A(2) 'selection or arrangement' and author's own intellectual creation')

NO — Is it a "Table or Compilation"?

YES — Was it created on or after 1.1.83

NO — It will be some other kind of copyright work? (CDPA s 1 eg collage, sound recording)

Is it 'original'? branch:

YES — Was it created on/before 27.3.96

- YES — Copyright under the Database Regulations
- NO — Also protected by database right if created on/after 1.1.83

Is it a "Table or Compilation"? branch:

NO —
- No protection as a copyright work for the database elements
- No database right protection
- Consider confidentiality as a means of protection

YES — Was it also created on/after 1.1.83?
- YES — May attract copyright under the CDPA 1988
- NO — No copyright protection for database as such
  - will attract database right protection if created on/after 1.1.83

Was it created on/before 27.3.96
- YES — Does it satisfy the "old" copyright test? (skill, labour, experience)
  - YES — Protection as a copyright work under the CDPA 1988
  - NO — No copyright protection
- NO — Was it also created after 1.1.83?
  - YES — Database right under the Database Regulations
  - NO — No database right protection

Was it created on or before 1.1.83 branch:

YES — It will attract database right protection

NO — No database right protection. Consider copyright

Was it created on/before 27.3.96 branch:

YES —
- The work will not attract copyright/database right.
- Consider confidentiality as a means of protection

NO —

There is conflict between the Database Regulations and the Database Directive. Under the Database Directive the new "originality" test should apply to all copyright for databases. Under the Database Regulations, this has only been implemented for those which are literary works.

It will not attract database right.

Index

References are to paragraph numbers; italic references are to page numbers of Appendices.